PICTURING HISTORY

American Painting 1770–1930

PICTURING HISTORY

American Painting 1770–1930

EDITED BY
WILLIAM AYRES

Chief Contributor: Barbara J. Mitnick
Foreword by Michael Kammen

Essays by Ann Uhry Abrams, Kenneth Ames,
Matthew Baigell, Bruce W. Chambers,
Wendy Greenhouse, Gail E. Husch, Barbara J. Mitnick,
Barry Schwartz, Mark Thistlethwaite, Ron Tyler

RIZZOLI
NEW YORK

in association with
Fraunces Tavern Museum, New York

This book accompanies the exhibition *Picturing History: American Painting, 1770–1930,* William Ayres, Project Director, Barbara J. Mitnick, Curator, organized by Fraunces Tavern Museum, New York City, with a grant from the IBM Corporation and additional funding from the National Endowment for the Arts, a federal agency.

Exhibition venues: IBM Gallery of Science and Art, New York City, September 28 to November 27, 1993; The Corcoran Gallery of Art, Washington, D.C., January 29 to April 2, 1994; Dallas Museum of Art, Dallas, Texas, May 1 to July 10, 1994; Center for the Fine Arts, Miami, Florida, August 6 to November 13, 1994.

Fraunces Tavern Museum is owned and operated by, and FRAUNCES TAVERN® is a registered service mark of, Sons of the Revolution in the State of New York, Inc.First published in the United States of America in 1993 by Rizzoli International International Publications, Inc. 300 Park Avenue South, New York, New York 10010

Library of Congress Cataloging-in-Publication Data

Picturing history : American painting, 1770–1930 / edited by
    William S. Ayres ; foreword by Michael Kammen ;
    introduction by William S. Ayres.
        p.   cm.
    Includes bibliographical references and index.
    ISBN 0-8478-1745-8
    1. Painting, American. 2. History in art. I. Ayres, William S.
ND1441.P53   1993
758'.9973'0973—dc20   93-10437
                                             CIP

Developmental Editor: Kathryn Grover
Designed by Abigail Sturges
Editor: Charles Miers
Compositor: Michael Bertrand
Proofreader: Mary Christian

Printed and bound in Italy

Front jacket: Emanuel Leutze and Eastman Johnson, *Washington Crossing the Delaware,* plate 124. Back jacket: Thomas Hart Benton, *New York History,* plate 132. Page 1: Frederic Church, *Hooker and Company Journeying Through the Wilderness from Plymouth to Hartford, in 1636.* 1846. 40 ¼ x 60 ⅜" (102.3 x 152.9 cm.). Wadsworth Atheneum, Hartford, Connecticut. Pages 2–3: Robert Weir, *Landing of Henry Hudson,* detail of plate 39. Pages 4–5: Dennis Malone Carter, *Molly Pitcher at the Battle of Monmouth,* detail of plate 13.

Contents

Previous Pages:
1. Thomas Cole. *Present.* 1838. 40 x 61"
(100.0 x 152.5 cm.). Mead Art Museum,
Amherst College, Amherst,
Massachusetts; museum purchase.

2. Peter F. Rothermel. *The Banishment
of Roger Williams.* ca. 1850. 35½ x 28½"
(88.7 x 71.2 cm.). The Rhode Island
Historical Society, Providence.

Foreword

MICHAEL KAMMEN

It has long been commonplace for skillful historians to think of themselves as artists, or to achieve recognition as "artists" etching with words. That aspiration characterized such prominent mid-nineteenth-century romantic historians as William Hickling Prescott and Francis Parkman, as well as many of their contemporaries. Alternatively, this book looks seriously at the work of artists who aimed to record or to envision history. If they romanticized the past, so did the prestigious historians who were their peers. Examining the artists' careers may suggest to us that a tension existed between pursuit of the romantic and the authentic, though in reality the tension lies more in our perceptions than in their work. These artists did not regard authenticity and romanticism as incompatible or incongruous values. The former had to do with historical veracity as they understood it; the latter involved the spirit and emotional significance of what they depicted, not to mention its meaning for Americans in search of historically informed self-knowledge—as individuals and also collectively as a people.[1]

Although history presented as an art form has a venerable tradition—one that has been revisited with rhythmic regularity—we are less accustomed to thinking of art as a literal mode of historical memory and commentary. Doing so might seem non-aesthetic, or even anti-aesthetic. But the wistful laments that opened and closed the nineteenth century, when men and women contemplated the condition of historical art, remind us that a pantheon of history painting is precisely what some Americans sought to establish. "What appears yet wanting," warned the critic George Murray in 1812, is "a *national gallery* of the works of American artists consisting of subjects from our own history."[2]

Still, because influential artists of the antebellum period viewed the United States as Nature's Nation, they were inclined to privilege nature above history and regarded the former as our great feature, the latter as something from which we had been mercifully liberated. It was not unusual for history, especially Old World history, to be depicted as a story of regress rather than progress. Hence Thomas Cole's majestic pair titled *Past* and *Present*, both painted in 1838 (plates 1 and 3). The past renders a lively and glorious medieval tournament, with knights jousting in the foreground and a mighty castle behind them. The present offers a dismal castle lying in ruins, an intimation of mortality and a civilization in decline. Piles of stone heaped up by man—even the sites of heroic encounters—could not compete with the sublime spectacle of timeless and unsullied nature.

Nevertheless, some American artists *did* look to heroic encounters and achievements in their native land, and especially, though not entirely, from the more recent past. To appreciate the themes and subjects that most intrigued those artists, we might think in terms of a decahedron, a solid figure offering ten faces, or facets, of our early past. First, there are the "landings" of Columbus and other intrepid explorers, such as de Soto, La Salle, and Hudson. Second, there are highly dramatic episodes involving white contact with Indians, such as William Penn and his legendary treaty, or Pocahontas saving others and experiencing her own salvation at the hands of concerned Christians. Third, there are the patient Pilgrims: embarking from Holland, covenanting on the *Mayflower*, landing at Plymouth, and eventually giving thanks for a sustaining harvest. Fourth (and most detailed), there is the life of George Washington as an officer both young and mature, being domestic at Mount Vernon, presiding at the Constitutional Convention, retiring from civic life, and then returning to heed the call

3. Thomas Cole. *Past.* 1838. 40 x 61" (100.0 x 152.5 cm.). Mead Art Museum, Amherst College, Amherst, Massachusetts; museum purchase.

of duty. Fifth, there are strategic land battles followed by victorious surrender scenes from the War for Independence. Sixth, there are memorable naval battles that span the years from 1779 until 1862, featuring John Paul Jones and "Old Ironsides," or the USS *Constitution.* Seventh, there is the Mexican War, precipitated by President Polk in order to fulfill our continental destiny during the later 1840s. Eighth, there is the institution of slavery, but painted in such a way as to accentuate the positive—conducting the *last* sale held in New Orleans or promulgating the Emancipation Proclamation. (Ultimately, you see, we did the right thing.) Ninth, there are assorted episodes from the Civil War, military "moments" of haunting violence. And then, completing our decahedron, the life and death of Abraham Lincoln, steadfast statesman and Christlike martyr.

There is more, much more, which the following essays describe and explain; but it seems equally important to inventory those important aspects of our history that are conspicuously missing and to speculate why they went unrecorded. The reasons are more complex than facile assumptions might suggest. For example, myths abound in our decahedron, but they are anecdotal myths that can be personified by a heroic individual, such as Princess Pocahontas, President Washington, or the prescient Lincoln. Some of our most consequential historical myths, however, are less susceptible to personification in a single canvas and do not appear: the genius of American politics for customarily escaping the kinds of ideological conflicts that so afflicted Europe; the United States as a place of opportunity, equality, and glorious individualism; the Virgin Land awaiting diligent newcomers who would make it forever fruitful on independent family farms and thereby feed the world.[3] We have personal myths and we have cosmic myths. Some of the latter, however, seem to have been too complex, or perhaps double-edged, for painters to daub in two dimensions and six colors. So they didn't.

History as *event* lends itself more readily to the painter's craft than history as *process*, as everyday life, or even as manifest in popular national slogans—such as "peace and plenty"—that appeared on pitchers and mugs, in speeches and banners, but seemed insufficiently iconic for the grandeur that proper historical art was expected to achieve.[4] How to envision the Bill of Rights, for instance, or passage of the great post–Civil War amendments (the Thirteenth, Fourteenth, and Fifteenth) is equally problematic. So, too, were civic events that involved criticism of cherished goals, or failures of nerve, or episodes that did not mobilize some sort of national consensus. Consequently we lack images of the Loyalists (Tories), the Anti-Federalists, Shays' Rebellion, the Hartford Convention (when New England contemplated secession in 1814), the women's rights convention at Seneca Falls, New York (1848), John Brown's dramatic raid at Harper's Ferry in 1859, or the hotly contested impeachment of President Andrew Johnson in 1868. We tend not to immortalize what is retrospectively embarrassing, inconclusive, or divisive.

Also missing are some occurrences deemed positive yet extremely difficult to depict, not because they are high ideals or abstractions (like the Bill of Rights) but because their principal embodiment is a document such as a treaty, a bill of sale, or a statement of national

4. David Gilmour Blythe. *Libby Prison.*
1863. 24 x 36" (60.0 x 90.0 cm.).
Museum of Fine Arts, Boston; bequest of
Martha C. Karolik for the Karolik
Collection of American Paintings,
1815–1865.

policy (the Northwest Ordinance of 1787, the purchase of Louisiana and later Alaska, the Supreme Court's landmark opinion in *Marbury v. Madison*). The absence of the Alamo, the Battle of San Jacinto (facilitating independence for Texas in 1836), Custer's "Last Stand" (1876), or even the great gold rush to California in 1849 is only moderately hard to understand.[5] Imaginative artistic renderings of them do exist; but our sensibilities have subsequently been heightened where imperialism, greed, and the land rights of native Americans are concerned. Out of sight can sometimes mean out of mind—almost.

Ralph Ellison, one of our greatest authors, has written eloquently about the role of memory and amnesia in American culture. He has observed that by "seeking to move forward we find ourselves looking back and discovering with some surprise from whence we've come":

> Perhaps this is how it has to be. For given the circumstances of our national origins, given our vast geopolitical space and the improvised character of our society, and given the mind-boggling rapidity of our national growth—perhaps it is understandably difficult for Americans to keep in touch with what has happened to them. At any rate, in the two hundred years of our national existence a great deal has been overlooked or forgotten. Some developments become obscure because of the sheer rush and density of incidents which occur in any given period of time; others fade through conscious design, either because of an unwillingness to solve national dilemmas or because we possess such a short attention span and are given to a facile waning of our commitments. Then too, having had no adequate model to guide us in establishing what we told ourselves was to be a classless society, it has often been difficult for us to place people and events in a proper perspective of national importance. So it is well that we keep in mind the fact that not all of American history is recorded. And in some ways we are fortunate that it isn't, for if it were, we might become so chagrined by the discrepancies which exist between our democratic ideals and our social reality that we'd soon lose heart. Perhaps this is why we possess two basic versions of American history: one which is written and as neatly stylized as ancient myth, and the other unwritten and as chaotic and full of contradictions, changes of pace, and surprises as life itself. Perhaps this is to overstate a bit, but there's no denying the fact that Americans can be notoriously selective in the exercise of historical memory.[6]

When we give careful consideration to American historical art, we survey a fascinating but contested field that involves the politics of culture. Advocates of a national culture in nineteenth-century America expected it to be consistent with a democratic ethos, yet little of our historical art has been done in a vernacular style. Most of the paintings grandly glorify heroes rather than the common man or woman.[7] They celebrate the republic and some of its ideals, but not vox populi or popular sovereignty. (George Caleb Bingham's *County Election* [plate 59] is a notable exception.) They supply images of manifest destiny but rarely depict the environmental and human cost of achieving that destiny. Nor do they ordinarily notice the degradation of democracy when immigrants and working-class Americans were brutally repressed by government in cooperation with corporations during the later decades of the nineteenth century.

A distinguished historian of the Civil War era, David M. Potter, has argued that for most of the nineteenth century the nature and meaning of American nationalism were not seriously contested in the United States. A remarkable consensus existed concerning our selection as a chosen people with a providential mission to spread our superior values and political system.[8] If Potter's assessment is correct about that consensus, then it helps to explain why there are so few "nay-sayers" or critics among the artists and icons in this book. In such paintings as *Libby Prison* (plate 4), David Gilmour Blythe consistently called attention to racism and political injustice, and *The Banishment of Roger Williams* by Peter F. Rothermel (plate 2) reminds us of Puritan intolerance toward dissent. But these iconoclastic statements are easily overlooked, and their contextual meaning is not readily grasped.

It has been fashionable in recent years to refer to pictures as "texts" that can be read and understood. In order to do so, however, we require contextual information about the human agency that informs the pictorial panorama (along with social and political forces, ideological tendencies, military conflicts, religious impulses, aesthetic values and visions) as well as about the artists and the circumstances in which their paintings were made—what once was called the "climate of opinion." Mark Twain pointed this out in a droll yet basic way in 1883 while discussing a (fanciful) historical painting that enjoyed great popularity in the former Confederacy. The picture by E. D. B. Julio was titled *The Last Meeting of Lee and Jackson* (plate 5). Twain happened to see it on display in Washington, D.C., and wrote in *Life on the Mississippi*:

> Both men are on horseback. Jackson has just ridden up, and is accosting Lee. The picture is very valuable, on account of the portraits, which are authentic. But, like many another historical picture, it means nothing without its label. And one label will fit it as well as another:
>
> First Interview between Lee and Jackson.
> Last Interview between Lee and Jackson.
> Jackson Introducing Himself to Lee.
> Jackson Accepting Lee's Invitation to Dinner.
> Jackson Declining Lee's Invitation to Dinner—with Thanks.
> Jackson Apologizing for a Heavy Defeat.
> Jackson Reporting a Great Victory.
> Jackson Asking Lee for a Match.

It tells one story, and a sufficient one; for it says quite plainly and satisfactorily, "Here are Lee and Jackson together." The artist would have made it tell that this is Lee and Jackson's last interview if he could have done it. But he couldn't, for there wasn't any way to do it. A good legible label is usually worth, for information, a ton of significant attitude and expression in a historical picture.[9]

Despite his wry tone, Twain was serious, and well he should have been. How often have we gone back to review an old favorite in some museum or gallery, only to learn that its title has been changed for some carefully researched reason. Sometimes the new and different title, or the reasons for its alteration, may actually affect our perception of the painting or of the artist's rationale for undertaking it. The same is true, oddly enough, of parodic versions of famous historical works. Who can ever again gaze with an innocent eye at Emanuel Leutze's *Washington Crossing the Delaware* (plate 30) after seeing Peter Saul's riotous spoof (1976) bearing a similar title? Our response to *Penn's Treaty with the Indians* by Benjamin West (plate 6) likewise changes after seeing Red Grooms's *William Penn Shakin' Hands with the Indians* (1967) and listening to Grooms acknowledge that he chose the subject "more because of Mr. Benjamin West than Mr. Penn. . . . The atmosphere in his paintings is so thick it looks more like 20 thousand B.C. than just a few hundred years ago."[10]

Such parodies and resonances, along with the quips that accompany them, remind us that we must wear metaphorical bifocals when we view these paintings. We should do so, as it happens, for multiple reasons. How *does* one look at a pictorial cliché? As a text? As a document? As an artifact? The answer, quite clearly, is that we must see such paintings simultaneously as works of art (some of them good and some not so good) and as icons that reveal national or sectional values and assumptions. We also need bifocals in order to perceive the pictures both as contemporaries did *and* with our own more farsighted vision—critically yet with added complexity. The artist, for example, may have been responsible for innovations (such as vernacular clothing or human models of the correct nationality or ethnicity) that *we* take for granted but were actually quite bold a century and a half ago—and were done in order to achieve greater authenticity.[11]

We must also remain alert for distinctions *within* the genre that is so casually called history painting because the mode is not monolithic. Was the artist an actual witness to the events depicted on canvas? Or did the painter rely upon secondhand accounts, oral or written, that stimulated the iconic imagination? What was the artist's attitude toward history itself? Documentary or romantic? Authentic or mythic? Prior to the 1880s historians and artists shared common assumptions about presenting the past, especially the national past. It

5. E. D. B. Julio. *The Last Meeting of Lee and Jackson.* 1869. 102 x 74" (255.0 x 185.0 cm.). The Museum of the Confederacy, Richmond, Virginia.

could legitimately be heroic, mythic, providential, and deliberately romanticized. After the 1880s, however, those aesthetic criteria were, if anything, nostalgically accentuated by the likes of Howard Pyle and N. C. Wyeth, whereas history as a professional discipline sought to become more scientific than mythic, more factual than visionary.

When we press the button that accelerates images to fast forward, however, we face dilemmas and perplexities that must be answered by each one of us individually. In our own time, for instance, enthusiasm for heroic moments and historical anecdotes is supposed to be infra dig, out of fashion. In reality, though, most of us enjoy anecdotes and yearn for heroes we can genuinely admire. We want to derive pleasure from the past even as we wish to learn from it. Robert Penn Warren put it well in his shrewd meditation upon the Civil War: "The asking and the answering which history provokes may help us to understand, even to frame, the logic of experience to which we shall submit."[12]

6. Benjamin West. *Penn's Treaty with the Indians.* 1771–72. 75½ x 107½" (191.8 x 273.1 cm.). The Pennsylvania Academy of the Fine Arts, Philadelphia; gift of Mrs. Sarah Harrison (the Joseph Harrison, Jr., Collection).

Preface

WILLIAM AYRES

Before John Trumbull's *Declaration of Independence* took its permanent place in the Rotunda of the United States Capitol, it was placed on temporary view at the American Academy of the Fine Arts in New York City. On October 5, 1819, the first day of its exhibition, thousands lined up and paid to see it. It was an "unprecedented professional and financial triumph"— and a media event of the first magnitude for its time. "To suppose that any native American can go back in recollection or his imagination to the period when this great event took place, and not feel a deep interest in the actual view of the personages by whom it was achieved," one newspaper exclaimed, "would be a species of reproach which we are not willing to cast on any fellow citizen." The painting then traveled to Boston, Philadelphia, and Baltimore, where it was exhibited to overflow crowds: more than twenty-one thousand people came to view the work before it was installed in Washington, again accompanied by great fanfare.[1]

Some thirty years later, in 1851, Emanuel Leutze's *Washington Crossing the Delaware* achieved an even larger critical and popular success. Admission was charged to see it, too, when it was shown at New York's Stuyvesant Institute. The *Knickerbocker* reported that "crowds . . . throng to see it by day and by night," the number queueing to view it ultimately exceeding fifty thousand. The New York press could not find enough superlatives to describe the work. It was variously labeled "the grandest, the most majestic, and most effective painting ever exhibited in America," "altogether the noblest painting exhibited in this country for many a year," and "the best painting yet executed on an American subject."[2] Even Henry James, not prone to praise, was profoundly moved by his visit:

No impression . . . was half so momentous as that of the epoch-making masterpiece of Mr. Leutze, which showed Washington crossing the Delaware in a wondrous flare of projected gaslight and with the effect of a revelation. . . . I live again in the thrill of that evening. . . . We went down, after dinner, quite as if going to the theater . . . but Mr. Leutze's drama left behind any paler proscenium.[3]

Critics asserted that *Washington Crossing the Delaware* "should be viewed and studied by every American," and the *Georgetown Advocate* offered a reason why. The painting had peculiar power over viewers, the *Advocate* observed; it engraved on their minds important historic truths and noble patriotic sentiments. "It had that kind of historic interest which seemed to send a thrill through the system and carry the mind back to the time when Washington, at the head of the Continental troops, worn down by want and sickness and dispirited by the successes of the enemy, thought it necessary to make a daring attempt to save the great cause in which the future of the country was involved."[4]

Nineteenth-century Americans continued to be impressed and instructed by history paintings, but after the Civil War they encountered them more often in the form of prints made after the painters' images and, even more, in books using them as the basis for illustrations. Earlier artists, including Trumbull and Leutze, had issued ambitious print editions, and later painters such as Peter F. Rothermel, Alonzo Chappel, Tompkins H. Matteson, and Dennis Malone Carter were even more successful in marketing their works for reproduction as prints. But by far the widest dissemination of American history pictures took place with the burgeoning of the nation's publishing industry, particularly from the 1870s into the first quarter of the twentieth century, with images created by artist-illustrators such as J. L. G. Ferris, John Ward Dunsmore, Howard Pyle, and N. C. Wyeth becoming familiar to every American schoolchild.

By the end of the 1920s, however, traditional American history painting—the line tracing its ancestry to Benjamin West and John Trumbull—seemed to have played itself out. The horrific devastation of the First World War had made many Americans, including artists, doubt some of the time-sanctified verities, including not only what lessons could or should be drawn from history, but what history actually *was.* Some, like George Bellows, had already spread the gory details of the cruelty of war on canvas (plate 7). Others had retreated from the pretense of presenting mimetic images—for instance, Edwin Austin Abbey, who used historical detail more for its theatrical appeal and pageantry than for any lessons it might arguably contain (plate 8). N. C. Wyeth visualized American history in his dreams, and painted t that way (plate 120). Walt Kuhn and Thomas Hart Benton found more power and significance in larger historical forces and movements than in specific acts of valor by canonized secular heroes (plates 131 and 132); their approach would provide a basis for the revival of history painting by the WPA and other New Deal agencies in the mid-1930s.

Since the Second World War, as Kenneth Ames points out, the earlier image-creating and image-supporting roles of history painting have been largely subsumed by other visual media, including photography, movies, and, most dramatically, television. Still, even today, our notions of many of the "great" moments that both define and describe American history arguably have been influenced more by these pictorial images than by any written text. It is impossible for many of us to form mental notions of, say, the first Thanksgiving, the signing of the Declaration of Independence, or the battles of the Revolution without conjuring up the forms in which Trumbull, Leutze, Ferris, Pyle, and others have depicted them.[5]

Nonetheless, as Mark Thistlethwaite observes here, grand paintings of American historical events have been out of fashion in intellectual circles for at least a century. Modernists have disliked history painting for being too realistic in style. Realists have criticized its tendency toward myth-making. Historians have declared it simplistic in general and wrong in particulars. Fans of photography have judged it lacking in verisimilitude. Aesthetes of various stripes have excoriated it for being little more than "mere" illustration or for aiming its appeal to the common denominators of popular taste rather than to

7. George Bellows. *The Germans Arrive.*
1918. 49½ x 79¼" (123.7 x 198.1 cm.).
Private collection.

8. Edwin Austin Abbey. *Columbus in the New World*. 1906. 87 x 120″ (221.0 x 304.8 cm.). Yale University Art Gallery; the Edwin Austin Abbey Memorial Collection, New Haven, Connecticut.

more educated and refined sensibilities. From its position at the apex of the Pyramid of Virtues, as articulated from the fifteenth to the eighteenth century by commentators from Alberti to Sir Joshua Reynolds, history painting in the eyes of many writers slid to the nadir of critical estimation by the end of the nineteenth and the beginning of the twentieth century, when respected writers termed its best examples "painted anecdote[s]," even "stupid atrocities."[6]

Recently, however, American history paintings have begun to attract a more sympathetic look from several quarters. Beginning in the 1970s, coinciding with the upsurge of popular interest in history at the time of the Bicentennial of the American Revolution, art historians, historians, sociologists, and American studies specialists have explored the genre from numerous vantage points. Some have concentrated on individual painters, others on depictions of specific persons or events, on paintings from a particular period, on the processes of memory and commemoration themselves, or on those people and subjects bypassed by American history painting. These scholars, including the essayists in *Picturing History*, have consistently been concerned with the social, political, and cultural contexts in which history paintings were created and initially viewed. In essence, they argue that an American history painting is at least as likely to reveal information about its creator and the time during which it was created as about the past realities it ostensibly presents.

If these writers share a general point of view about history painting, they also share several particular sub-stantive conclusions. For instance, they maintain that history paintings, far from being slavish recorders of "fact," are often creative and inventive. Gail Husch shows here how American history paintings in the mid-nineteenth century expressed the values of antebellum millennialism and republicanism. Barry Schwartz demonstrates how the image of Lincoln was altered over time to serve larger social purposes.

In such senses, these and other scholars assert, most American history paintings are broadly political. Their creators and disseminators advocated through them a way of looking at events for their prescriptive value. Ann Uhry Abrams has found this tendency present in some of the genre's first American expressions, the mural series in the United States Capitol begun by John Trumbull. By the Mexican War, as Ron Tyler shows, creators of history pictures were singularly sensitive to the ideology and priorities of the government in power.

American history painters tended to be conservatives, not radicals. And in their insistence on the value of clear narrative content and mimetic pictorial devices, they were stylistically conservative as well. They were also optimists, typically presenting their view of American history in pleasant shapes and cheerful colors. As Barbara Mitnick demonstrates here, this optimism arose at least partially from what the American public wanted to see. The vast majority of these artists, after all, created pictures for a living, for profit. American majoritarian cultural discourse determined where that profit could most likely be found.

But by the same token, as Matthew Baigell notes,

9. Lilly Martin Spencer. *War Spirit at Home (Celebrating the Victory at Vicksburg)*. 1866. 30 x 32¾" (76.2 x 82.6 cm.). The Newark Museum, Newark, New Jersey; purchase 1944 Wallace M. Scudder Bequest Fund.

10. Robert Stuart Duncanson. *Uncle Tom and Little Eva*. 1853. 27¼ x 38¼" (69.2 x 97.2 cm.). Detroit Institute of Arts, Detroit, Michigan; gift of Mrs. Jefferson Butler and Miss Grace R. Conover.

groups not at the center of discourse were often minimized, excluded, or poorly treated in these works. Nor were these groups represented in significant numbers among history painters. Almost no women painters specialized in the genre: Jennie Brownscombe is the notable exception (plates 14 and 126); only a few other women, such as Sarah Paxton Ball Dodson and Lilly Martin Spencer (plate 9), occasionally painted historical subjects. African-American artists producing paintings of historical scenes before 1930 were even rarer, largely due to the negligible opportunities available to black artists before the New Deal; those works that were created, such as Robert Duncanson's *Uncle Tom and Little Eva* (plate 10), nonetheless demonstrate the

strength of their vision. Certain native American groups had a well-developed tradition of recording historical events (plate 11), but before the 1930s their works were not widely disseminated outside the communities that produced them.

Until now, despite the resurgence of interest in the subject, no comprehensive exhibition devoted to American history painting has been presented. Fraunces Tavern Museum's *Picturing History: American Painting, 1770–1930*, which this publication accompanies, was thus organized to bring together these iconic views of the national past. The museum invited Barbara Mitnick, who had been guest curator of its 1989 exhibition *The Changing Image of George Washington*, to serve again

11. Irving Couse. *The Historian (Indian Brave Recording General Mackenzie's Fight with the Cheyenne)*. 1902. 35 x 46" (87.5 x 115.0 cm.). Private collection.

in that capacity. The original motivation for undertaking the *Picturing History* project came from the museum's desire to explore in more depth its own considerable collection of history paintings. Assembled over many decades by the museum's parent organization, Sons of the Revolution in the State of New York, the museum has large numbers of paintings by each of three artists, John Ward Dunsmore (plate 116), Harry Ogden (plate 12), and Henry Hintermeister (the last outside the time frame of this exhibition). Individual examples by several others are also in the collection; among these, two are particularly well known: Thomas Pritchard Rossiter's *Signing of the Constitution of the United States* (plate 93) and Dennis Malone Carter's *Molly Pitcher at the Battle of Monmouth* (plate 13). Both these paintings have excited the attention of many visitors, particularly those who recall the images from school texts. The museum's interpretive materials point out that these works were painted by artists who were born too late to have witnessed the events they portrayed and who relied upon longstanding European artistic conventions to give their protagonists a heroic cast. Nonetheless, many people leave the museum feeling that they have been in the presence of veritable "snapshots" of historical events.

This is not an isolated phenomenon. In history museums and historic sites across the nation, people tend to respond to history paintings as if they are eyewitness accounts. Visitors to the Patrick Henry Memorial in Virginia are awed by the size, majesty, and power of Peter F. Rothermel's *Patrick Henry before the Virginia House of Burgesses* (plate 51); Emanuel Leutze's grand and imposing *George Washington at the Battle of Monmouth* (plate 31) affects viewers similarly at Monmouth County Historical Association in New Jersey, as do Henry Sargent's *Landing of the Pilgrims* and Jennie Brownscombe's *First Thanksgiving* (plate 14) at Pilgrim Hall in Plymouth, Massachusetts. It is from these much later depictions of focal events that people receive their most lasting impressions, accurate or not. Decades after they were painted, these pictures still successfully accomplish what their creators set out to do—both consciously and unconsciously—to communicate, long after the

12. Harry Ogden. *The Star-Spangled Banner, Francis Scott Key Composing Our National Anthem, September 13, 1814.* N.d. Watercolor and goauche on paper. 26¾ x 21¼" (66.9 x 53.7 cm.). Fraunces Tavern Museum, New York.

13. Dennis Malone Carter. *Molly Pitcher
at the Battle of Monmouth.* 1854. 42 x 56"
(105.0 x 140.0 cm.). Fraunces Tavern
Museum, New York.

Overleaf:
14. Jennie A. Brownscombe. *First
Thanksgiving at Plymouth.* 1914. 28 x 44"
(70.0 x 110.0 cm.). The Pilgrim Society,
Plymouth, Massachusetts.

fact, a point of view about a certain person or event in particular and the American past in general. *Picturing History* examines this phenomenon by identifying and exploring the individual, social, and cultural contexts in which history paintings were created, placing them in a perspective in which their significance to American culture at large can be seen and assessed.[7]

On the other hand, to insist that American history paintings are important *only* as cultural artifacts of the time they were created would be as misguided as to take them at face value as factual representations of the events they purport to portray. For they operate both backward and forward in time. The backward-projecting documentary and commemorative functions are obvious, for earlier historical events are their narrative focus. Their forward-projecting function is more elusive, but arguably even more central. For in most

cases, as the following essays show, artists intended history paintings to convey both straightforward and subtle moral and spiritual messages to those who would later gaze upon them. They are rarely, if ever, philosophically neutral.

The black-or-white, good-versus-bad, morally didactic quality of history paintings is largely responsible for the antithetical reactions they may generate today. These works captivate people seeking the "eternal" verities they promote. They alienate relativists who reject such exclusive assertions as well as critics who believe that art should be morally neutral and express artists' individual inner states, not tell stories or promote causes. This inherent tension makes the study of American history paintings fascinating not only for what the paintings tell us about the past but for what they also reveal about the present—and about ourselves.

PICTURING HISTORY
American Painting 1770–1930

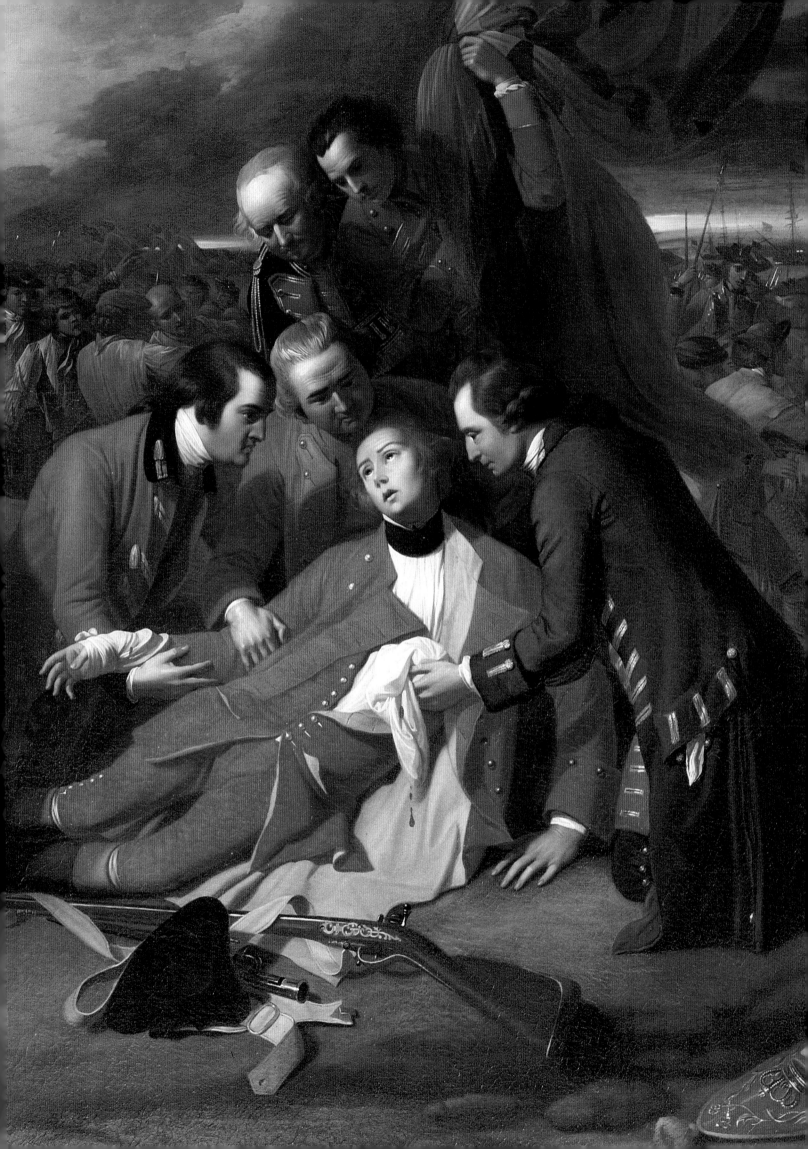

The History of History Painting

BARBARA J. MITNICK

The greatest work of the painter is the istoria.

> Leon Battista Alberti,
> Della pittura (1436)

In 1770 Benjamin West, an American-born painter living in England, created a large painting intended to commemorate an event that had occurred only eleven years earlier. On September 13, 1759, the British general James Wolfe had died in battle on the Plains of Abraham outside Quebec during the French and Indian Wars, a series of struggles between Great Britain and France over control of the North American interior.

West created *The Death of General Wolfe* (plate 17) as his major submission to the 1771 exhibition of England's Royal Academy. But King George III, clearly enamored of West's earlier history paintings—he would appoint the artist Historical Painter to the King only a year later—did not purchase the work.[1] Reportedly, George III felt West had compromised the dignity of the general's death by depicting modern military costume in the painting. According to John Galt, an early nineteenth-century biographer of West, the painter had in fact been admonished, as he created the work, to avoid contemporary detail: Dr. Robert Hay Drummond, Archbishop of York and one of West's patrons, had visited West's studio with Sir Joshua Reynolds, then president of the Royal Academy, where both told the painter, apparently in no uncertain terms, to "adopt the classic costume of antiquity."[2]

West is said to have replied that the scene took place in an area of the world "unknown to Greeks and Romans" and that, to do justice to his subject, he must therefore paint what he understood to be the truth. "The same truth that guides the pen of the historian should govern the pencil of the artist," Galt quoted West to have told them. "I consider myself as undertaking to tell this great event to the eye of the world; but if, instead of the facts of the transaction, I represent classical fictions, how shall I be understood by posterity!"[3]

According to the art historian Edgar Wind, Reynolds and other members of the Royal Academy "insisted with some justice that heroism is not an everyday occurrence, and they had feared that the presentation of heroic death in everyday dress would destroy respect for the hero in the spectator and deprive the latter of that feeling of reverence and astonishment, that sense of the extraordinary and marvellous, with which he ought to approach heroic deeds."[4] For centuries, the moral superiority of heroes had been signified by clothing them in the costumes of antiquity, but West was adamant. Though he was not the first to defy this convention, he wanted to merge the growing interest in historical veracity with the earlier heroic traditions of painting designed to present and transmit high moral content.

Nevertheless, in a conciliatory gesture, West is said to have assured Drummond and Reynolds that if they still disapproved of *The Death of General Wolfe* when it was finished, he would "consign it to the closet."[5] In the end, Galt reported that Reynolds was so impressed by the completed painting that he rescinded all prior reservations. "Mr. West has conquered," Reynolds is claimed to have declared. "He has treated his subject as it ought to be treated. I retract my objections against the introduction of any other circumstances into historical pictures than those which are requisite and appropriate." Reynolds further predicted that West's picture would "not only become one of the most popular, but occasion a revolution in art."[6]

This approach was not universally followed

Benjamin West. *The Death of General Wolfe*, detail of plate 17.

throughout Europe, however. In France (where, ironically, accurate costume had become an accepted feature of theatrical productions by the late eighteenth century), painters were slow to accept period dress in history painting; there, as James A. Leith has observed, academic art was still viewed as propaganda, a visual means of fortifying the authority of the state and of improving society.[7] Historical paintings in the grand style were often monumental works of heroic subjects, intended to inspire and uplift. They were also a reaction against the frivolity of the previously fashionable rococo style, which emphasized erotic imagery and had found great favor among the aristocracy. French critics had accordingly begun to call for painting to evince "moral and patriotic themes."[8]

As West was painting *The Death of General Wolfe* in London, Jacques-Louis David had just begun a career in Paris of painting figures in classical garb in settings of his own invention. His *Death of Socrates* (plate 15) shows a different attitude toward historical accuracy. Based on an episode in the fifth scene of Diderot's proposed pantomime drama of the event, David's painting represents Socrates surrounded by his students. He sits on a bed preparing to drink the hemlock, an act representing his rights as a free man who, though continuing to express respect for the rule of law, finds his independent views to have been declared unacceptable.[9]

Since the Renaissance, analogies had been drawn between antique and Christian themes, and some eighteenth-century writers had attempted to equate the death of Socrates with the Crucifixion of Christ.[10] Yet David may have modified his depiction of the event to accord instead with the wishes of a member of the Trudaine family, the patron of the work, whose mission was to establish that "Socrates, like Seneca, was proof that a high standard of morality could be achieved beyond the confines of Christianity."[11] David apparently received research assistance on the depiction, but he is said to have found the answers to his questions so complicated that he virtually ignored them. Instead, he looked to the works of earlier neoclassical artists to construct the event as his patron wished. David may have modeled the uplifted hand of Socrates after Raphael's *School of Athens* and may have adapted the work's sense of patterning from Poussin's first set of *Sacraments*.[12]

On viewing the painting in Paris, Sir Joshua Reynolds declared it the finest production of its kind.[13] In 1771, the very year in which West exhibited *The Death of General Wolfe* at the Royal Academy, Reynolds had emphasized in a series of discourses on art that the painter "must sometimes deviate from vulgar and strict historical truth, in pursuing the grandeur of his design."[14] Yet Reynolds, who could see both sides of the argument, had that year also approved the realism of West's *Death of General Wolfe*, even as he supported and later applauded the neoclassicism of Jacques-Louis David.

These works by West and David, and Reynolds's praise of them, represent the struggle of diverse tendencies in history painting, evident by the end of the eighteenth century and pronounced in secular historical representation in the United States by the end of the nineteenth. The roots of these tendencies lie in ancient

15. Jacques-Louis David.
The Death of Socrates.
1787. 59 x 78" (147.5 x
195.0 cm.). The
Metropolitan Museum of
Art, New York; Wolfe Fund.

16. Masaccio. *The Tribute Money*. ca. 1427. 100 x 235" (250.0 x 587.5 cm.). Brancacci Chapel, Santa Maria del Carmine, Florence.

and Renaissance times. And at other historical moments, the confluence of painters, patrons, and theorists of art helped establish these often-competing traditions as they defined the genre of history painting.

In ancient Egypt, rulers demanded that god-kings be glorified pictorially; in ancient Rome, the triumphs of the empire were depicted, and have survived, primarily in carvings on stone. In the Middle Ages, historical representation, mainly through sculpture, mosaics, and frescoes, was viewed as assisting the Church's effort to foster divine salvation. The illiterate could "read" and be inspired by these otherworldly and spiritual messages and in some degree could absorb biblical stories through art.

The placement of history painting at the apex of all artistic endeavor originated in fifteenth-century Renaissance Italy. Leon Battista Alberti, an architect by profession and a pioneering Renaissance theoretician, encouraged the pursuit of history painting in *Della pittura*, a guide for artists he published in 1436. Alberti emphasized the importance of the *istoria*—roughly, "history" or "story," or, as one scholar has put it, "a significant human action." Alberti used the term to identify an art of monumentality and a projection of emotion, not simply a work large in size or a mere illustration of an event. He declared the *istoria* to be "the chief business of a serious painter."[15] He stated further, "The *istoria* which merits both praise and admiration will be so agreeably and pleasantly attractive that it will capture the eye of whatever learned or unlearned person is looking at it and will move his soul."[16]

Alberti is thought to have learned from Latin authors that the artists of antiquity "sought to bestow an ideal beauty upon their works," and his interest in the *istoria* was clearly related to his interest in antiquity.[17] One modern translator of *Della pittura* has noted that Alberti encouraged "antique themes with human gestures to portray and project the emotions of the actors" and em-

phasized that "no doubt Alberti's education and his desire to impress the prospective patron account in large measure for his emphasis on antiquity."[18]

The ideals of the ancients enjoyed a significant revival in Italy during the Renaissance, an era that continued to emphasize the primacy of religious belief. The theme of civic virtue, for example, was taken up by one of the great humanists of the day, Leonardo Bruni. Bruni, who also served in the curia of Pope Boniface IX and Pope Innocent VII, began work on a *History of the Florentine People* in 1415, and in 1428, during his term as chancellor of the City of Florence, he composed an oration equating Florence with ancient Athens.[19]

This rebirth of interest in the antique affected not only the subject matter of painting but also its stylistic conceptions. Donatello's sculptural representation of anatomically accurate figures standing in poses reminiscent of classical *contrapposto* was an early expression of this influence, as was the balanced and harmoniously conceived architecture of Brunelleschi. The influence of the antique soon affected painting as well. Figures took their places in religious, military, and mythological narratives within accurate settings composed according to the newly "invented" scientific perspective. The Church and wealthy noble families patronized artists creating these new works. The fine arts began to take their place among the liberal arts, and the artist, no longer regarded as an artisan manipulating materials to produce simple "handiwork," became a man of ideas.

The Florentine painter Masaccio revolutionized history painting with *The Tribute Money* (plate 16), painted in about 1427 as part of a series of frescoes commissioned for the Brancacci Chapel of Santa Maria del Carmine. *The Tribute Money* displays the New Testament account of Christ sending Peter to catch a fish, retrieve the tribute (or tax) money from its mouth, and then pay the tax collector.[20] Masaccio's fresco aimed to inform and inspire the churchgoer by presenting a "continuous narra-

17. Benjamin West.
*The Death of
General Wolfe*.
1776 version. 75 x
110" (187.5 x 275.0
cm.). William L.
Clements Library,
University of
Michigan, Ann
Arbor.

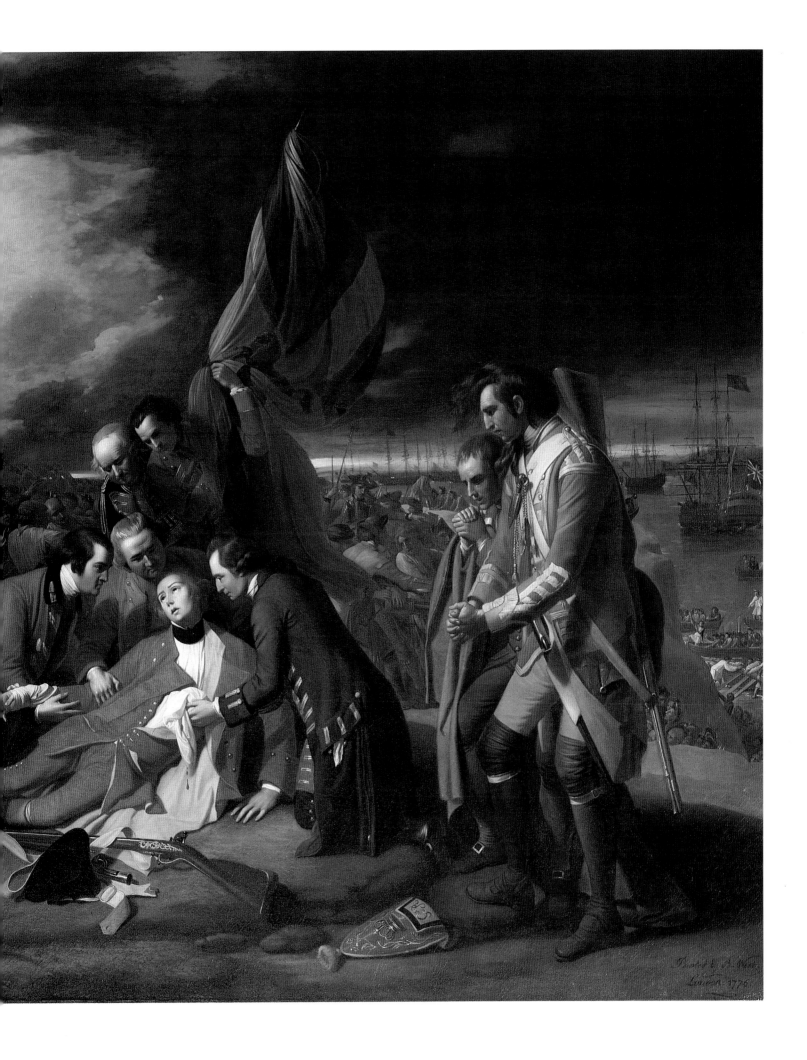

18. Sandro Botticelli. *The Birth of Venus*. ca. 1480. 69 x 110" (172.5 x 275.0 cm.). Uffizi Gallery, Florence.

tive," a series of related events in biblical history. But the impulse to represent the scene accurately is evident in the work's scientifically measurable perspective, its anatomically correct figures, and its depiction of costume that early Renaissance thinkers considered appropriate to an ancient context. Masaccio died at the age of twenty-seven, before *Della pittura* was written, but his understanding of human anatomy and the laws of perspective clearly influenced Alberti's theory, which in turn guided other artists of the Renaissance.

The depiction of military events earned its place in *istoria* with Paolo Uccello's *Battle of San Romano*, believed to have been commissioned by Cosimo de' Medici in 1456 as part of the decorative scheme for the bedroom of Lorenzo de' Medici.[21] The Medici family and its circle of humanists also commissioned Sandro Botticelli's *Birth of Venus* (plate 18), a painting that exemplifies the perception that mythology, the literature of the ancients, was a legitimate subject for history painting. Intended to decorate the interior of the Villa di Castello, *The Birth of Venus* depicts the goddess as she is borne on a shell from the sea, According to E. H. Gombrich, Botticelli's mythological iconography was inspired by the Neoplatonic writings of the humanist Marsilio Ficino, who believed the goddess symbolized both virtue and humanity. Venus's image, associated with erotic love, was reconciled to the humanism of the fifteenth century by being linked instead with Christian love, charity, and "the birth of beauty."[22] Classical form, which had influenced painting since the fourteenth century, and classical content were thus permitted to merge.

Another significant development in the genre is em-bodied in Raphael's *School of Athens* (plate 19), commissioned by Pope Julius II for his private apartment in Rome, the Stanza della Segnatura. According to Giorgio Vasari, the sixteenth-century biographer of artists, *The School of Athens* depicted a "scene of theologians reconciling Philosophy and Astrology with Theology: wherein are portraits of all the sages in the world disputing in various ways."[23] Diogenes appears with his cup, Aristotle with the *Ethics* in his hand, Plato with the *Timaeus*. The Duke of Mantua, the architect Bramante, Zoroaster, and Raphael himself are also portrayed in the painting. The antique is venerated as the picture extols the triumphant "rebirth" of antiquity: the philosophers of ancient Greece are shown to occupy the same ground as the geniuses of the Italian Renaissance.

Within less than a century, from Masaccio's *Tribute Money* to Raphael's *School of Athens*, both the forms and content of grand-style history painting were established. Encouraged by the theoreticians of the early Renaissance and supported by the Church, its donors, and the nobility, Renaissance artists sowed the seeds of modern history painting as they generated the tensions that stimulated its growth.

History painting was elevated to new heights of critical estimation in 1668, when French theoretician André Félibien enunciated an actual hierarchy of subject matter and placed the genre at its summit. In his *Conferences de l'Académie Royale de peinture et de sculpture pendant l'année 1667*, Félibien asserted that still life (*nature morte*) was the lowest form of painting; next he placed landscape, then the depiction of animals (positioned higher because they are animate), then portrai-

19. Raphael. *The School of Athens.*
1509–11. Baseline 303" (757.5 cm.).
Stanza della Segnatura, The Vatican,
Rome.

ture, and finally what he referred to as the *grand peinture*, his term for history painting. To Félibien, the history painter was virtually the earthly counterpart of God: as God's most perfect creation was man, the painter who portrays human figures in history was thus the next step from creation.[24]

In Félibien's estimation, the painter Nicolas Poussin was the epitome of artistic virtue, a new Raphael who had assimilated the best that the artists of antiquity had to offer.[25] Poussin's *Israelites Gathering the Manna* (plate 20) was to Félibien the supreme example of unity of action and of the apt portrayal of expression, drawing, and proportion. The Church was still the most important patron of art in seventeenth-century France, yet Poussin received only one major commission from it, an altarpiece for St. Peter's through Cardinal Barberini, nephew of Pope Urban VIII. Poussin's career illustrates instead the growing importance of private patronage. Such patrons as Cassiano dal Pozzo and later Jacques Stella and Paul Fréart de Chantelou amassed impressive painting collections during this period, and Chantelou in particular was enamored of Poussin's work. His support gave Poussin financial and aesthetic independence, which had no small effect on his art. The broad and relaxed composition of *The Israelites Gathering the Manna* may reflect this sense of freedom.

Later French painters emulated Poussin's neoclassicism, a feature that, by the end of the eighteenth century, distinguished their history paintings from those of their English counterparts. Even though Poussin's work shows, as one art historian has put it, a "passion for accuracy," Poussin substituted what appears to be a European countryside for the biblical desert in *The Israelites Gathering the Manna*, a practice widely regarded as acceptable poetic license in the effort to create a historical scene that would please its patron.[26]

Only two years after the appearance of Poussin's *Israelites Gathering the Manna*, the Spanish artist Diego Velázquez produced *The Surrender at Breda* (plate 21), often thought of as the first modern history painting. Although the legacy of heroism and grandiose representation of the earlier period informed this monumental work, Velázquez placed a new emphasis on more accurate settings, historical accounts, and life models.

Painter to King Philip IV since the early 1620s, Velázquez concentrated on works of history and mythology after being freed from the demands of patrons who preferred religious themes.[27] In 1634 he began work on paintings for Philip IV's new palace, the Buen Retiro. For the walls of the great Hall of the Realms, the original throne room, Velázquez painted *The Surrender at Breda* (also known as *Las Lanzas*, The Lances), as part of a series related to Philip's military victories.[28] The painting depicts the 1626 Spanish triumph over the Dutch at Breda, the highly fortified gateway to Holland.[29] Velázquez's painting captures the spirit of the battle, a victory won after a long winter of conflict, and accurately depicts the topography of the battleground. But the artist enhanced the appearances of the Spanish soldiers, who by at least one account were battle-weary

20. Nicolas Poussin. *The Israelites Gathering the Manna*. 1637. 59 x 80" (149 x 200 cm.). Musée du Louvre, Paris.

21. Diego Velàzquez. *The Surrender at Breda [Las Lanzas]*. 1639–41. 102¾ x 144½" (301.8 x 361.2 cm.). The Prado, Madrid.

and miserable at the time of the Dutch surrender.[30] Pictured with lances in the midst of a surrender ceremony, the soldiers in the painting symbolize the strength of the Spaniards. But the defeated Dutch troops are not shown kneeling in an act of submission, as was formerly the convention, and Spanish commander Ambrosio Spinola instead lays his hand on the shoulder of the vanquished Justin of Nassau rather than immediately taking the city's keys. Velázquez thus transformed the surrender into an act of "clemency and magnanimity," reflecting the seventeenth-century desire (not always fulfilled) for courtesy in such circumstances.

Scholars have suggested that Velázquez saw the scene as a drama, a fleeting moment of history, and intended through the painting to transform the whole "dreary history of surrender scenes in art." By making Spinola a gracious and charitable victor, Velázquez revealed his belief that "victories of arms make a king powerful; clemency and magnanimity made him great."[31] In *The Surrender at Breda*, Velázquez successfully melded accurate detail with the heroic purposes of history painting (and the interests of his patron).

Still, though eighteenth-century writers of historical literature made an attempt to "approach traditional heroes with an air of familiarity," it remained an "offense against good taste" to paint heroes who looked too much like themselves, who were represented as familiar figures. As Wind has noted, "While the Academicians refused to depict ordinary men as heroes, the new historians re-

fused to believe in heroes who could not be depicted as ordinary men."[32] It was a problem in need of a solution, and the "test case"—indeed, the painting that eventually had the greatest impact on the subsequent course of the genre—was West's *Death of General Wolfe*.

Born in Pennsylvania in 1738, West studied with a local artist before becoming a portrait painter in Philadelphia. In his twenties he traveled to Europe and studied for three years in Italy, where he was reportedly impressed by the anatomical correctness of the classical subjects depicted by Anton Raphael Mengs and Gavin Hamilton.[33] In 1763 he settled in London, where his accomplishments as a history painter ultimately earned him not only the position of Historical Painter to the King but also, in 1792, appointment as second president (following Reynolds) of the Royal Academy of the Arts.

Throughout the 1760s, West painted works depicting classical subjects, such as *Agrippina Landing at Brundisium with the Ashes of Germanicus* and, for the collection of George III, *The Departure of Regulus* and *The Oath of Hannibal*. His 1770 *Death of General Wolfe*, replicated three times, successfully mediated the tensions between "truth" in history painting and heroic grandeur.

West certainly relied upon grand-manner conventions in some aspects of the work. Its composition, as historian Simon Schama has noted, resembles more a religious lamentation in the form of a pietà than a scene at the conclusion of a battle, and, indeed, West had been exposed

37

22. John Singleton Copley. Study for
*The Death of the Earl of Chatham in the
House of Lords.* 1779. 21 x 25½" (52.5 x
63.7 cm.). National Gallery of Art,
Washington, D.C., gift of Mrs. Gordon
Dexter.

Facing page:
23. John Singleton Copley. *The Death of
Major Peirson, 6 January 1781.*
1782–1784. 99 x 144"
(247.5 x 360.0 cm.). The
Tate Gallery, London.

to sculptural lamentations during his Italian travels.[34] But his own patriotism appears to have inspired his interest in historical accuracy; West may have found sources for his depictions of clothing in costumes with appropriate period detail designed for eighteenth-century dramatic productions in both England and France.[35] Velázquez had depicted contemporary military dress in *The Surrender at Breda*, but West was the first in eighteenth-century England to give pictorial expression to what art historian Allen Staley has identified as "a slackening of the belief in the moral superiority of classical antiquity."[36]

The waning of this conviction was apparent in the fact that critics and patrons of the day were receptive to *The Death of General Wolfe*; its replicas were never "consigned to the closet" but found ready buyers—including, ultimately, King George III himself, who appears to have come around to the value of accurate detail much as Reynolds had. Like other European heads of state, George III found in historical painting an apt vehicle to record and celebrate the military victories of his empire. And, reaffirming Félibien's seventeenth-century hierarchy, Reynolds in his late eighteenth-century discourses on art declared history painting to be the highest form of subject matter to which an artist could aspire.[37]

Despite the success of West's *Death of General Wolfe*, David's *Death of Socrates,* a classically inspired representation intended to edify and inspire the viewer without recourse to historic fidelity, was equally well received. History painters of the last two hundred years thus inherited a genre that embraced both these intentions, which were more often than not opposing.

John Singleton Copley tried to build on West's foundation. After a successful early career primarily in portraiture, increasing hostility between Britain and the American colonies brought a decline in Copley's portrait commissions in Boston, and his family ties to England made it uncomfortable for him to remain in Massachusetts. By the time Copley reached London in 1774, West's *Death of General Wolfe* had been exhibited and accepted by critics and patrons, and he learned that West had profited greatly from the engraving produced after the work. Undoubtedly, Copley was also well aware of Reynolds's recently published views on history painting. It was clear that paintings combining national historical subjects with graphic power would be popular.[38]

In 1778, the year Copley painted his unusual *Watson and the Shark*, William Pitt, Earl of Chatham, collapsed in the House of Lords during a debate on the war with America. This event stimulated Copley to create a monumental documentary history painting that included a major group portrait. Despite the lack of a patron, he spent more than two years creating drawings of all the participants in the scene and establishing the nature of the composition. *The Death of the Earl of Chatham in*

24. John Trumbull. *The Sortie Made by the Garrison of Gibraltar*. 1787. 15⅛ x 22⅛" (37.8 x 55.3 cm.). The Corcoran Gallery of Art, Washington, D.C.; museum purchase, Gallery Fund.

25. John Vanderlyn. *The Death of Jane McCrea.* 1804. 32 x 26½" (80.0 x 66.2 cm.). Wadsworth Atheneum, Hartford, Connecticut; museum purchase.

the House of Lords (plate 22) seems to lack the drama of West's *Death of General Wolfe*, and sales of prints of the work did not match Copley's expectations. Yet it did much to establish Copley's reputation in London.

The Death of the Earl of Chatham also reflects Copley's interest in portraying figures, settings, and costumes accurately, and like West he melded his own sense of narrative to the "truth" of the event. At the same time, the lighting, balance of composition, and gestures all show the influence of the neoclassicists. The painting prompted noted London art entrepreneur John Boydell to commission *The Death of Major Peirson, 6 January 1781* (plate 23), which Copley completed by 1784. In this painting as well, Copley interpreted the actual event somewhat loosely for the sake of the composition, although the fact that he prepared seventeen sketches and studies for the work suggests his overall intention to document the event carefully. Yet Copley also saw instructive, even propagandistic, potential in a work that showed Peirson, a British officer, being killed as his compatriots endeavored to subdue the invading French in a battle on the Isle of Jersey.

A number of West's American students, including John Trumbull, developed the history painting genre in the United States after the Revolution. While still in England, Trumbull had painted scenes of European history. Reportedly at the suggestion of West, who had lost a commission to Copley from the London Court of Common Council to paint *The Siege of Gibraltar*, Trumbull created several versions of *The Sortie Made by the Garrison of Gibraltar* (plate 24).[39]

Trumbull's choice of the daring sortie and destruction by fire of the Spanish forces showed his interest in depicting scenes involving personal heroism. Knowing the appeal of such depictions to the British audience, Trumbull created the painting without a commission to do so, because he believed it would help establish his reputation. According to art historian Jules Prown, "Trumbull said he was offered 1200 guineas for the picture (an extraordinarily high sum, if accurate), but he declined, thinking, incorrectly, as it turned out, that he would realize greater profit by exhibiting the picture, taking a subscription for prints, and then selling the painting later."[40]

Trumbull's three-part composition—showing the attack at left, the dying Spanish officer Don José de Barboza at center, and a group of British officers at right—may possibly have been influenced as well by Copley's *Death of Major Peirson*. Evidence also suggests that Trumbull relied on antique sculpture as models for some of the figures.[41]

Trumbull's great contribution during the late eighteenth and early nineteenth centuries was his role in establishing the subject matter of grand-style American history painting, an opportunity that neither West nor Copley, both permanent residents of England, had tak-

en. In the 1780s, Trumbull, again on his own, began to devote his energies to the portrayal of events of the War for Independence. He produced *The Death of General Warren at the Battle of Bunker's Hill, June 17, 1775* (plate 133) and *The Death of General Montgomery in the Attack on Quebec, December 31, 1775,* whose basic composition recalls that of West's *Death of General Wolfe.*[42] Both works exhibit the neoclassical influence to which Trumbull had been exposed during his travels in France in the late 1780s. But the accuracy of the portraiture and costume reveals the heritage of Benjamin West.

John Vanderlyn was similarly interested in neoclassical composition, as well as in figures whose delineation resembles the balance and harmonious movement of antique sculpture. Born in 1775 in Kingston, New York, Vanderlyn studied art at the Columbian Academy in New York, worked as Gilbert Stuart's assistant in 1796, and traveled to Paris later that year to study under François André Vincent at the École des Beaux-Arts. In 1804, while still in France, Vanderlyn painted *The Death of Jane McCrea* (plate 25), inspired by the story of an American woman who traveled through enemy lines during the Revolution to find her English fiancé. McCrea had been shot by two Mohawk Indians, who took her scalp to British General John Burgoyne for a reward. For Americans, the painting was a symbol of the national suffering under British aggression, a subject that inspired not only Joel Barlow's poem *Columbiad* but other contemporary poems and ballads.[43]

Like West before him, Vanderlyn chose a contemporary subject for history painting, but unlike West his inspiration was clearly the antique and French neoclassical traditions. When it was completed in 1804, *The Death of Jane McCrea* was accepted for exhibition at the Paris Salon. According to art historian Samuel Y. Edgerton, the work was "the first indigenous American history [painting] ever to be accepted" for this annual exhibition; it was viewed as "sufficiently Davidian in composition and anti-English by implication to win academic approval."[44] Edgerton has also suggested that Vanderlyn's figure of McCrea may have been based on Niobe or Hersilia stretched between Romulus and Tatius. Other scholars, such as Kathleen Pritchard, have equated McCrea's pose with antique marble figures in the *Kneeling Venus* and those of the Indians with antique fauns or the figures in David's *Oath of the Horatii.*[45] After its exhibition at the Salon, Vanderlyn shipped *The Death of Jane McCrea* to New York for exhibition at the Academy of Fine Arts, where he hoped it would contribute to an elevation of taste in America.

Still, Americans in the early nineteenth century were groping for a satisfactory definition and national character for the fine arts. This goal remained elusive even into the 1820s. In a lecture at the New York Atheneum in 1826, Samuel F. B. Morse declared, "As in national character we combine the various traits of the many nations of which we are composed, so in regard to the Fine Arts we have as yet no decided character, no truly distinctive American school of Art."[46] Indeed, the scarcity of American patrons inhibited the development of such a school. No national church could emerge as a source of support for American artists, and few private collectors existed in the early nineteenth century. Public patronage (primarily by the federal government) was virtually the only source of support.

An apparatus for training artists began to emerge by the 1820s, and with it a theoretical posture that reiterated the principles Reynolds and Félibien had earlier propounded. In a review of the second annual exhibition of the recently founded National Academy of Design (over which Morse presided), Daniel Fanshaw asserted that "that department or that work of art should rank the highest which required the greatest exercise of mind, or, in other words . . . mental is superior to manual labor."[47] Fanshaw divided the highest category of artistic endeavor into three parts—the Epic, the Dramatic, and the Historic. Poussin's *The Sacraments* he termed "dramatic," while Copley's *Death of the Earl of Chatham* was a "historic" work, one Fanshaw defined as portraying a "fact, an event; its characters may be ideal, provided truth is observed in time, place and custom, and . . . it records an event which has happened; the event, not the persons are principal."[48]

The nature of patronage also began to broaden. Vanderlyn's *Death of Jane McCrea* was reportedly purchased by Robert Fulton, whom Barlow had commissioned to illustrate his *Columbiad*. Fulton turned the task over to Vanderlyn, who created the final composition.[49] As West had created *The Death of General Wolfe* to show at the Royal Academy in England, American artists began to produce works that might be featured in the annual exhibitions of the National Academy of Design in New York and, later, of such organizations as The American Art-Union, formed in 1839.[50] A network of art dealers and entrepreneurs also arose, inspired by the vision of profit from paintings of historical subjects and engravings produced after them.

In the nineteenth century, the heritage of accurate representation West had established found a receptive audience in the United States, where portraiture had long emphasized specificity and actual fact. One 1843 issue of *Graham's Magazine* expressed this preoccupation with truth. "To falsify the truth of history in paintings is no less a crime, if willful, no less proof of total incapacity, if accidental, in an artist, than the same defects would be in a writer," the author declared.[51]

By the middle of the nineteenth century, another European influence began to be felt in paintings of American historical scenes as American artists trained in Düsseldorf began to exhibit their works. Art historian William H. Gerdts has noted that this cultural exchange with the painters of the German city "was the single most essential ingredient for the fullest expression" of history painting in this country.[52] Beginning in 1826, after Wilhelm von Schadow became director of the Düsseldorf Art Academy, the school began to teach the principles of a strict form of neoclassicism, influenced by the paintings of early nineteenth-century Nazarenes based in Rome and infused with the sensibility of religious art of the fifteenth-century Italian Renaissance. Artistic training particularly emphasized the neoclassicism of Raphael and Jacques-Louis David.[53]

Americans began to arrive in Düsseldorf about 1840, but few seemed interested in the religious, allegorical, and other works that found favor at the academy. They came mainly for the formal training in drawing from the antique and from life and in painting in the grand manner.[54] Paintings by the Düsseldorf artists became available in the United States in 1849, when John Godfrey Boker opened the Düsseldorf Gallery of Fine Arts in New York.[55] One of the American artists whose works Boker often exhibited was Emanuel Leutze, who had been born in Germany and brought to America as a child. Leutze had returned to study history painting at Düsseldorf and went on to paint important works of American and Columbian history as well as scenes from English Tudor and Stuart periods. Although by midcentury several history painters had begun to include humanized historic characters and elements of genre, Leutze chose to continue the grand-style tradition begun in America by earlier painters. With the benefit of the discipline and emphasis on color of his Düsseldorf training, he was able to paint dramatic canvases, several of which he sent to America for exhibition.[56]

Several influences must have been present when Leutze painted his famous *Washington Crossing the Delaware* of 1851 (plate 30). The painting demonstrates his awareness of the grand-style approaches of West, Copley, and Trumbull. Leutze also appears to have equated Germany's contemporary struggles with the American fight for independence. Barbara Groseclose has called the painting "both a historical symbol and a brilliant metaphor for psychological encouragement." The *Literary World* pronounced it "incomparably the best painting yet executed for an American subject."[57] Crowds flocked to see the painting when it was sent from Düsseldorf for exhibition at Goupil's Gallery in New York. It was later exhibited to similar acclaim at the Capitol's Rotunda.

Later American history painters composed works according to the tradition encouraged by Benjamin West or Jacques-Louis David or, like Leutze, created paintings that combined these influences. And with Leutze, they created a veritable archive upon which much of our understanding of the past is based.

The Landing of the Fathers

Representing the National Past in American History Painting, 1770–1865

WENDY GREENHOUSE

The breaking waves dash'd high
On a stern rock-bound coast,
And the woods against a stormy sky
Their giant branches toss'd;
And the heavy night hung dark
The hills and water o'er
When a band of exiles moor'd their bark
On the wild New England shore.[1]

The perilous landing of the Pilgrim Fathers on Plymouth Rock, as enshrined in Felicia Hemans's famous poem of 1826, offers an apt metaphor for the arrival of national history as the premier subject of American history painting: both subject and medium were as fraught with perils as they were apparently inevitable. While the portrayal of events from the history of the New World is associated with the founding of American history painting, full critical and popular acceptance of such subjects took more than half a century. That this is not entirely obvious has much to do with the fact that such landmarks of American history painting as Benjamin West's *Penn's Treaty with the Indians* (plate 6), John Trumbull's *Declaration of Independence* (plate 42), and Emanuel Leutze's *Washington Crossing the Delaware* (plate 30) have evolved into ubiquitous monuments virtually synonymous with the events they depict.

The dominance of national history in American history painting partly awaited the development of conditions that fostered artistic life in general. A growing taste for images of the more imaginative sort—from ideal landscape to religious, literary, and historical subjects—went hand-in-hand with the gradual accumulation of the apparatus of artistic sophistication: art academies,

regular exhibitions, interested private patrons, critics and journals, art unions and reproductive engravings, and opportunities for study abroad. But acceptance of national fathers as the preeminent subject of American history painting depended additionally on factors that stand outside the traditional context of American art history, among them a changing conception of the American past and the rise of national history subjects in European painting.

Founding fathers actually figured in American history painting from its birth. Though working in England, Benjamin West and John Singleton Copley, themselves the founding fathers of American history painting, made their mark by depicting recent events that had occurred on their native soil. These artists' distinctly American self-identity in the midst of English artistic and political life contributed to their openness not only to a new range of specific subjects, but, through their portrayal, to a redefinition of the genre itself. In the eighteenth century, history painting was rigidly codified to include only subjects thought to communicate universal truths and models of moral conduct—specifically, classical and biblical history or modern history rendered as classical allegory.[2] With his *Death of General Wolfe* (plate 17), West effected a "revolution in the art" of history painting by using the artistic conventions of the grand manner to ennoble an unconventional subject, an event that was not only obviously contemporary but set in distant backwaters of the British Empire. The image combined an unprecedented degree of accuracy in the rendering of costume and the figures' facial features with a largely apocryphal arrangement of officers that evokes the deposition of Christ. In its reverential and referential

26. Charles Willson Peale. *George Washington at the Battle of Princeton.* 1779–1782. 95¼ x 61¾" (238.1 x 154.4 cm.). Princeton University Libraries, Princeton, New Jersey.

27. Benjamin West. *The Death of the Chevalier Bayard.* 1772. 87¼ x 70½" (221.7 x 179.1 cm.). Her Majesty Queen Elizabeth II.

treatment of its subject, *The Death of General Wolfe* evinced the global importance of events in the remote New World—in this case, the battle that decided the British dominance of North America—and offered a model for their dignified treatment in grand-manner history painting.[3]

Later in his remarkable career, West's conspicuous position as official history painter to King George III deterred him from portraying the great events of the American Revolution, a plan that he encouraged his student John Trumbull to pursue in his stead.[4] But beginning in 1772 with *The Death of the Chevalier Bayard* (plate 27), West pioneered another new source of subjects: national history from the Middle Ages through the seventeenth century.[5] By the mid-eighteenth century, the medieval period, traditionally regarded both as morally barbaric and visually uninteresting, was beginning to interest not only historians and antiquarians but architects, authors, and artists. The American history painters in England used it as the opportunity to expand the possibilities of history painting by applying the genre to unprecedented subjects. West's series of works illustrating the career of Edward III, painted for the king in the 1780s, applied a new level of historical rigor to the depiction of this largely unfamiliar period of history. In the twelfth-century English ruler, with whom George III personally identified, West found an *exemplum virtutis* to rival

time-honored heroes of antiquity, such as Regulus and Germanicus, whose stories he had already pictured.

West's national history paintings expanded the bounds of appropriate subject matter for history painting without challenging the genre's traditional emphasis on the character of the great hero as a model for posterity. By contrast, John Singleton Copley's *Charles I Demanding in the House of Commons the Five Impeached Members* (plate 28) commemorated a specific, significant *event*: the moment when the conflict between the absolutist monarch and an assertive parliament solidified and the path toward civil war seemed set. Every educated Englishman recognized the scene as a turning point in the development of constitutional government; thus the scene spoke to a collective consciousness of the history of a people, rather than to individual moral sensibility. Copley's choice of subject and approach reflected growing popular interest in national history and in the pictorial re-creation of important moments that shaped it. Significantly, while West's Edward III series was a commission from a traditional patron of history painting, the king, Copley created his *Charles I* for the art audience of the future as it emerged in the second half of the eighteenth century: a middle- and upper-class public willing to pay to attend exhibitions of works of art.[6]

By the end of the eighteenth century, national history

achieved unprecedented popularity in English history
painting. The illustrations in Robert Bowyer's ambitious
edition of David Hume's *History of England*, published
in 1812, foreshadowed dramatic changes in history
painting that would occur in the next few decades.[7]
While Hume's text was a rather dry, analytical recount-
ing of events, the illustrations brought out the dramatic
moments and gave full play to the stories and emotions
of individuals, particularly women. Thus, for example, a
rather static image of Oliver Cromwell demonstrating
his respect for English law and convention by refusing
the crown was overshadowed by a larger engraving after Robert Tresham's *Daughter of Cromwell Urging Him
to Repentance* (plate 29), an imaginative rendering of a
moment devoid of historic significance but replete with
emotional conflict and deathbed drama. In Britain and
Europe, the national past had come into its own as a
saga as colorful and riveting as the historical fiction it
was beginning to inspire.

In America, the sensationalism of English Romantic
history painting had little relevance for the successors of
West and Copley. Artistic and intellectual conditions in
the new republic were notoriously unfriendly to the fine
arts in general and history painting in particular. Both
critics and supporters applied a stringent test of moral
utility to imaginative art, whose appropriate role in the
new republic—if any—was to promote national unity,

30. Emanuel Leutze. *Washington Crossing the Delaware*. 1851.
149 x 255" (372.5 x 637.5 cm.). The Metropolitan Museum of Art,
New York; gift of John S. Kennedy.

civic identity, and moral conduct.[8] This sober outlook perpetuated the influence of West and the tradition of didacticism and stylistic neoclassicism, and it reaffirmed the traditional dominance of the portrait, which now seemed peculiarly suited to the aim of using history as uplifting example. Charles Willson Peale's *George Washington at the Battle of Princeton* (plate 26), for instance, was commissioned in the hope that it would not only preserve the appearance of the great hero, but that "the contemplation of it may excite others to tread in the same glorious and disinterested steps which led to public happiness and private honor."[9] John Trumbull most fully applied this formula in the realm of history painting: his grand project to commemorate the American Revolution presented the birth of the new nation as a rational, "bloodless" operation of abstract principle and legal procedure.[10] Even Trumbull's battle scenes adhere faithfully to the formula used so successfully by both West and Copley for such works: personalizing the conflict in the noble death of an heroic exemplum. As in West's *Death of General Wolfe* and Copley's *Death of Major Peirson* (plates 17 and 23), Trumbull's *Death of General Warren at the Battle of Bunker's Hill* (plate 133) pictures the demise of the hero rather than the conflict itself, thus downplaying the significance of the historical event in favor of the didactic value of the individual's conduct.

The survival of this conservative approach was the product not only of artistic conditions and attitudes, but of a distinctly American attitude toward the national past. From the outset, as Trumbull's history paintings suggest, Americans invested their history with a sense of noble mission. In Europe and Britain, the era of romantic nationalism saw the birth of popular identification with centuries-old national histories. But in America national self-identity had always included a consciousness of the brief national past. In particular, in Puritan New England, later the birthplace of the founding school of national history writing, settlements were established in the conviction of a providential appointment with destiny. The Puritan "errand into the wilderness" was the resolution of the divine plan for humankind, and it made America, according to J. H. Plumb, "the tribunal before which all history was to be judged."[11] The founding of God's righteous empire on American shores was invested with awful momentousness, representing the end of human history and the birth of a post-historical world truly modeled on the divine plan. New England Puritans Cotton Mather and William Bradford's arguments to this effect amount to the first histories of America produced on these shores.[12] Since then, as Frank Wesley Craven has noted, "the American community has consistently looked to its origins for an explanation of its distinctive qualities and thus for an indication of what its future should hold."[13] In this sense, history has always been integral to American culture—informing even the characteristic American impulse to focus on the future.

The special sense of mission had a direct impact on the imaging of the American past as it emerged in the first half of the nineteenth century and is reflected in two major preoccupations that dominate American history painting. The first is the almost too obvious theme of American superiority, often embodied in an individual hero as the representative of national virtue (or at least the hegemony of largely Protestant whites).[14] The past was so heavily invested with the burden of national superiority that it was virtually unthinkable to picture it negatively—as was demonstrated by the severe criticism that met Leutze's *George Washington at the Battle of Monmouth* (plate 31), perhaps the era's sole image of the father of his country in an undignified moment.[15] Whether Americans pictured themselves landing on these shores, battling the British for independence, or conquering the wilderness, invariably they appear as the upholders of superior values, forwarding a cause vindicated by subsequent events and national mission.[16]

The second, though not equally universal, preoccupation of antebellum portrayals of the American past is the theme of original moment. The very limitation necessarily imposed by the medium's single frame, in fact, peculiarly favored the American tendency to conceive the national past in terms of significant individual birth-events. A series of dramatic departures, landings, arrivals, and discoveries, symbolic touchstones of the nation's destiny, implied that America itself was an apocalyptic revelation to mankind.[17] Of John Trumbull's four panels for the Capitol Rotunda, only *The Declaration of Independence* describes an initiatory moment, but all four of the panels that later joined them fit this formula. John Vanderlyn's *Landing of Columbus* and William Henry Powell's *Discovery of the Mississippi by De Soto, A.D. 1541* (plates 48 and 49) both deal with literal arrivals; Robert Walter Weir's *Embarkation of the Pilgrims at Delft Haven, Holland, July 22nd, 1620* (plate 47), in which the Pilgrims reaffirm their pact with God, anticipates their arrival in his kingdom more than it sounds the theme of departure; and even John Gadsby Chapman's *The Baptism of Pocahontas at Jamestown, Virginia, 1613* (plate 46) pictures a spiritual, if not a physical, arrival: the Indian princess's acceptance of the blessings of Christianity prefigures the spiritual transformation of an entire continent.

Landings, in fact, are the subject of some of the earliest portrayals of the national history produced in the new republic. In 1800 Boston engraver Samuel Hill created a humble and inaccurate image of the landing of the Pilgrim Fathers for an invitation to the first meeting of the Sons of the Pilgrims.[18] Henry Sargent, a pupil of West, undertook an ambitious painting of the subject in

31. Emanuel Leutze. *George Washington at the Battle of Monmouth.* 1857. 52 x 87" (130.0 x 217.5 cm.). Monmouth County Historical Association; Freehold, New Jersey; gift of the descendants of David Leavitt.

32. Peter F. Rothermel. *The Landing of
the Pilgrims at Plymouth Rock.* 1854.
41⅛ x 54⅞" (102.8 x 137.2 cm.). Kirby
Collection of Historical Paintings,
Lafayette College, Easton, Pennsylvania.

33. Frederick Kemmelmeyer. *First Landing of Christopher Columbus.* 1800–1805. 27⅜ x 36½" (69.0 x 91.25 cm.). © 1992 National Gallery of Art, Washington, D.C.; gift of Edgar William and Bernice Chrysler Garbisch.

1815. Mrs. Hemans's famous poem, published in 1826, provided the direct inspiration for the culminating image of the Pilgrims' arrival, Peter F. Rothermel's painting of 1854 (plate 32). By that point, the landing of God's elect at Plymouth Rock stood on its own as a powerful symbol of original mission for Americans. The voyage of the *Mayflower,* as recounted in one typical children's history of New England, assumes epic significance as we "behold . . . the political and religious destiny of all America, lodged in one frail ship, tossed on the angry waves of a stormy ocean!"[19] Equally popular among artists was the landing of Columbus, in depictions ranging from Frederick Kemmelmeyer's fanciful view (plate 33), showing the Europeans dressed like Jacobean dandies, to the works of academically trained artists in search of themes appropriate to the American setting. For example, among Robert Walter Weir's first efforts as a professional painter was a *Landing of Columbus in America,* which he exhibited repeatedly at the Pennsylvania Academy of the Fine Arts in the 1820s. Even the career of Washington could be treated in terms of the arrival theme. Emanuel Leutze's famous painting of mid-century was long preceded by Thomas Sully's *Passage of the Delaware* (1819), in which a heroic Washington calmly oversees the river crossing that will lead to victory over the British at Trenton.

Artists essayed these subjects in the face of the con-siderable discouragement that met most efforts in the field of history painting in the first third of the nineteenth century. Both Sargent's *Landing of the Pilgrim Fathers* and Sully's *Passage of the Delaware,* executed in the sanguine expectation that Americans were ready to patronize grand-scale imagery of the sanctified events associated with their nation's founding, suffered the fate that awaited most ambitious history paintings of the period. Anticipated government support failed to materialize; public exhibition proved unremunerative, and the artists parted with their enormous works at considerable loss.[20]

The failure of such projects was less the result of a lack of interest in the national past than of the new republic's lack of sophistication in artistic affairs—in particular the absence of a mass market for art and the means to reach it. But it is also a measure of some of the problems presented by a national past both brief and still relatively uncelebrated. Although laudatory biographies of Washington appeared in his own lifetime and the history of the Revolution was being chronicled by the close of the century, the writing of American history as a synthetic epic awaited the passing of the Revolutionary generation after the first third of the nineteenth century. Meanwhile, history painters and their elite public found it difficult to make the national past the subject of dignified visual representation. The example

53

34. Paul Delaroche. *Cromwell and Charles I*. 1831. 92 x 120" (230 x 300 cm.). Musée des Beaux-Arts, Bordeaux.

of Benjamin West notwithstanding, American history seemed too deficient, either in visual color or chronological distance, to picture. The fidelity to historical detail demanded in the portrayal of events as recent as the Revolution was incompatible with commemorative grandeur. Washington Allston, for instance, flatly refused to paint a work for the U.S. Capitol's Rotunda on the grounds that American civil history was too dull and commonplace to be the stuff of high art.[21] Critics of Trumbull's *Declaration* agreed, disparaging his painting both because of liberties the artist took with historical fact in deference to the higher truth of the "silence and solemnity of the scene" and because the contemporary dress and repetitive portrait heads gave an inappropriately prosaic effect to a public monument to the nation's founding.[22]

Well into the nineteenth century the perceived incompatibility of historical veracity and pictorial effect continued to confound artists. In some aspects of his *Baptism of Pocahontas*, wrote one critic in 1841, Chapman "may have sacrificed the picturesque for the sake of historical truth, to which he has endeavored to adhere."[23] Despite their "noble themes," such images of national history as Vanderlyn's *Landing of Columbus*, declared another critic, "have less affinity with the more lofty poetry of art" than the "universal" subjects of neoclassical sculptors.[24] Such comments reflected an underlying anxiety that conventional history painting was simply inappropriate to the recording of the nation's history and that the American past itself was too brief and colorless to be the subject of great art. No less a booster of American subjects in art than the American Art-Union

bemoaned "the limited and unpicturesque character of American History,"[25] a history lacking not merely length but the accumulated layers of association that lent a rich mellowness, a patina of romantic antiquity, to European culture and landscape alike. The slender material heritage of what meager history Americans could claim was fast disappearing, so that, as one critic noted in *Morris's National Press*, "one of the greatest difficulties the historical painter has to contend with . . . is to adhere to . . . the *minutiae* and detail of everyday life, as it existed in the period where his subject is located."[26] Critic Charles Lanman was one of many voices arguing that the cause of high art in America could only be served if her artists disregarded the narrow strictures of nationality in subject matter and looked abroad.[27]

There was little argument about what exactly constituted the important events of American history. Like the landings of Columbus and the Pilgrim Fathers, the subjects of Trumbull's Revolutionary paintings were familiar as seminal historical moments that embodied national ideals. But there seemed few other comparable moments in a history so brief: "After taking out the Indians and the Puritans, what is there left besides the contentions of deliberative assemblies and the mathematical evolutions of the wars with Great Britain and Mexico?" conceded the American Art-Union regretfully.[28]

The problem of defining distinctly American historical subject matter continued to stimulate history painters into the decade of the Civil War. In the first third of the nineteenth century, however, discussion was largely shaped by two factors. The first was the idea of the United States as a nation of the future, in which the role of a national past, if any, was undefined.[29] The Founding Fathers' Enlightenment concept of America as a tabula rasa, a nation blessedly unburdened by a history, a constitutional experiment unprecedented in human experience, was reinforced by the pressing practical needs of the new republic.[30] The second factor was the result of the first: most Americans knew relatively little of their national past. The teaching of American history at the elementary level, for instance, did not enter the public school curriculum until the 1820s,[31] and British school texts, which naturally ignored American history, dominated well after that date.[32] College curricula continued to present classical and European history as the proper education for sons of the elite; the first chair in American history, occupied by Jared Sparks at Harvard, was not founded until 1839.[33] By comparison with the rich antiquity of classical and European history, the American past appeared meager indeed. Some Americans looked for compensation in nature, discovering in their continent's geologic antiquity a worthy parallel to the Old World's millennia of human settlement.[34] Charles Willson Peale's *Exhumation of the Mastodon* (plate 36) was an early picturing of the idea that America was not really "the new world" but "coeval with the oldest"[35]; the mission of Peale's pioneering museum, a repository of natural history specimens, was soon taken up by numerous museums and historical societies organized as much for the purpose of housing minerals, fossils and bones, and Indian artifacts as for enshrining recent heroes and founders.[36]

Ignorance of the national past, then, was by no means the result of indifference. America's "prolonged protest against the dominion of antiquity"[37] took the form of a backward glance. As the nation became more interested in the problem of defining national culture, inevitable comparisons with the Old World heightened concerns that America's very youth and lack of a past contributed to its apparent inability to support an artistic life worthy of its achievements in other endeavors. The race to salvage and preserve material evidence of the national history now counterbalanced the nation's characteristic headlong rush into the future. By 1838 almost every state in the union boasted a state historical society, while numerous similar organizations with local and regional focuses added to the competition for collectible materials in their eagerness to "seize on and seal up every worthless reminiscence of our colonial and revolutionary time," in the scathing view of one observer.[38] As the Revolution passed into hallowed memory, a series of significant anniversaries, including the silver jubilee of independence in 1826 and the centennial of Washington's birth in 1832, along with the increasing institutionalization of the Fourth of July celebration (widely celebrated since the end of the previous century), gave Americans opportunities to wax nostalgic about an increasingly mythologized past.[39] The conception of the national history underwent a subtle transformation, one that prepared the way for the popularity of American history in painting. As Americans became increasingly anxious about the future of their nation, they

35. Jacob Eichholtz. *An Incident of the Revolution.* 1831. 48½ x 66" (121.2 x 165.0 cm.). Museum of Fine Arts, Boston; Karolik Collection.

36. Charles Willson Peale. *The Exhumation of the Mastodon.*
1806–1808. 50 x 62½" (127.0 x 158.8 cm.). The Peale Museum,
Baltimore City Life Museums.

looked to their past for reassurance and for guidance. At their most pessimistic, Americans saw the birth of their nation as a golden age from which they had since fallen; at their most optimistic, they formulated their goals for the future in terms of fulfilling the promise and maintaining the standards set by the nation's founders.[40] In either case they took the nation's history as the text of their argument. Issues that had preoccupied the founding generation—whether America truly had a history, whether having one was not burdensome or even irrelevant to a new and unique nation—gave way to a passionate enthusiasm for antiquity.[41] The problem of defining the national past continued, but history—as obsession, object of veneration, or mode of perception—became a firmly entrenched feature of the national consciousness and culture. In 1842 the librarian of the American Antiquarian Society announced approvingly that "fashion has taken up antiquity,"[42] while Ralph Waldo Emerson, one of few voices to protest, condemned the "retrospective" attitude of a generation, which rather than experiencing nature directly, "builds the sepulchres of the fathers [and] writes biographies, histories, and criticism. The foregoing generations beheld God and nature face to face; we, through their eyes."[43] By midcentury, the dooming nature of an obsessive attachment to the past was the theme of a novel set in contemporary New England, Nathaniel Hawthorne's *The House of the Seven Gables*. Yet Hawthorne himself acknowledged that a past was necessary to the development of culture.[44]

In literature, American romantic fascination with the national past manifested itself earliest in poetry and fiction. American biography and historical chronicle were already well established, but as distance cast a hazy charm over the past, America's early days inspired a more imaginative literature, from Washington Irving's romances of Dutch colonial New York to James Fenimore Cooper's tales of the Revolutionary era. The possibilities for recasting the American past as the stuff of romantic fiction stimulated painters to explore alternatives to grand-manner stylistic conventions and standard subject matter; Thomas Cole and John Quidor, for example, interwove history with landscape and literary genre, respectively. Such experimentation across the boundaries of artistic categories reflects an openness to the interpretation of the nation's past fueled by the hunger to establish a national antiquity.[45]

It also owed much to the powerful example of Sir Walter Scott, whose historical fiction was transforming not only the genre but the very nature of historical interpretation and re-creation on both sides of the Atlantic.[46] Scott's Waverly novels, which brought the past alive for the present and emphasized wistfully the unbridgeable separation between the two, gave a certain legitimacy to local subject matter that bolstered calls for more assertive pride in America's albeit brief past. Historical novels began a dizzying rise in numbers and favor, but the penchant for color and drama also breathed new life and popularity into biography, that staple of American historical writing. Such popular and influential works as Parson Weems's *Life of George Washington* and Washington Irving's *Life and Voyages of Christopher Columbus* were plundered by enterprising history painters in their hunger for new, suitably national historical subjects by which they could tap a burgeoning market of avid readers of history.[47]

By the 1830s European artists offered Americans models for the kind of reinterpretation of the national past already suggested by historical fiction.[48] Abroad, the once-rigid distinction between history and genre had rapidly disintegrated; British and French artists portrayed historical situations in terms of their impact on ordinary, generic people or produced intimate, behind-the-scenes genre paintings of the lives of actual historical figures. These range from decorative exercises in the rendering of historical dress and interior architecture, as in Richard Parkes Bonington's pictured glimpses into the private lives of French royalty, to resonant—if altogether imagined—historical "scenes." In his *Cromwell and Charles I* (plate 34), for instance, Paul Delaroche telescopes the momentous drama of the Puritan Revolution into a private final encounter between the regicide and his victim. American artists, while eschewing the personal tragedy and dark drama that Europeans tended to emphasize in depicting their own history, were quick to absorb the example of history as genre. Jacob Eichholtz's *An Incident of the Revolution* (plate 35) was one of the earliest attempts to personalize the past by portraying an incident derived from biography rather

than from the public record of the nation's birth. The story, an American version of the legend of King Alfred in the neatherd's hut, is utterly irrelevant to the history of the Revolution. But it offered an intimate view, complete with appropriate historical dress, of Washington and his generals, as well as a thoroughly contemporary American lesson in social equality. Eichholtz's work found later competitors in a host of paintings showing scenes from the private lives of great national heroes, particularly Washington. Such works share little of the romantic, escapist delight in the past for its own sake that frequently colors their European counterparts. Rather, they function self-consciously as moral sermons on personal character and patriotic example; in such familiar works as Junius Brutus Stearns's views of a domesticated Washington as bridegroom and as farmer (plates 106 and 108), Thomas Pritchard Rossiter's *Washington and Lafayette at Mount Vernon, 1784* (plate 37), and Carl Schmolze's *Washington Sitting for His Portrait to Gilbert Stuart*, the father of his country serves as an uplifting, unifying symbol of national virtue in his private, rather than more familiar public, role. Domesticity humanized this larger-than-life hero, who offered a safer embodiment of the American everyman than the Jacksonian mob. In the end, however, such American works of historical genre fulfilled the same high-minded, didactic function as conventional depictions of public events.

The "genrefication" of history went well beyond images of time-tested heroes, however. The impulse to define and describe the national character that animated American enthusiasm for the "thoroughly American productions" of such genre painters as William Sidney Mount also encouraged the picturing of generic Ameri-

37. Thomas Pritchard Rossiter and Louis Mignot. *Washington and Lafayette at Mount Vernon, 1784.* ca. 1859. 87 x 146½" (221.0 x 372.1 cm.). The Metropolitan Museum of Art, New York; bequest of William Nelson.

38. William T. Ranney. *Veterans of 1776 Returning from the War.* 1848. 34⅛ x 48⅛" (85.3 x 120.3 cm.). Dallas Museum of Art, Dallas, Texas; the Art Museum League Fund, Special Contributors, and General Acquisitions Fund.

can historical types. Rufus Choate, for instance, argued that stories of ordinary people from the American past could be a means of uniting an increasing fractured republic.[49] Some, like the valiant heroine of Leutze's *Mrs. Schuyler Firing Her Wheat Fields* (1852), were the subject of minor legend; others, like the four ragtag soldiers pictured in William T. Ranney's *Veterans of 1776 Returning from the War* (plate 38), were anonymous embodiments of collective American character or virtue who helped bring hallowed memory down to everyday accessibility.[50] In the Civil War era, idealized portrayals of Revolutionary times, such as Daniel Huntington's *Lady Washington's Reception* (1861) and Rothermel's *State House on the Day of the Battle of Germantown* (plate 40), which celebrates the compassion of the Philadelphia ladies who nursed American prisoners of war, exploited national history as an inspirational reference during trying times.

The great national histories of the period share this underlying preoccupation. In the three decades that preceded the Civil War, Americans for the first time chronicled their past in a sweeping saga of the United States as the climax of world civilization's march of freedom and progress, a frank apologetic for the doctrine of Manifest Destiny and the inevitable triumph of white, Protestant culture. In 1835 George Bancroft published the first volume of his *History of the United States,* which prompted one enthusiastic reviewer to declare that until that point the United States had possessed no "authentic . . . creditable and connected relation of the events which have led to its existence among the na-

tions of the earth."[51] Composed in what a modern historian has characterized as "the eagle-screaming tradition of countless Fourth of July orators,"[52] Bancroft's history became the model for many others that followed in the next two decades. Meanwhile, the other great practitioners of this first real school of national historical writing, notably William Prescott, and, later, John Lothrop Motley and Francis Parkman, wrote histories of European nations and of the French and Spanish conquests of the New World—subjects in which they found American "affiliations or parallels"—for the same purpose as Bancroft's New England–centered history: to "point the moral of American superiority and adorn the tale of American escape from contamination."[53] Antebellum Americans were as interested in European history as in their own. Yet, although they increasingly recognized the connections between the two, they were committed to interpreting the European past, whether in prose or painting, in negative terms that implied a satisfying contrast to American superiority.[54]

In a society in which the reading of history had always been accepted as a morally edifying pursuit, the popularity of written history spilled over into the far less widely accepted arena of the visual arts. Painters borrowed the legitimacy of historians by portraying scenes from their writings, identifying their textual sources in exhibition catalogues in an apparent effort to interest viewers already familiar with the written versions of the same subjects. Leutze, who painted no fewer than six history paintings inspired by Irving's biography of Columbus, was only one of many artists to picture

39. Robert Walter
Weir. *The Landing
of Henry Hudson.*
ca. 1838. 68 x 108"
(170.0 x 270.0 cm.).
David David
Gallery,
Philadelphia.

scenes specific to that popular work; William Prescott's histories provided the texts for Rothermel's and Leutze's images of the Spanish conquests. More important than mere textual borrowing, however, was the impulse of writers and painters alike to conceive American history in grandly epic terms. Only this approach, the product of a history now amenable to romantic generalization, can explain the respectful enthusiasm with which Americans embraced the patriotic bombast of such works as Bancroft's *History* and Leutze's *Washington Crossing the Delaware*. As history painters looked to historians to legitimize their genre as well as to suggest specific, familiar subjects, writers enlivened their histories by assimilating techniques associated with the visual arts: colorful visual detail, descriptive "portraits" of characters, the *tableau vivant*.[55] Among painters, the original moment, in scenes of discovery, exploration, or settlement, remained a favorite motif, although the range of subjects to which it could be applied had widened since the beginning of the century.[56]

The grand-manner treatment of great public events typified by Leutze's *Washington Crossing the Delaware* represents a climax of the tradition perfected by West and his circle and perpetuated, albeit with faint popular support, in the intervening generation. In the case of Leutze and the many American history painters who followed him to Düsseldorf in the 1840s and 1850s, this tradition received a fresh infusion from the example of German artists, as William H. Gerdts has demonstrated.[57] Carl Friedrich Lessing, in particular, offered both ideological and formal inspiration in the picturing of national history as a dynamic symbol for contemporary aspirations. In Leutze's hands, a heroic Washington leading his forces to triumph over British tyranny served as a symbol of Düsseldorf's struggle for freedom against her Prussian rulers.[58] In the American context, however, the revolt against oppression was transmuted into the quest for unity. In the increasingly fractured political environment of the 1850s, the father of his country embodied—at least for northerners—the righteous cause for which thirteen contentious colonies had come together under a common banner, just as Leutze's Washington, towering over a crowded boatful of soldiers on the Delaware's icy waters, visually unites the motley band.[59] While secessionist-minded southerners referred to the Revolution as a precedent justifying their proposed revolt against Yankee oppression, other Americans took an increasingly conservative view of the national origins, downplaying the radicalism of 1776 in favor of the consolidation of union in 1787.[60] The American past had come to serve a variety of causes as Americans tailored their interpretations of both national and local history to specific, topical concerns.

Hence, throughout the period, symbols of national union such as Washington found their counterparts in historical subjects with more regional identifications. By

40. Peter F. Rothermel. *State House on the Day of the Battle of Germantown.* 1862. 34½ x 47½" (87.6 x 120.7 cm.). The Pennsylvania Academy of the Fine Arts, Philadelphia; bequest of Henry C. Gibson.

41. John Blake White. *General Marion Inviting a British Officer to Dine.* American Art-Union print. 1840. The Anne S. K. Brown Military Collection, John Hay Library, Brown University, Providence, Rhode Island.

the 1830s, the South and, to a lesser extent, the West were in revolt against New England's traditional dominance of the interpretation of American history, and state and local history were on the rise.[61] Thomas Birch's *Landing of William Penn* (ca. 1849), Weir's *Landing of Henry Hudson* (plate 39), and related works offered regional echoes of more familiar, and by now "hackneyed,"[62] embarkation scenes; John Blake White's *General Marion Inviting a British Officer to Dine* (plate 41), engraved for the Apollo Association in 1840, and *Mrs. Motte Directing Generals Marion and Lee to Burn Her Mansion to Dislodge the British* (a precursor to Leutze's *Mrs. Schuyler Firing Her Wheat Fields*) suggested that the histories of zones other than New England offered lessons from which the entire nation could profit. In recognition of growing regional self-identity and local pride, artistic accomplishment was set aside in favor of geographical diversity in the choice of the four artists to complete the decoration of the Capitol's Rotunda, as well as their subjects; most of the resulting paintings, in fact, came in for criticism on the basis of not being sufficiently "national."[63] Indeed, although Joseph Sill of Philadelphia commended the Pilgrims' landing, a subject then being undertaken by Rothermel, as a "great National Subject," Weir claimed a place in the Capitol for his own *Embarkation of the Pilgrims* on the somewhat defensive grounds that "there should be at least one picture in our National Hall, whose subject should commemorate a event connected with the history of our eastern states; since they were the first to grapple in that struggle for liberty, the achievement of which, is our glory and boast."[64]

Paradoxically, the triumphant climax of the cult of national history was marked by a vigorous impulse of sectional partisanship. By the mid-nineteenth century, the most familiar events resonated with varied, sometimes contradictory meanings as Americans engaged in a lively dialogue with their past and its symbolic imagery. History had never been so important, nor more earnestly pressed into service to national self-pride. For history painters, this situation compounded long-standing tension between the conventions of their genre and the limited character of the American past. Their response was fractured into a clear distinction between the grandly epic, epitomized by Leutze's *Washington Crossing the Delaware*, and the prosaically anecdotal, in the increasingly popular format of historical genre. For historical genre, the stimulus of transformations in the writing of history and the pursuit of an always elusive public was complemented by the inspiration of European experiments in national history imaging. But for American artists, their past remained as separate and unique as the national destiny. Charged, in an era of doubt and conflict, with an urgent mission to inspire, uplift, and encourage, the national fathers had arrived in American consciousness and American art.

National Paintings and American Character

Historical Murals in the Capitol's Rotunda[1]

ANN UHRY ABRAMS

Eight large paintings depicting scenes from American history—John Trumbull's *Declaration of Independence, Resignation of General Washington, Surrender of Lord Cornwallis at Yorktown*, and *Surrender of General Burgoyne at Saratoga*, John Vanderlyn's *Landing of Columbus*, Robert Walter Weir's *Embarkation of the Pilgrims*, John Gadsby Chapman's *Baptism of Pocahontas*, and William Henry Powell's *Discovery of the Mississippi by De Soto, A.D. 1541*—line the circumference of the central hallway, the Rotunda, of the United States Capitol. During the nineteenth century, these compositions, each twelve by eighteen feet, were labeled "national paintings" because they presumably imparted illuminating messages about the history of the United States.[2]

Considering the issue of federally funded artwork, James Fenimore Cooper commented in 1834 that paintings in the Capitol building should convey "American character" even if some of the pieces lacked "the highest class of excellence."[3] The author's preference for content over quality mirrored a prevailing belief that art sponsored by the government was charged with instructing viewers about traditions and doctrines that upheld the federal union. Beneath such lofty objectives lay more mundane distractions. Then as now, artists and their patrons had to contend with special interests, administrative maneuvering, partisan debates, and bitter rivalries. Even when espousing such high-minded aspirations as placing "American character" in visual terms, congressmen were bound by the exigencies of "politics as usual."[4] The eight Rotunda paintings should thus be viewed as historical images frozen in a cultural, social, and political time warp, for as such they provide excellent insights into the priorities and prejudices of the early nineteenth century.

John Trumbull and New Nationhood

Construction of the United States Capitol stretched over seventy years. The first portion, designed by William Thornton in 1793, was set aflame by British forces during the War of 1812. After the peace, Benjamin Latrobe, the fourth architect to supervise the project, began the slow process of reconstruction but resigned in 1817. The Boston architect Charles Bulfinch assumed the post, expanded his predecessors' plans for a central rotunda to connect the two legislative chambers, and included within the new design eight wall panels reserved for paintings. Quite likely Bulfinch was influenced by his friend John Trumbull, with whom he often corresponded.[5]

Trumbull had long dreamed of assembling his historical compositions into a "Hall of Revolution." As a student in Benjamin West's London studio during the 1780s, the former colonel in the colonial army began the series that included *The Death of General Warren at the Battle of Bunker's Hill, June 17, 1775* (plate 133), *The Death of General Montgomery in the Attack on Quebec, December 31, 1775*, and *The Declaration of Independence*. In hopes of installing his "Hall of Revolution" in the new Capitol building, Trumbull appeared before the House of Representatives in January 1817, carrying samples of his work along with letters of recommendation from former presidents and other influential politicians.[6] Although the legislators admired the artist's paintings, some held strong reservations about whether the federal government should sponsor fine arts projects of any description. But because the majority believed that paintings representing scenes from the American Revolution would have a positive "moral effect" on future generations, both houses of Congress passed a joint resolution authorizing Trumbull to paint four murals.[7]

John Trumbull, *Declaration of Independence*,
detail of plate 42.

65

42. John Trumbull, *Declaration of Independence in Congress, at the Independence Hall, Philadelphia, July 4th, 1776.* 1786–1819. United States Capitol Art Collection, Washington, D.C.; photograph courtesy Architect of the Capitol.

Despite his initial success in receiving congressional confirmation, Trumbull's good fortune soon abated. Several legislators disapproved of his plan to charge an admission fee of twenty-five cents when exhibiting the completed *Declaration of Independence* (plate 42) in New York, Philadelphia, and Baltimore. It was improper, they insisted, to mix public funding with personal profit.[8] This rebuke was mild compared to the outcry that ensued after the pictures appeared in the Rotunda. John Holmes of Maine complained that those "paintings, which cost 32,000 dollars were not worth 32 cents," while John Randolph of Virginia rendered his oft-quoted remark that *The Declaration of Independence* should be called a "shin piece" because it displayed so many legs.[9] In reality, the legislators were less troubled by aesthetic deficiencies than by the artist's failure to convey the lofty "moral effect" that they had expected, for orators, authors, and politicians had clothed the events that Trumbull was attempting to represent in such hyperbole that no visual re-creation would have been satisfactory.

Trumbull's pictures should have pleased the legislators, however, because they received the blessings of the most prominent of the Founding Fathers who were then still alive—Thomas Jefferson, John Adams, James Madison, and James Monroe. While Minister to France in 1786, Jefferson had advised the artist on how to construct his first version of *The Declaration of Independence;* Adams also made suggestions for that composition, and both he and Jefferson wrote letters of recom-

mendation to Congress in 1817; Madison, as outgoing president, specified how each subject should be delineated; and incoming President Monroe formally initiated the project.[10] Not only had Madison, Monroe, Adams, and Jefferson been key players in the events Trumbull was commemorating, but they were highly instrumental in the formation and implementation of the new republican government that the murals celebrated.

More than any of Trumbull's other paintings, *The Declaration of Independence* suggests a complex package of American ideals.[11] The stage-like setting features Thomas Jefferson, Benjamin Franklin, John Adams, Roger Sherman, and Robert Livingston standing before the desk of John Hancock, while other delegates to the Continental Congress, packed in a semicircular formation around the Assembly Room, witness the signing. Attached to the central wall of the symmetrical chamber are crossed flags behind a drum, adding a flourish of patriotic zeal to the otherwise sedate gathering. Trumbull went to great lengths to obtain exact likenesses of each participant in order to place in visual terms Madison's dictum that a republic "derives all its powers directly or indirectly from the body of the people."[12] By making certain that "body" was composed of distinct individuals, the well-researched portraits in Trumbull's *Declaration of Independence* announce that the United States was founded by an assembly of sovereign citizens resolving their grievances through rational debate.

Even though Trumbull first painted the subject in 1787—before the guillotines were erected in Paris—his composition acquired heightened meaning after the French Revolution ended in anarchy and eventual dictatorship. For a generation of Americans who remembered the French "Terror" as a frightening abomination, there was solace in envisioning the beginnings of the United States as a methodical process of change by proclamation. Writing in 1818, a correspondent for the *Commercial Advertiser* described Trumbull's *Declaration* in terms of its didactic effect:

> No inhabitant of this country can view it without experiencing a deep sense of the hazards which the members of that illustrious assembly thus voluntarily assumed—of the anxiety, the sufferings, the triumphant success, by which that most important transaction was followed. Before this great and decisive step was taken, the people of the States considered themselves as only struggling against oppression—from that moment forward they contended for existence.[13]

As this declaration indicates, Trumbull's *Declaration* transmitted an amplified message for viewers in 1818. Packed with portraits of the Founding Fathers, Trumbull's visual recapitulation of the assembly at Independence Hall recalled the seminal event of nationhood, thus acquiring a patriotic distinction usually reserved for the flag or for other emblems of national significance. Hence, when the artist tried to exhibit the work as if it were a commercial curiosity, those who regarded the event as "sacred to American feelings" were infuriated.

Trumbull's *Resignation of General Washington* (plate 43) imparts an analogous sense of national purpose and rational process. The static formality of the composition mirrors the legendary dignity attributed to the ceremony in the Maryland State House during which Washington resigned his military commission to resume his duties as a gentleman farmer, inspiring the so-called "Cincinnatus" legend that became a cornerstone of the Washington myth.[14] To illustrate the pacifism of Washington's choice, Trumbull pictured a tranquil assembly crammed with an orderly assortment of dignitaries and family members. The formality of this gathering prompted Representative John Holmes of Maine to call the *Resignation* "a piece of the most solemn daubing" he had ever seen.[15] The solemnity that bothered Holmes is the very effect Trumbull must have intended, for many years later he commented that he believed the general's resignation to be "one of the highest moral lessons ever given to the world [demonstrating that] Washington aspired to . . . that glory which virtue alone can give, and which no power, no effort, no time, can ever take away or diminish."[16] In the aftermath of the War of 1812, as the new United States attempted to develop a peacetime economy, Trumbull's explication of the national "Father's" rejection of military glory served as a grave reminder that the entire nation wanted to cultivate its own land and avoid further fighting.

Even Trumbull's two compositions representing action on the battlefield—the British surrenders at Saratoga and Yorktown—denote peace, not war. While his well-known "grand-style" paintings, *The Death of General*

43. John Trumbull. *The Resignation of General Washington*. 1822–24. United States Capitol Art Collection; photograph courtesy Architect of the Capitol.

44. John Trumbull. *The Surrender of General Burgoyne at Saratoga.* 1822–24. United States Capitol Art Collection; photograph courtesy Architect of the Capitol.

Warren and *The Death of General Montgomery*, would certainly have made a more dramatic addition to the Capitol panorama, such reminders of war would have been highly inappropriate because they demonstrate heroism in the context of human loss. Instead Trumbull and his advisors chose to signify combat in peaceful terms. Tranquility permeates *The Surrender of General Burgoyne at Saratoga* (plate 44). Guns have been silenced, the sky is blue, the flag flies proudly over the American headquarters, and the full panoply of participants—and non-participants—crowd in upon Horatio Gates, the American general who ushers the British general and his men toward a tent, where they will share refreshments. Behind this gesture of goodwill is the assumption that officers serving a republic are forgiving and gracious; thus, the American Revolution was a contest governed by honorable rules of fair play.

A similar aura of harmonious cooperation pervades *The Surrender of Lord Cornwallis at Yorktown* (plate 45). The American general Benjamin Lincoln holds center stage on his white horse as Washington (shown approaching from the right rear) allowed his second-in-command to accept the surrender, a display of the commander-in-chief's personal humility and the enemy's public humiliation. Trumbull emphasized this significant maneuver by converging several diagonal "lines" in the composition on Washington, who is also connected this way to General Lincoln in the foreground.[17] In addition, the artist diminished the stature of the defeated British by placing them on the ground decidedly beneath their victorious counterparts. Although troops of three nations—Britain, France, and the United States—were present at Yorktown, Trumbull depicted only the American flag. The assembled French on the left side carry no Fleur-de-Lys, perhaps because the political situation in France had altered so dramatically by the 1820s that Trumbull deemed it unwise to picture either the Bourbon standard or the Tricolor. Only Britain's white flag of surrender waves over the defeated troops, leaving the Stars and Stripes as the unchallenged emblematic victor.

Trumbull designed all four Rotunda paintings on a horizontal and vertical grid to denote "orderly process," a concept often employed by eighteenth-century authors to suggest temperance, moderation, and stability.[18] Stasis and calm prevail in the symmetrical linear pattern and rectangular interior spaces of *The Declaration of Independence* and *The Resignation of General Washington*, those two events that were chosen to exhibit the legal foundations of the United States and peace-loving attitudes of its first president. Similarly, the balanced compositions in *Burgoyne* and *Cornwallis* convey a sense that the Revolution itself was an agreeable endeavor devoid of violence and brutality. The theatrical backdrop of billowing clouds (that essential component of "grand-style" battle pieces) not only contributes a swirl of motion to the otherwise stagnant surrender scenes, but it defines the fighting between Britain and its former colonies as a systematic confrontation enlivened by a burst of controlled emotion.

Viewed together, Trumbull's murals reiterated perceptions of national purpose held by most Americans of the artist's generation and certainly by the Founding Fathers, whose endorsement and advice helped shape the ideological framework. The message was simple but forceful: independence had its roots in the methodical procedures of an elected assembly; victory resulted from fair play on the battlefield; the commander-in-chief preferred peaceful endeavors over military service. Thus interpreted, the paintings are meant to inspire appreciation of a fearless, well-regulated republican government which maintains a coherent federal union. They contain, in fact, the very "moral effect" that the mandate from Congress specified.

Romanticism and Regional Pride

Although Trumbull easily won the approval of a relatively unified Congress in 1817, no such accord existed a decade later when the legislature resumed discussion of the four remaining Rotunda panels. Not only were lawmakers now polarized by divisive political and regional squabbles, but a new generation of younger artists was petitioning Congress in hopes of winning a commission. None was more aggressive than Samuel F. B. Morse, who had recently demonstrated his competitive spirit by openly opposing Trumbull's American Academy of the Arts and spearheading the group that ultimately formed the National Academy of Design. In 1826 Morse made a move to stave off Trumbull's plan by petitioning New York Congressman Gulian C. Verplanck to request that Congress conduct a thorough search for four of the "principal Historical Painters of our country" instead of choosing just one artist to fill the remaining panels, a suggestion endorsed by the House Committee of the Library the following year.[19]

When Congress finally addressed the matter in early 1828, partisan politics surrounding the upcoming presidential contest between Andrew Jackson and John Quincy Adams transformed an ostensible discussion of art into a political donnybrook. Rather than examining the abilities and training of possible aspirants, the House centered its debate around potential subjects, not so much for their "American character" but to protect the interests of voters back home. Adams's New England supporters, for example, promoted the battle of Bunker Hill to counter the wave of southern and Democratic fervor backing Jackson's victory at New Orleans; westerners lobbied to gain support for the battle of Lake Erie.[20] At

45. John Trumbull. *The Surrender of Lord Cornwallis at Yorktown.* 1787–1828. United States Capitol Art Collection; photograph courtesy Architect of the Capitol.

one point, Edward Everett of Massachusetts urged Congress to remember its "obligation to teach a valuable lesson to posterity" by rejecting military encounters in favor of episodes from the nation's "civil history." In this atmosphere of chauvinistic bombast, suggestions to encourage scenes of "valor and heroism" from the colonial past, such as Penn's treaty with the Indians and the landing of the Pilgrims, only succeeded in magnifying regional defenses.[21] Two days of wrangling effectively buried considerations of artistic merit beneath the tangle of local and partisan concerns, thus tabling the resolution.

In the eight years that elapsed between the aborted resolution of 1828 and the actual commissions of 1836, Morse and other artists—including John Vanderlyn, Thomas Sully, Thomas Cole, John Gadsby Chapman, Henry Inman, and Robert Walter Weir—petitioned Congress, often hinting of their willingness to interpret a favorite regional theme. When the issue again reached the House floor in January 1834, a putative discussion about art once more devolved into a political morass.[22] To escape additional controversy, the House scuttled further public discussion and quietly passed a bill in 1836 that awarded the coveted commissions to Vanderlyn, Chapman, Weir, and Inman, and left the choice of topics up to the individual artists with only vague stipulations that they select "subjects serving to illustrate the discovery of America; the settlement of the United States; the history of the Revolution; or the adoption of the Constitution."[23]

Cooper's idea of "American character" may have been a paramount consideration in the commissioning pro-cess, but in the absence of published debates we have only the resulting paintings to indicate that the winning artists were backed by influential congressmen and accordingly agreed to depict subjects of regional significance.[24] This last factor was confirmed by a brief article in *The New York Mirror,* which disclosed that John Vanderlyn would depict the landing of Columbus (a "mighty event, big with the fate of the worlds"); John Gadsby Chapman would delineate "scenes in Virginia" that illustrated "the colonization of that portion of America"; Robert Walter Weir would represent "the departure of the pilgrims" to found "an empire *on a rock . . .* which no storm can overthrow"; and Henry Inman would picture pioneers "with cheerful faces . . . journeying on the way which Daniel Boon [*sic*] trod, and which is now the beaten path to wealth and power." Congress, the writer insisted, chose artists who "have done honour to themselves and to their country by their selection of subjects . . . [that] commemorate four distinct seeds, from which have arisen plants uniting and forming a great tree."[25] This author no' doubt understood the four subjects as parts of a composite saga of national beginnings, the genesis chapter of American history filled with a complete package of contemporaneous sociopolitical ideals. In so doing, he applauded the inclusion of different continental and regional legends of origin, those "four distinct seeds" from which grew the American family tree.

The first "seed" to bear fruit was John Gadsby Chapman's *Baptism of Pocahontas at Jamestown, Virginia, 1613* (plate 46), representing an apocryphal scene from

46. John Gadsby Chapman. *The Baptism of Pocahontas at Jamestown, Virginia, 1613.* 1837–40. United States Capitol Art Collection; photograph courtesy Architect of the Capitol.

47. Robert Walter Weir. *The Embarkation of the Pilgrims at Delft Haven, Holland, July 22nd, 1620.* 1837–43. United States Capitol Art Collection; photograph courtesy Architect of the Capitol.

the earliest days of Virginia's colonial history.[26] Begun in 1837 and installed in 1840, Chapman's painting illustrates one aspect of the quasi-historical Pocahontas legend first told in John Smith's *Generall Historie*, published in the early seventeenth century. In this account of his explorations, Smith told how Pocahontas saved him from her father's tomahawk, made numerous efforts to protect the English settlement, married John Rolfe, was "instructed in Christianitie," journeyed to England with her husband and infant son under the title of "Lady Rebecca," and met a "religious and godly end" before she could return to her native land.[27] Although there is ample evidence to indicate that Smith may have fabricated or exaggerated his *Generall Historie* to recruit settlers for the Virginia Company and elevate himself as a singular leader of the early colony, the account is still revered in Virginia because many of the state's prominent families (most notably the Bollings and Randolphs) trace their ancestry to the son of Pocahontas and John Rolfe.[28]

By the time Chapman painted his composition, the natives of Pocahontas's tribe were virtually extinct, and those few who remained had been pushed westward beyond the fringes of settlement, where struggles for territorial rights continued in the wake of the Jackson administration's removal of native tribes from the eastern United States.[29] Against this background of frontier skirmishes and Indian uprooting, those prominent Virginians who proudly claimed descent from Thomas Rolfe needed to legitimize their own interracial heritage while simultaneously justifying the displacement of so

many native tribes. One answer lay in reaffirming Pocahontas's voluntary adaptation of the English religion and way of life.[30]

Chapman's painting provides visual documentation that the Indian maiden eschewed her "savage" past and embraced Christianity.[31] Dressed in "pure" white, the Anglicized native kneels on a raised platform in the center of the Jamestown chapel while the Reverend Alexander Whiteaker performs the baptismal rite. Her husband, John Rolfe, is poised slightly behind her, and the imposing figure of Virginia Governor Thomas Dale— wearing heavy armor—stands at the left. The assortment of native Americans on the right are a curious lot, some attired for battle, others swathed in flowing drapery. A majestic Nantequas, Pocahontas's favorite brother, stands right of center; her cousin, the villainous Opechancanough, looms ominously in the shadows; an unidentified sister with her baby lounges near the foreground; and her uncle Opachisco bursts into the church from the far right. These stereotypical portayals of native Americans pose a jarring intrusion into the placid sea of "civilized" white faces, a juxtaposition of ceremonial piety and "savage" primitivism confirming missionary claims that in order to coexist with Euro-Americans, Indians must convert to Christianity.

A few weeks after Chapman's *Baptism* was installed in the Rotunda, a reporter for Washington's *Daily National Intelligencer* commented that the "subject appears . . . to have been an unfortunate one for an historical painting, being more local and individual than national."[32] In anticipation of such allusions to the regional character of his subject, Chapman addressed the issue in a brochure published in conjunction with the Capitol installation. Pocahontas, the text explained, "appeals to our religious as well as our patriotic sympathies, and is equally associated with the rise and progress of the Christian church, as with the political destinies of the United States."[33] In other words, by depicting the apocryphal baptism, Chapman was interpreting the "Mother of Virginia" not as a brave "creature of the forest" but as an American Joan of Arc who helped procure the land for the British and embody its dominant religion among the "heathens." The ceremony (said to have taken place ca. 1613–1614) also asserts that Protestantism first reached the North American shores in Virginia, not in Massachusetts as New Englanders claimed.

Perhaps the best indication that Chapman's *Baptism* was a historical manifesto for the Anglican heritage of Virginia comes from a sermon delivered by Stephen G. Bulfinch (son of Charles Bulfinch, former Architect of the Capitol) at Washington's Unitarian Church in 1843, shortly after Robert Walter Weir's *Embarkation of the Pilgrims at Delft Haven, Holland, July 22nd, 1620* (plate 47) was installed in the Rotunda. The minister specified that "those kneeling Puritans" who represent the religion of New England hang alongside Chapman's *Pocahontas* "which exhibits the priestly vestments of Episcopalian worship," while the yet-to-be-finished *Landing of Columbus* "will present in contrast yet in harmony with, the symbols of the Roman Catholic belief. It is well," Bulfinch continued, "that these varying denominations should thus meet, in the memorials of the great and good by whom each has been honored, and in the Legislative palace of our Union."[34]

With Bulfinch's sermon as an introduction, one can have little doubt that Weir's painting spoke for the interests of New England. Viewers lauded the painting as a symbol of regional pride when it appeared in Boston prior to its installation in the Capitol. "There are few sons of New England sires," exclaimed a writer for the Boston *Critic*, "who can look upon this picture without emotion—or . . . without feeling a stronger sense of his duties as a patriot, citizen and a Christian."[35] Clearly, New Englanders felt comfortable with Weir's depiction of the Pilgrims praying on the ship deck before their departure from Delft Haven. Not only were they depicted as Protestant worshipers, thus playing to the nativist, anti-Catholic sympathies of some offspring of the original settlers, but they were fair Anglo-Saxons from whom many old-guard New Englanders boasted their descent. At the apex of the semicircular configuration of men, women, and children is the ruling elder, William Brewster, holding a Bible opened to the beginning of the New Testament. Grouped around him are John Winslow,

William Bradford, and Miles Standish along with their wives and an assortment of other voyagers added for human interest and historical verisimilitude.[36]

When creating this assembly of distinguished worshipers, Weir may well have taken his cue from Daniel Webster's oration delivered at Plymouth during the 1820 bicentennial of the Pilgrims' landing. Using the venerated ancestors as his touchstone, Webster told the audience that the first settlers came to the "chosen land" not for commercial betterment but to escape religious intolerance. Through great sacrifice and numerous hardships, Webster explained, the hallowed ancestors spread Christianity, universal education, and constitutional government into formerly "savage" areas.[37] By the mid-1830s, New Englanders were repeating the ideas Webster and other orators expressed during the Pilgrim bicentennial to demonstrate that because the Puritans migrated solely for religious reasons, they were vastly different from the "tumult of an Irish mob, sweeping through the streets" of Boston in search of economic advantages.[38] This recurring denunciation—replete with vicious anti-Catholic rhetoric—resounded from the podiums of New England and spawned fears that descendants of the original settlers were losing their cultural and political hegemony to the uncontrollable mobs.

To distinguish the emigrants of 1620 from the unwashed masses, Weir transformed his Pilgrims into idealized replicas of nineteenth-century New Englanders by giving them fair complexions and dressing them in fine woolens, silks, and feathered hats. So attired, these prosperous and devout ladies and gentlemen appeared as the worthy progenitors of the religious, moral, social, and economic ideals their descendants were then attempting to propagate throughout the United States.[39] Or, as Bulfinch pointed out in his sermon following the installation of Weir's mural in the Capitol, the painting represents New England Protestantism by depicting the "exiles" as pious, educated, and orderly Saxons united in their quest for religious liberty.[40]

John Vanderlyn's *Landing of Columbus* (plate 48), installed in the Rotunda in 1847, also contains a complex palimpsest of messages, foremost being the supposition that the arrival of the Spanish party in the Caribbean initiated a chain of events that ultimately produced the United States. A writer for the *Daily National Intelligencer* repeated that assumption after seeing the painting in Vanderlyn's Paris studio. "No subject can be more interesting to the American than the landing of Columbus," he exclaimed, "the discovery of a world, and that world emphatically ours."[41] As this chauvinistic appraisal indicates, most Americans cared little that Columbus never set foot on their continent; they preferred to accept him as the prime instigator of national prosperity and expansion. Washington Irving perpetuated that myth when he wrote in his popular *Life and Voyages of*

Christopher Columbus (1828) that the admiral started the process "of conciliating and civilizing the natives, of building cities, introducing the useful arts, subjecting every thing [*sic*] to the control of law, order and religion, and thus of founding regular and prosperous empires."[42] By picturing Columbus as a towering hero, Vanderlyn contributed to the herculean image that had been evolving since the late eighteenth century.[43] In the center of his composition, a tall, broad-shouldered, fair (though graying) Columbus holds a standard of the combined kingdoms of Aragon and Castile, his eyes cast upward in prayerful gratitude. Members of his crew surround him, one carrying a simple metal cross, others bearing banners adorned by the green crosses of Ferdinand and Isabella, and still others bowing in reverential homage to their leader. Around this assembly, scantily clad natives dart across the beach, peep from behind trees, or throw themselves on the ground; sailors move around the water's edge, some searching for promised treasures.

As Chapman's and Powell's Rotunda paintings testify, Vanderlyn's depiction of half-clothed "savages" was the standard way to delineate "civilized" whites confronting the native population. However, in *The Landing of Columbus*, Indians appear to be subdued and almost transparent, leading the viewer to focus upon the admiral and his entourage who occupy center stage. Although a preliminary study indicates that the artist originally planned to spotlight a less docile assortment of natives in the foreground, he ended up reducing these

Indians to shadowy peripheral presences, peering at the Christian rite transpiring on the shore as if they were already vanishing into the wilderness to make way for advancing "civilization."[44] The painting contains evidence of other mid-nineteenth-century stereotyping as well, most notably North Americans' distrust of their Latin neighbors. "The Spaniards were not only cruel to the poor Indians," related a primer of 1829, "but they were cruel also to Columbus who had made them so rich."[45] To suggest the sinister nature of some explorers in contrast to the noble Columbus, Vanderlyn pictured two Spanish sailors crawling along the ground in search of gold and showed members of the landing party bartering with the natives along the shore.

The Landing of Columbus can be considered a complementary pendant to the Chapman, Weir, and Powell murals, or perhaps a hub from which the other three paintings radiate. Just as Michelangelo focused his Sistine ceiling on God-the-Father begetting the universe by touching Adam's hand, so Vanderlyn perpetuated a similar myth of origin by picturing Columbus stepping onto American soil to initiate the flow of "civilization" to Massachusetts, Virginia, and the beckoning West.

The last of the Capitol's Rotunda paintings—William Henry Powell's *Discovery of the Mississippi by De Soto, A.D. 1541* (plate 49)—was not installed until 1855. Powell replaced his teacher Henry Inman, who died in 1846 before his mural of Daniel Boone crossing the Alleghenies could be completed. A House committee decided

48. John Vanderlyn. *The Landing of Columbus.* 1837–47. United States Capitol Art Collection; photograph courtesy Architect of the Capitol.

49. William Henry Powell. *Discovery of the Mississippi by De Soto, A.D. 1541.* 1848–55. United States Capitol Art Collection; photograph courtesy Architect of the Capitol.

to choose a new topic before selecting the young Cincinnati-born artist, thus altering the procedure that had allowed the other seven artists to name their own subjects within the broader parameters of congressional guidelines.[46] Instead of Boone, who lived well into the nineteenth century, the congressmen chose de Soto to represent the American West. Not only did this hero hark back to the distant past with no connection to more recent territorial disputes, but his sixteenth-century explorations of the continent seemed to fit more appropriately with the other three legends of founding already hanging in the Rotunda.[47]

Powell's composition is indeed a theatrical spectacle. De Soto—riding a prancing white steed and dressed as a Renaissance courtier—arrives with a procession of horsemen flourishing colorful banners. The half-clothed Indians who await him have discarded their weapons, the tribal elder even presenting a peace pipe to signal submission. While the natives accept their white conquerers with gestures of peace and compliance, the shadowy Spaniards aligned along the lower half of the composition are surrounded by emblems of war (cannon and rifles), avarice (shovels and a treasure chest), and religious domination (a wizard-like priest and strong-armed men raising a huge cross), thus adhering to the then-prevailing notion that the settlers of Latin America were fundamentally dishonest. Such additions must have appealed to Congress's western constituency.

Reaction to the midcentury Rotunda paintings was as negative as it had been when Trumbull's murals were unveiled two decades earlier. Congressmen railed about the artists' inability to capture the "sanctity" of historical events, while art critics were disappointed in the leaden renditions obtained from such a well-publicized competition. A writer for *The Literary World* in 1848 complained that "National" pictures "should have been strictly limited to actual scenes in the actual history of the United States" and that "the subject itself should have been at all events an actual point of history."[48] In other words, artistic license was somehow improper if applied to "actual" historical "facts," assuming, of course, that such "facts" could be reproduced in a work of art.

History Revisited

Notwithstanding general dissatisfaction with the paintings themselves, the Rotunda murals constitute a summary of America's founding as conceived at the time they were created. A comparison of the paintings by Trumbull with the four from midcentury reveals some interesting insights into the "history lessons" the artists were attempting to impart.

All eight paintings share a conviction that creation of the United States was preordained. Great moments in history were merely scenes in a drama destined to end with the best of all republics possessing the greatest degree of piety, liberty, and freedom.[49] Illustrating that fragile balance between the imperfect past and the glorious future, the eight rotunda paintings depict historical turning points or events about to happen. Columbus journeys between the old world and the new, the Pilgrims are similarly poised between Europe and America, Pocahontas moves from her aboriginal background into a Europeanized culture, and de Soto opens the untamed West for European settlers. The same pivotal transitions occur in the four Trumbull paintings: Jefferson and his colleagues break ties with England, Washington advances from military service into civilian life, and the two British surrenders mark the termination of foreign domination over the thirteen American colonies and signal the founding of a new republic. While condemning the bellicosity and authoritarianism that forced America's European ancestors to emigrate, the murals glorify perpetuation of old-world social, legal, and cultural institutions to justify eradication of "savagery" and mastery of the wilderness. Interpreted as such, the genesis cycle in the Capitol's Rotunda constitutes a history lesson about the dependence/independence dichotomy that characterizes the relationship between Europe and its offspring.

A second unifying theme is the belief that the United States is a government of the people.[50] Each of the paintings portrays a large crowd gathered to witness a ceremony—the legal procedure of signing a document, the military formalities of receiving a surrender or relinquishing a commission, the religious sacraments of prayer and baptism, the imperial rites of conquest. Not only does the entire population participate in governmental affairs, but the orderly assemblies in which they gather are directed toward a mutually beneficial goal. The notion of "due process," most precisely delineated in Trumbull's legislative chambers and battlefield surrenders, is also implicit in the well-structured rituals of the *Pocahontas* and *Pilgrim* paintings and the organized construction of the exploration parties in the "discovery" scenes. Leaders—whether clergymen or conquistadors, generals or elected representatives—maintain order simply by applying wise and moderate counseling. Democracy thus pictured appears as a tempered participatory government devoid of the revolutionary excesses then exploding throughout Europe.

While all the Rotunda murals share broad conceptual similarities, in formal terms the four paintings commissioned in 1836 are the antitheses of Trumbull's rational symmetry. Figures merge and jumble, curves and diagonals predominate, horizontals and verticals—not to mention parallel lines—are rare. And there are thematic differences as well. In place of Trumbull's communal ceremonies of statehouse and battlefield, these scenes in a chapel, on shipboard, on a Caribbean beach, or on the banks of the Mississippi celebrate the valor and achievement of the individual. Temperate deliberations by statesmen and generals have given way to passion-

ate crusaders venturing into the hazardous unknown: Columbus defies current wisdom to pursue his own course, the Pilgrims leave familiar surroundings to face unanticipated perils, Pocahontas denounces her aboriginal past to embrace the ways of strangers, and de Soto charges into the wild and dangerous forests to spread European "civilization" into uncharted lands. Fervid convictions propel these heroes to the brink of melodramatic excitement and adventure, a fitting historical "lesson" for a nation facing a standoff between North and South, a skirmish for western lands, a struggle to handle increased immigration—all challenges their forefathers never anticipated.

Trumbull emphasized the orderly process of nation building, but the four later paintings, conceived amidst a ground swell of evangelical ardor, stressed the Christian character of America's founding. While the emblems in Trumbull's paintings—flags, uniforms, swords, documents—are entirely secular in character, religious objects—Bibles, baptismal fonts, crosses—are scattered through the murals by Weir, Chapman, Vanderlyn, and Powell. Pilgrims led by clergymen pray for a safe voyage; Pocahontas takes Anglican vows; priests accompany the exploring parties of Columbus and de Soto. For a nation founded to preserve the separation of church and state, the Christian content of the second set of Rotunda paintings seems curiously inappropriate when viewed today. But during the antebellum years, Christian values and national purpose were believed to be inseparable.[51] From the more obvious religious services taking place in *Embarkation of the Pilgrims* and *Baptism of Pocahontas* to the diminished references to "Papism" in *Landing of Columbus* and *Discovery of the Mississippi by De Soto*, missionary Protestantism prevailed. One would scarcely suspect that Columbus or de Soto were Catholic, for the priests and monks in both entourages have been relegated to the shadows while knights and noblemen surround the conquering hero. By neutralizing the Catholic presence and emphasizing the cross (a symbol shared by all Christians), the early Spanish explorers appear properly reverential yet divorced from overt associations with Rome. At the same time, the Pocahontas and Pilgrim paintings exude simple Protestant piety as worshipers in humble settings communicate directly with God. Aboard the rugged vessel about to depart from Delft Haven or in the primitive chapel at Jamestown, the placid atmosphere assures visitors to the Capitol that the United States had been initiated under the protective covenant of an austere, independent, and essentially democratic worship.

The eight paintings became permanent installations beneath the Capitol dome, but instead of representing Cooper's "American character," four reflect the ideology of republicanism filtered through the memories and minds of the Founding Fathers, and four convey the

50. The Capitol Rotunda. Photograph
courtesy National Graphics Center, Falls
Church, Virginia.

partisan ambitions, regional interests, and cultural bias- es of a generation divided by sectional tensions. In the cavernous Capitol entrance, these rituals of American history—government by law, rule by an assenting ma- jority, military security, Christianity, continental expan- sion, and the Euro-American triumph over the native population—stand as reminders of the way nineteenth- century Americans perceived their society (plate 50).[52] Absent from those perceptions were ethnic or racial groups then excluded from the mainstream, particularly African Americans, no doubt because the issue of slav- ery was so divisive that neither legislators nor artists dared even suggest it. If Cooper's notion of "American character" meant interpreting history by further enshrin- ing these prevailing beliefs, then the eight paintings in the Capitol's Rotunda bear witness to an age that has both shaped and haunted future generations.

"Freedom's Holy Cause"

History, Religious, and Genre Painting in America, 1840–1860

GAIL E. HUSCH

In the mid-nineteenth century, countless observers remarked, the United States whizzed along on a train called Progress, its head spinning as the present flashed by in a whirl of newspaper extras. "We are always in a restless fever of agitation," an American journalist wrote in 1845. "We forget what is past and bend forward to what is future."[1] Such technological miracles as the train, the steam engine, and the telegraph collapsed the perceived boundaries of space and time. In record numbers Americans pulled up stakes and, lured by expanding territories and promises of prosperity, headed West. The population grew, supplemented by immigrants with unfamiliar habits, languages, and customs who swelled the voting ranks.

A nation with so much to absorb its attention would seem to have had little time to waste on bygone people and events. In fact, the United States, like the rest of the Western world in the nineteenth century, was obsessed with history. Most people believed that each successive age sent its unique influence, as one American journalist explained, "down the stream of time to the world's vast future."[2]

American artists at midcentury shared this fascination with the past and its influence on an unfolding future. The numerous scenes of American history they produced in these years are obvious testaments to an interest in exploring the nature of national destiny, but ostensibly unrelated subjects also carried within them indications of an intense concern with the onward "stream of time." Many genre scenes of contemporary American life cast backward looks toward a still-compelling past. Many paintings of biblical prophecy were tokens of fearful yearning toward a fast-approaching future. Historical, genre, and biblical paintings reveal their complexity when they are explored in each other's company and within the web of social, political, and religious concerns that animated Americans at midcentury.

Frances William Edmonds's *Image Peddler* (plate 52) visualizes the relationship between America's past accomplishment and its future potential. A grandfather in old-fashioned knee breeches expounds on a plaster bust of George Washington for the patriotic edification of his grandson, who wears a Continental army uniform. Washington was the paradigm of what Americans had come to accept as the Revolutionary generation's mythic courage and spirit of self-sacrifice. This is the lineage, Edmonds asserts, from which young America springs, and it must nurture the present in order to shape the future. Remembrance of this lineage was crucial. "Now that we have grown to be a mighty nation," the contemporary commentator Lewis G. Clark advised, ". . . let us not forget the blessed boon for which [our forefathers] fought and suffered. . . . Look at the great legacy which has been left to us by these brave spirits—free institutions [and] the blessings of civil and religious liberty."[3]

Clark wrote these words in appreciation of another painting that conjured the memory of past heroism, Tompkins H. Matteson's *Spirit of 1776* (plate 53): he in fact renamed the painting "Freedom's Holy Cause." Widely distributed in the form of prints, *The Spirit of 1776* depicts a young Continental soldier gallantly leaving his home to take up arms for freedom. His aged parents hand him his weapons, his sister buckles his armor, and a boy fills his powder horn. An infant sleeps in the lap of his mother, who holds a newspaper dated July 4, 1776. As in *Image Peddler*, the lifetime and promise of the young nation is embodied in the imagery of an intergenerational family, from very old to very young, from the past to the future.

But the benefits of freedom won by "The Spirit of

51. Peter F. Rothermel. *Patrick Henry before the Virginia House of Burgesses*. 1851. 84 x 66" (210.0 x 165.0 cm.). Patrick Henry Memorial Foundation, Brookneal, Virginia.

52. Francis William Edmonds. *The Image Peddler.* ca. 1844. 33 x 42" (82.5 x 105.0 cm.). The New-York Historical Society, New York.

1776" were not to be taken for granted, Clark warned: the nation's future happiness and prosperity were conditional. The blessings of liberty earned by the Revolutionary generation would continue only if the nation followed a similar course of justice and piety. "Let us . . . wisely use the blessing of Liberty vouchsafed to us by a gracious and overruling Providence, through the instrumentality and patriotism of our forefathers, that it may long be continued to us;" Clark admonished, "and that we may become the moral magnet of attraction to the whole world."[4]

Matteson's *Spirit of 1776* was just one of many scenes of American Revolutionary history produced in the 1840s and 1850s. Such paintings as Emanuel Leutze's *Washington Crossing the Delaware* (plate 30) and Peter F. Rothermel's *Patrick Henry before the Virginia House of Burgesses* (plate 51) also served to reinforce in the public mind America's right to claim a special understanding of liberty and to qualify for the role of moral magnet. Such pious tributes to an idealized American past, designed to inspire personal emulation and encourage patriotism, provided unifying national memories for a disparate and often contentious society. But these reminders to "wisely use the blessing of Liberty" also served as goads to national righteousness

and beacons of future triumph—or so their creators and patrons hoped.

According to this conception of history, the United States was anointed to carry the ameliorating effects of technology, democracy, and Protestantism westward into the wilderness. As one observer wrote in 1851, "In Democracy . . . we see the hope of the world. . . . This will be but the beginning, as the great secular agent of Christianity in bettering man's earthly estate. . . . The distinct utterances of Holy Writ . . . all point to a coming 'Golden Age,' to a second and still brighter Eden on Earth."[5] Many Americans believed that their nation led the entire world towards a state of universal peace, liberty, and prosperity—the realization of the biblical millennium on earth and in real time. Literally, the millennium is the thousand-year period mentioned in Revelation 20:1–3 that is to succeed the Second Advent and precede the Last Judgment, when Satan is chained in the bottomless pit and Christ reigns triumphant. Many antebellum Americans, however, understood the millennium to be a gradually attainable period of universal harmony during which Christ ruled in spirit but not in flesh.

Asher B. Durand clearly visualized this ideology of American leadership in *Progress* (plate 54). In Durand's expansive landscape, the passing of the Indian and

53. Tompkins H. Matteson. *The Spirit of
1776.* ca. 1845. 25 x 30" (62.5 x 75.0
cm.). Private collection.

54. Asher B. Durand. *Progress.* 1853. 48 x 72" (120.0 x 180.0 cm.). The Warner Collection of the Gulf States Paper Corporation, Tuscaloosa, Alabama.

his primeval environment is evident in the tangled left foreground. As the composition moves us back in space—and forward in conflated time—the emblems of progress become visible. Trains, telegraphs, and steamboats are nestled comfortably, like the farmers and their livestock, in a pastoral setting dotted with rustic but sturdy cottages. A church steeple stands guard. A serpentine diagonal in the right of the painting, aided by receding telegraph lines and poles, draws viewers into the distance, toward the brilliant glow of the sun on the horizon. This light holds within it the promise of the consummation of prophecy in the earthly Good Time.

Other midcentury artists displayed their yearnings for an American-led world of peace and prosperity in more abstract terms. Junius Brutus Stearns completed *The Millennium* in 1849, and Jasper F. Cropsey depicted Isaiah's prophetic vision in his *Millennial Age* of 1854 (plate 55), a composition based on an 1851 painting he titled *The Spirit of Peace* (plate 56).[6] Both Cropsey paintings present an idyllic coastal landscape dotted with palm trees and bathed in golden light, and in both a central architectural element contains symbols of Isaiah's vision, most particularly the lion, lamb, and child coexisting in harmony.

Two wispy columns of incense—Cropsey's personal metaphor for pious faith—rise from the altar in *The Millennial Age* and mingle to form gentle clouds in an otherwise perfect sky. A shepherd, a woman with a distaff, and three young boys are gathered in the central foreground. The seated youth in the middle holds a harp,

the instrument of prophecy, and his companions write on sheets of white paper. The arcadian mood of the landscape is projected into the future through these children, whose poetic voices continue the work of prophesying history and recording its fulfillment. Cropsey's *Spirit of Peace* and *Millennial Age* are timeless and abstract conceptions of the spiritual, emotional, and physical experience of God's sanctified kingdom, symbolized as a reincarnation of the Edenic paradise.

To many antebellum Americans, each episode in their nation's history—but most particularly the successful struggle for independence—had a spiritual and prophetic role to play in the arrival of this kingdom on earth. The heroes of 1776 had fulfilled their millennial destiny. It was up to modern Americans to do the same.

The self-imposed responsibility to be the world's moral center and to lead it into the millennium weighed heavily on the minds of many thoughtful Americans, who in poems, essays, sermons, and speeches of the 1840s and 1850s constantly found themselves morally inadequate to the generation of the Founding Fathers. "Fulfilling the Founder's expectations and preserving their achievements," Michael Kammen has written, "was the most persistent theme in the decades after 1832."[7] According to Ernest R. Sandeen, many were "desperate for reassurance that their nation had not strayed from the path laid out for them by providence."[8]

Some Americans believed that the continuing practice of slavery was a serious challenge to the achieve-

55. Jasper F. Cropsey. *The Millennial Age.* 1854. 38 x 54" (95.0 x 135.0 cm.). Newington-Cropsey Foundation, Hastings-on-Hudson, New York.

56. Jasper F. Cropsey. *The Spirit of Peace.* 1851. 44 x 67" (110.0 x 167.5 cm.). The Woodmere Art Museum, Philadelphia; bequest of Charles Knox Smith.

ments of 1776 and the nation's providential mission. Others warned that arguments over slavery fomented disunion and thus betrayed the past as they threatened the nation's future. Many perceived materialism, selfishness, ambition, or pride as modern American vices incompatible with the revolutionary virtue of self-sacrifice for the common good. As George H. Callcott observed, "Men of both sides in every dispute—tariff, improvements, expansion, slavery, secession—argued in terms of retaining the faith of the founding fathers or of renewing that faith."[9]

A number of specific events in the late 1840s and early 1850s brought these general concerns into sharper focus and caused many to wonder just how far the nation was straying from the millennial path laid out by the heroes of 1776. Secular and religious journalists noted a growing anxiety among Americans provoked by such "signs of the times" as the Irish potato famine of 1845 to 1846. The famine, which drove thousands to the United States and reinforced already existing concerns about the assimilation of immigrants into American life and the democratic process, caused many to consider the nature of providential judgment. The country undertook its first foreign war, severing diplomatic relations with Mexico in March 1845, declaring war in May 1846, and signing a peace treaty in July 1848. The war with Mexico encouraged territorial acquisition and westward expansion, intensified conflict over the spread of slavery in the United States, and exacerbated dangerous rivalries between North and South. Before exploding into civil war, sectional conflicts threatened disunion; they colored the election of 1848 and all electoral politics thereafter. The Compromise of 1850, designed to assuage tensions, only intensified them: its infamous Fugitive Slave Act incensed radical abolitionists and disgusted many moderate antislavery sympathizers. In 1848 and for several succeeding years a series of liberal and nationalistic revolutions rocked Europe; the Italian, French, German, and Hungarian struggles excited American sympathy while causing some to question their slaveholding nation's role as beacon of liberty to the world. The discovery of gold in 1848 unleashed an epidemic of gold fever, which, in 1849, coincided with the nation's worst epidemic of cholera since 1832.

Each of these situations forced Americans to examine with unusual fervor their country's moral rectitude and to wonder what the future held. Did the prosperity of the United States, its burgeoning democracy, its expanding borders indicate divine pleasure, they wondered, or did its materialism, its militarism, and its slaveholding invite divine wrath? Fear of cataclysmic civil strife vied in the popular mind with visions of perfect unity. The American antebellum mind, as historian James H. Moorhead has explained, balanced precariously "between progress and apocalypse."[10] "The future," a journalist noted in 1848, "sometimes lowers, sometimes brightens, ominous-hopeful before us."[11]

In the years around 1850, journalists noted that contemporary events in the United States and abroad had stimulated popular interest in the study of biblical prophecy. Many Americans interpreted war, revolution, famine, cholera, and the increased struggle over slavery as apocalyptic omens. Commentators perceived a general mood of heightened expectation, a popular sense that the divine plan was heading more quickly than usual towards some kind of ultimate resolution. As one journalist explained in April 1850, "The course of events has . . . been adapted to awaken curiosity and excite investigation [in the subjects of biblical prophecy]: and the extraordinary occurrences of the last two years, aroused an almost universal apprehension that other great changes were at hand."[12]

The prophetic books of the Old and New Testaments—Isaiah, Jeremiah, Ezekiel, Daniel, Revelations—provided clues to the nature of these great changes, to the meaning of current events, and to the providential design of history. Presbyterian minister Albert Barnes, a popular biblical expositor, observed that in times of crisis human beings instinctively searched secular history and the scriptural record of prophecy "to see whether these very events may not be shadowed forth in some symbol till now not understood."[13] To Barnes and devout Americans like him, "these very events"—the ones then occurring as well as their historical antecedents—had already been woven into the cosmic web of divine history. A Christian's duty was to perceive, as far as human myopia would allow, the will and plan of Providence revealed in the events around him and to contribute to the fulfillment of this plan. Unusual concern with the fulfillment of divine history is apparent in the great number of apocalyptic paintings that appeared in the United States in the years around 1850. Frederic Edwin Church, for example, produced *The Plague of Darkness* in 1849 and *The Deluge* in 1851, James H. Beard painted *The Last Victim of the Deluge* in 1849, and Asher B. Durand exhibited *God's Judgment upon Gog* (plate 57) in the spring of 1852.[14]

In *God's Judgment upon Gog*, Ezekiel is depicted standing with prophetically outstretched hand on a ledge overlooking an abyss and presiding over the destruction by beasts and birds of prey of the errant Prince Gog and his armies. Gog's oppression of the peaceful people of Israel and his disdain for God's law invited divine wrath. Most commentators noted how unusual this violent Old Testament subject was for the typically more pastoral Durand. According to the artist's son, the subject was "prescribed by, and painted for, Mr. Jonathan Sturges," a New York merchant and art patron.[15] Sturges's apparent piety as well as his interest in the important issues of the day suggests why he might have been drawn

57. Asher B. Durand. *God's Judgment upon Gog.* 1852. 60¾ x 50½" (151.9 x 126.2 cm.). The Chrysler Museum, Norfolk, Virginia; photograph by Scott Wolff.

to a subject of divine retribution. Sturges's obituary reported that "in religion Mr. Sturges was a member of the Reformed church" and that he "was a stanch [*sic*] supporter of Republican institutions and was a recognized leader of the anti-slavery movement."[16]

Sturges's apparent interest in liberty must have been stirred in the 1840s and 1850s when the issues of American slavery and European revolution burned red-hot. In her journal entry for February 2, 1852, Sturges's daughter Virginia commented on two important events outside the domestic sphere that must have been important topics of family discussion: Napoleon III's coup d'état and the Hungarian revolutionary Louis Kossuth's American visit (Kossuth was called, among other things, the "Washington of Hungary"). "Kossuth [is] now among us pleading the cause of his downtrodden fatherland," she wrote, "and this year sees France once more in the pow-

er of a Napoleon who is advancing towards his throne through throngs of victims to a longing for liberty they have never seen."[17]

The social and political upheavals that intersected at midcentury raised questions in American minds about their ultimate purpose in the providential scheme. John Greenleaf Whittier, in a poem entitled "The Peace of Europe," lamented the European situation in apocalyptic language.[18] The poem scorned the idea that—as her kings and priests claimed—peace and order reigned in Europe. Not, Whittier scoffed, while patriots and fighters for liberty were locked in foul dungeons and princes, kaisers, priests, and czars once more held carnival. The "White Angel of the Lord"—symbol of a "better day"— would never, Whittier warned, grace any land—European or American—where slavery ruled. Whittier hoped that the voice of Liberty "might pierce the ear/of princes, trembling while they hear/a cry as of the Hebrew seer/ REPENT! GOD'S KINGDOM DRAWETH NEAR!" In May 1852, in a letter to William Lloyd Garrison, Whittier envisioned a great clash of opposing forces, "the conflicts and skirmishes which are preparing the way for the great battle of Armageddon—the world-wide, final struggle between freedom and slavery." Whittier had no doubt of "the certain victory of the right."[19]

The bitter animosity engendered by the passage of the Fugitive Slave Act of 1850 was, to many Americans, particularly compelling evidence of the forthcoming struggle between freedom and slavery. Harriet Beecher Stowe's *Uncle Tom's Cabin*, begun in 1851, was written to protest the law and to present graphically the evils of slavery. In her "Concluding Remarks," Stowe asked her readers to consider the awful consequences if the United States did not repent its injustice and cruelty. The Union could not be saved, she warned, and the promised day of grace would never come. Stowe described the unique character of the present age as it struggled for universal liberty, and she prophesied a grave national fate:

> A mighty influence is abroad, surging and heaving the world, as with an earthquake. And is America safe? Every nation that carries in its bosom great and unredressed injustice has in it the elements of this last convulsion. O, Church of Christ, read the signs of the times! . . . Can you forget that prophecy associates . . . the *day of vengeance* with the year of his redeemed. . . . injustice and cruelty shall bring on nations the wrath of Almighty God![20]

The language of doom and promise Stowe and Whittier used in their literary reaction to contemporary events offers a compelling parallel to the apocalyptic imagery of Durand's painting. Questions of human and divine government are as fundamental to *God's Judgment upon Gog* as they are to Whittier's "Peace of Europe" and Stowe's *Uncle Tom's Cabin*. In an 1873 address Sturges denounced tyranny and oppression and asserted that justice and humanity were the commandments of God. His assertion implies a belief that those who ignored such commandments—like Prince Gog or present-day kings—naturally invited divine retribution. Perhaps, given his apparent antislavery position, Sturges also saw that the American government was at war with its own legacy of liberty and, consequently, with God's plan. Straying from the providentially ordained path of virtue and justice broken by the heroes of 1776 could only invite divine retribution; following its course was humanity's only hope.[21]

Yet even the bleak vision of human accountability offered in *God's Judgment upon Gog* holds the promise of a millennial outcome. After God vanquished Gog, he restored the Israelites to divine favor.[22] The promise of future calm is apparent in the blue sky, golden light, and quiet landscape glimpsed in the painting's background. A critic for *The Literary World* recognized the visual and thematic importance of this vista. "We are glad to escape over that mighty multitude of death-doomed men to the peaceful sunlight of the broad valley beyond," he wrote, ". . . It gives a point of relief to both the eye and the mind, without which the picture would only be a scene of carnage and terrible agony."[23]

Historical as well as biblical example spoke with particular eloquence to the anxieties and desires of a country consumed with change and faced with a growing sense of crisis, as the United States was by the late 1840s. When, as Kammen observed, "Americans have felt a buoyant sense of optimism about the present and future, they have been comparatively uninterested in their origins."[24] But when confused by the events of the present, modern Americans could find some measure of stability and moral compass by searching the past. The nation's Revolutionary era, now viewed as its heroic golden age, was a clear and unequivocal beacon in a rapidly changing world. Some used episodes from this era to validate the country's expansionist present and to bolster its faith in progress. But others invoked the hallowed past to admonish a nation they saw hurtling towards annihilation.

This serious questioning of the place of America's Revolutionary past in a rapidly changing present—all with an eye to America's ultimate destiny—is evident even in a genre painting such as George Caleb Bingham's *County Election* (plate 59), a view of American democracy in action. A stooped old man hobbles through the crowd of expectant voters and obsequious politicians who gather around Bingham's midwestern courthouse. The only figure who descends the courthouse stairs, he has just finished casting his vote. He bucks the upward diagonal sweep of the crowd and moves against the tide of a younger America.

The old man's identity is unequivocally indicated in a drawing (plate 58), in which the numerals "76" inscribed on his hat immediately label him as a Revolutionary veteran. Like the bust of Washington in Edmonds's *Image Peddler*, Bingham's veteran is a reminder of the country's heroic past, an evocation of the virtues dramatized in Matteson's *Spirit of 1776*. Although his fellow citizens ignore him, Bingham's veteran plays a significant role in the composition. He is literally at the visual heart of the painting: his figure marks the absolute center of the canvas; his upper body and especially his head are accorded a halo of space. "Old '76" is the axle around which all other activity revolves: his presence underscores the place of Revolutionary history in antebellum America and its perceived relationship to the contemporary democratic process.

This democratic process, as the figure of "Old '76" reminds us, was set in motion through the courage,

58. George Caleb Bingham. *Veteran of
'76*. 1851–52. Drawing. 11⅜ x 9" (29.0 x
22.5 cm.). The Saint Louis Art Museum,
Saint Louis, Missouri; lent by the People
of Missouri.

59. George Caleb Bingham. *The County Election*. 1851–52. 37⁷⁄₁₆ x 48¾" (90.1 x 123.82 cm.). The Saint Louis Art Museum, Saint Louis, Missouri.

virtue, and self-sacrifice of his Revolutionary generation. But do the modern voters who surround him—the benefactors of this sacrifice—possess similar moral standards and mental capabilities? Can they maintain the republic established by "Old '76" and his peers? To some Americans in the antebellum period, the spread of suffrage among more classes and types of white males and the rise of mass politics and public electioneering seemed a happy extension of the Revolutionary legacy. But many others were concerned that such developments placed reasoned, thoughtful government by the people in jeopardy.

The Irish voter (so identified in contemporary reviews of the painting and distinguished by his stereotypical pug nose, stocky physique, and red hair) who replaces "Old '76" at the head of the courthouse steps makes the focus of this question even more explicit. The assimilation of immigrants into the American democratic process was hotly debated in the 1840s and 1850s. While both the Whig and, particularly, the Democratic parties recruited immigrant voters, nativists argued that most Europeans were unfit by background and education to be natural heirs to Yankeedom's "Spirit of 1776." When people who lacked, in their opinion, the capacity for self-government were allowed to vote, "our institutions must totter and fall into that deep abyss, where lie the wrecks and ruins of ancient republics."[25] Such language underscores the deep-seated fear of national chaos and disintegration that haunted the progressive United States.

Is Bingham's *County Election* a nativist warning about the evils of immigrant voting, or does it celebrate the continuation of a process begun by "Old '76," his leaders, and his peers?[26] Does Bingham present his motley assortment of voters as evidence of democracy out of control or to indicate a diverse citizenry coexisting in freedom? These crucial questions are raised but not clearly answered in Bingham's painting, where signs of drinking, fighting, and election-day chicanery mix with examples of thoughtful discussion and quiet deliberation.

In *County Election*, Bingham acknowledges the complexity of American society and understands its urgent need to weigh present conditions against past accomplishments. Whatever Bingham's personal assessment of the state of American democracy at midcentury, the most revealing aspect of his *County Election* is its ambiguity. Driven by uncertainty and haunted by doubts, Bingham's generation asked questions whose answers they anticipated both with fear and hope. This tension is woven into the fabric of *County Election*.

Yet the painting is governed by an overriding visual order that contains the imperfect aspects of the modern American democratic process. Bingham—for all the painting's ambiguity—tilts the scales towards an affir-

mation of contemporary American republicanism. The clear rectangular space of the courthouse porch intersects with the broad-based triangular mass of bodies to create a monumental and stable structure that calls to mind Bingham's Whig concern with social order and unity. In the context of the sectional tensions then disturbing the nation, Bingham constructed an image of national harmony more hoped for than actually attained, one that suggested the millennial implications accorded American democracy.

More of the figures in the painting, a varied group marked by economic and social differences in dress and demeanor, are intent on their republican duty than on drinking or fighting. None pays much attention to the wily politician soliciting their votes. And the Irishman, peacefully assimilated into American society, exercises his voting "privilege" with dignity and seriousness. Bingham treats him with none of the caricatured excess that disfigured many midcentury images of Irish people.

Bingham's Irishman forces a comparison of the American political and economic situation to that of Europe. Memories of the famine that drove many Irish to the United States and of the revolutions that by 1851 had failed to overthrow authoritarian rule only reinforced what many Americans considered the exceptional nature of their national form of government and their country's providential mission of liberty.[27] The national mood evoked in *County Election*, where free Americans vote beneath a sky of what Elizabeth Johns has termed "Edenic beauty," is hearty, humorous, and undeniably peaceful.[28]

"Old '76," souvenir of the United States' own successful overthrow of despotism, is a mark of national pride in Bingham's *County Election*. He reminds modern viewers of their heritage, but, old and frail, he also warns them of their responsibility. *County Election* is not an unequivocal affirmation of the actual state of democracy in modern America. Yet it does offer hope that, given a thoughtful, self-controlled citizenry, the legacy of "Old '76" can and will be maintained.

The tension suggested in Bingham's *County Election* is even more palpable in Richard Caton Woodville's *Old '76 and Young '48* (plate 60), which offers no comfortable reconciliation between the days of General Washington and those of General Taylor.[29] Woodville, like Bingham, used a frail old veteran as symbol of America's earlier struggle "for Freedom's cause." The artist included other evocative details—the aged man's oval portrait as a youthful soldier in his Continental army uniform, a bust of George Washington, and a framed print of John Trumbull's *Declaration of Independence*.[30] The young officer, wounded in the Mexican War but in high spirits, regales his parents, young sibling, grandfather, and black household servants with stories of his recent adventures. His extended arm gestures in the direction of his grandfather's youthful portrait, indicating the gallantry that united them as American soldiers, while his eyes are fixed on the man's now-aged form.

American supporters of the war with Mexico employed references to the earlier, undeniably noble struggle in the service of their cause.[31] They argued that the United States was continuing the providential process of republican influence begun by the Revolution, extending the millennial benefits of liberty—and Protestantism—to a backward, Catholic people. As *The Home Journal* boasted in July 1848, "We vanquish in order to elevate. . . . It is a divine, rather than a mortal trait, thus to exert superior force—not to appropriate a triumph, but to diffuse a blessing. . . . The duty of maintaining uninjured . . . this matchless establishment, which God and our forefathers have given us, is of infinite responsibility."[32]

But antiwar activists just as frequently portrayed the Revolutionary War as a noble struggle for freedom in contrast to the Mexican War, an aggressive war of imperialism that they believed negated all that republics stood for.[33] Critics' of the war saw the spread of slavery, sectional divisiveness, and imperialism as serious threats to the nation's ability to carry on the legacy of the Revolutionary generation. They invoked and challenged the nation's identity as a new chosen people whom God destined to redeem humanity and usher in the millennial age. In January 1851, for example, D. H. Barlow decried America's propensity for "waging wars of spoliation on weaker powers." He warned, "I find myself glancing back at that old-time appalling doom of the 'chosen people of God.' I cannot but query, 'Are we, in very deed, to betray our transcendent trust, to falsify our lofty mission, and wantonly extinguish our unparalleled hopes?'"[34]

The troubled visage of "Old '76" as he listens with averted gaze to his grandson reflects something of this concern. Certainly Woodville's link to the glorious Revolutionary past does not, by carriage or expression, affirm victorious American exploits in Mexico. Woodville's image, like Bingham's *County Election*, raises but does not clearly answer the anxious query, "Fathers! have ye bled in vain?" which troubled the national conscience.[35]

Bingham and especially Woodville produced disquieting images of confrontation, in which the virtuous legacy of the Revolutionary generation is disturbingly frail and buffeted by modern issues of immigration, imperialism, slavery, and territorial expansion. But other artists chose to present this legacy as if it were still vigorous—as the youthful "Spirit of 1776" rather than the doddering "Old '76." Such paintings as Peter F. Rothermel's *Patrick Henry* (plate 51) manifested the "ominous-hopeful" tension of the times, reconstructing the drama and humanity of national history with such immediacy as to bridge any emotional rift between past and present. And such paintings reinforced America's preoccupation with its duty to organize the rights of man, using the visual language and tenor of biblical prophecy to underscore the nation's place in the providential plan.

Late in 1851, the Philadelphia Art Union commissioned Rothermel, the city's most highly regarded history painter, to produce a work that would be engraved for its subscribers and that would encourage "national spirit and national pride."[36] Completed by January 1852, Rothermel's painting commemorates the moment in May 1765 when Patrick Henry announced his resolutions in opposition to the hated Stamp Act before the Virginia House of Burgesses. One 1852 key to the painting described the scene:

> "Caesar had his Brutus!" Henry cried, "Charles the First his Cromwell, and George the Third _____." At this moment the speaker cried "treason!" and "treason, treason!" was re-echoed in every part of the House. Henry faltered not an instant, but rising to a loftier attitude, and fixing on the Speaker an eye of the most determined fire, he finished the sentence with the firmest emphasis—"may profit by their example! If this be treason, make the most of it."[37]

Henry, his right arm raised, dominates the vertical arrangement. He addresses the cringing figure of John Robinson, Speaker of the House, located in the upper left.[38] In the middle of the composition, the clerk of the House looks on in consternation while a member approaches to whisper "impeachment" in his ear. In the left foreground, Edmund Pendleton, a distinguished lawyer, extends his hand as if to silence the inflammatory Henry. Seated in front of Pendleton, Richard Henry Lee grips his chair and gazes out of the composition. All around, other figures stare, some infuriated by Henry's audacity, others galvanized by his courage. Women, alarmed by the cries of treason, are hurriedly leaving their seats in the gallery. A mysterious glove, its owner not identified by any visual clue, lies directly in the center of the painting's foreground and suggests that this is a moment of dangerous challenge.

Rothermel originally envisioned a horizontal format and a simpler composition for the painting.[39] The vertical orientation of the finished work emphasizes the drama of the moment while it plays havoc with the architectural reality of the House of Burgesses in Williamsburg. Rothermel placed women, who were not allowed into the chamber of the House, in an imaginary gallery. Like peripheral but presiding angels, brightly lit and in direct line of Henry's eloquently raised arm, they register alarm and interest in the proceedings and obliquely acknowledge a feminine contribution to Revolutionary struggle.

Rothermel also took liberties with the figure of Patrick Henry. The artist admitted that the red cloak was histori-

60. Richard Caton Woodville. *Old '76 and Young '48.* 1849. 21 x 26⅞" (52.5 x 67.2 cm.). Walters Art Gallery, Baltimore, Maryland.

61. Godefroid Guffens. *Rouget de Lisle
Singing the "Marseillaise."* 1849. 52 x 67"
(130.0 x 167.5 cm.). The Pennsylvania
Academy of the Fine Arts, Philadelphia.

cally inaccurate, and he gave Henry a powdered wig instead of a more likely, and more modest, brown one. The red cloak and white wig add a dimension of authority and dignity to the figure that a stricter realism might have muted.[40] Still, Rothermel clothed his hero in plain dark vest, breeches, and stockings, which contrast with the gorgeous apparel of most of the other Burgesses. Apparently, Rothermel wished to indicate certain aspects of Henry's public image—his modest egalitarianism and dislike of aristocratic privilege as well as the inherent nobility and grandeur of a born leader.

The theme of Rothermel's *Patrick Henry* affirms a fundamental tenet of American self-definition—the country's God-given custodianship of individual liberties—at a moment when Americans, concerned by developments in Europe, were particularly aware of their country's "providential" mission. On May 14, 1848, at the First Presbyterian Church in Philadelphia, the Reverend Barnes delivered a sermon that directly linked American history, European revolution, and prophetic fulfillment.[41] Barnes's title—"The Casting Down of Thrones. A Discourse on the Present State of Europe"— was taken from Daniel 7:9, a passage describing a vision of divine judgment and heralding the coming of the Messiah. Trying to make sense of the "surprising and unexampled" events then occurring in the world, Barnes wanted to "assign those events their appropriate place in the divine arrangement" by looking at the scriptural prophetic records for symbolic parallels. "If there is any single phrase that will best characterize the events now occuring [*sic*] abroad," Barnes explained, "it is 'THE

CASTING DOWN OF THRONES.'" Barnes made clear the debt that many Americans felt Europe (particularly France) owed them: "She has caught the love of liberty from our example . . . and seeks to enjoy a republic modeled after the fashion of our own." In his view, the American and European revolutions were all stages in the world's progress toward the millennium.[42]

Rothermel's painting similarly links his nation's successful eighteenth-century revolution to the mid-nineteenth-century European upheavals then running their course. This relationship, though implicit in the painting, becomes clearer when Rothermel's work is compared to an almost contemporary European painting. Mark Thistlethwaite has observed that Belgian artist Godefroid Guffens's *Rouget de Lisle Singing the "Marseillaise"* (plate 61) was one possible inspiration for Rothermel's *Patrick Henry*.[43] Dated 1849 and on view in Philadelphia since 1849 or 1850, Guffens's image was itself a reaction to the 1848 French revolution. It depicts that moment when young Rouget de Lisle first sang his new composition, "the celebrated Marseillaise hymn."[44] An article in *Graham's Magazine* attributed the popularity of Guffens's painting to its subject, which "appeals to that feeling so quickly aroused in every American heart . . . the hatred of tyranny and oppression."[45] Rothermel's Patrick Henry and Guffens's Rouget de Lisle are brothers united against tyranny. Both paintings focus on a brave young leader whose inspired face, upraised arm, and impassioned words send shock waves through his transfixed listeners.

Other midcentury American artists expressed, as

62. William W. Walcutt. *Pulling Down the Statue of George III at Bowling Green.* 1857. 51⅛ x 77⅝" (129.0 x 194.0 cm.). Lafayette College, Easton, Pennsylvania.

Vincent Colyer then put it, "deep interest in the great effort that has been going on these last few years, in Europe, for the good of mankind" and used images from American Revolutionary history to comment on contemporary European struggles.[46] Barbara Groseclose has clearly established this political context for Emanuel Leutze's *Washington Crossing the Delaware* (plate 30).[47] Leutze painted two versions of the scene between 1849 and 1851 in Düsseldorf, a hotbed of German liberalism and nationalism which helped foment the 1848 revolution. Groseclose has described Leutze's painting as "a brilliant metaphor for psychological encouragement," which Leutze designed expressly to rally demoralized German revolutionaries. Leutze depicted Washington leading his cold and hungry troops across the Delaware River in the dead of night on December 25, 1776, as they prepared to ambush the enemy at dawn. The episode, treated—like Rothermel's *Patrick Henry*—more dramatically than facts warranted, offered Washington as a modern Moses. He is a model of resourceful courage, undaunted even in the face of physical hardship and apparent defeat. Similarly, Arthur Marks has interpreted William W. Walcutt's *Pulling Down the Statue of George III at Bowling Green* (plate 62)—a scene of American colonists committing symbolic regicide in 1776—in light of both the French and the Hungarian situations.[48] Walcutt was one of a number of New York artists who volunteered to design decorative arches and tableaux in honor of the visit of Louis Kossuth, the Hungarian revolutionary leader, in late 1851.

Rothermel's *Patrick Henry* also shows its creator's—and the public's—interest in European revolution. Like Barnes's sermon, it too recognizes the apocalyptic implications the nineteenth century saw in these and all revolutionary struggles. The prophetic dimension of Rothermel's painting is manifest in the figures of Patrick Henry and the Speaker of the House, probably inspired, as Thistlethwaite has observed, by the prophet Daniel and King Belshazzar in Washington Allston's *Belshazzar's Feast* (plate 63). Patrick Henry—symbol of American mission and agent of divine admonition—warns the English monarchy of its impending defeat, just as Daniel prophesied the fall of Babylon. Poised against a dark and shadowy backdrop, with the same pose and fervor as Allston's Daniel, Henry gestures upward towards a brilliant, empty expanse of wall. Rothermel's speaker, like Allston's Belshazzar, draws back in alarm from the warning. *Graham's Magazine* described Rothermel's figure of Henry in language that emphasizes a message of divine justice: "The impassioned orator stands erect and self-possessed, his open hand aloft, as though a thunderbolt has just passed from his fingers."[49] Henry's pose and gesture are analogous to those of the prophet Ezekiel in Durand's contemporary *God's Judgment upon Gog*.

Just as Rothermel's *Patrick Henry* recognizes American leadership in the progress of freedom, it also suggests the still-unfolding nature of this progress. The casting down of thrones evoked in Barnes's sermon is implied in Patrick Henry's accusatory gesture. The stone structure that enframes and supports the symbol of British monarchy cracks beneath his divine eloquence, just as the statue of King George topples in Walcutt's painting. In *Patrick Henry* we can discern the first tremors of an apocalyptic earthquake destined to crumble all thrones and castles to dust. In it Rothermel has reconstructed, as Barnes put it, "an epoch in the history of the world—a step in the progress towards that period when 'thrones' are to be everywhere cast down, and when universal liberty shall prevail."[50]

This approaching millennium of universal liberty is implied in Rothermel's conception by the figure of Richard Henry Lee, who like Henry opposed the Stamp Act. While the cowering Robinson is small and almost lost in the shadows, Lee shares compositional weight with Henry. Both wear warm, richly colored drapery and are linked by subtle parallel gestures.

Yet, while all other eyes are pinned on Henry's powerful form, Lee has his back towards the excitement. Lee's gaze and position leads the painting out of Revolutionary America into the mid-nineteenth century and beyond. Although he focuses above it, an ominous shadow darkens the empty space before him. He grips the edge of the table and the arm of his chair with almost painful force. He concentrates on an internal vision inspired by the import of Henry's prophetic words and action. Rothermel's figure of Lee, his body frozen in tense anticipation as he gazes into the future, suggests the mingling of hope and fear so characteristic of these midcentury years. "Lee sees by a sort of prophetic intuition," wrote the reporter for *Graham's Magazine*, "the full import of this inspired oratory. His very face, under the magic of Mr. Rothermel's genius, is a long perspective of war, desolation, heroic deeds, and the thick-coming glories of ultimate civic and religious liberty."[51] Lee imagined the struggle and the sacrifices that would have to be endured. More important, he saw beyond to the blessings of liberty that would eventually be realized.

Rothermel's *Patrick Henry* is a double portrait of American prophecy in action, a warning and an encouragement for the modern world. Few Americans believed that "ultimate civic and religious liberty" had yet been attained, even in the progressive United States. Patrick Henry, a plebeian Daniel amid the richly aristocratic House of Burgesses, thunders a warning to the despotism embodied in the power of George III. He fills the timid with courage and literally points the way onward and upward. Henry is the prophet as the voice of divine warning, urging the present to act in order to save and sanctify the future. On the other hand, Lee the visionary seer is outwardly removed and ostensibly

63. Washington Allston. *Belshazzar's Feast.* 1817–43. 144⅛ x 192⅛" (360.3 x 480.3 cm.). The Detroit Institute of Arts, Detroit, Michigan; gift of the Allston Trust.

passive as he inwardly paints a glorious social millennium, to be realized after the inevitable period of violence and upheaval.

Some Americans clearly recognized the connection implied in Rothermel's painting between their country's history, its role in the modern world, and the spiritual destiny of humankind. In the late 1850s Joseph Harrison, Jr., a Philadelphia collector with a particular interest in scenes of American history, acquired Rothermel's *Patrick Henry* as well as Cropsey's *Millennial Age* and his *Spirit of Peace*.[52] "Liberty is like the Christian Religion," Harrison wrote, "and man must be regenerated before he can understand its spirit or feel its value." He gave the United States a preeminent role in this secular and sacred regeneration of humanity, but he also recognized the uncertainty of its outcome: "The United States has an important mission to fulfill in the world's progress, and well it will be for her and the world if nothing occurs to stop her on her onward course."[53] Harrison saw many obstacles to this onward course, particularly slavery and unbridled democracy, but he retained a fundamental hope in its eventual triumph.

Like many other mid-nineteenth-century white, well-to-do Americans, Harrison believed in the necessity of spiritual—specifically Protestant—regeneration as a prerequisite for successful republican government, which in turn was a prerequisite for the earthly millennium. And he, like many of his peers, saw America's unfolding

history as evidence of the nation's successful but as-yet incomplete mission. Harrison's own words suggest why he was drawn to both Rothermel's *Patrick Henry* and Cropsey's *Millennial Age*, and they indicate how American history and the fulfillment of biblical prophecy were intimately related in the antebellum American mind.

Even genre scenes—mediated images of contemporary life—could examine the role of history in the modern world and contemplate American destiny. Bingham's *County Election* and Woodville's *Old '76 and Young '48* plainly posed the question that haunted antebellum Americans and that reverberates in the Rothermel and Cropsey images: was the heroic legacy and millennial promise of the American Revolution surviving in the modern United States?

History painters such as Rothermel and Leutze, Walcutt and Matteson used all the eloquence of their art to convince audiences of the relevance and the vitality of this legacy. And such artists as Durand and Cropsey prophesied in paint the serious consequences of either ignoring or embracing it. History paintings like *Patrick Henry*, biblical subjects like Cropsey's *Millennial Age* and Durand's *God's Judgment upon Gog*, and genre scenes like Bingham's *County Election* complemented and reinforced each other in America's self-proclaimed scheme of providential progress. Merging secular and sacred, national and divine, they indicate how the nation's past served its present as compass of the future.

Historic Reportage and Artistic License

Prints and Paintings of the Mexican War

RON TYLER

When Richard Caton Woodville's *War News from Mexico* (plate 64) was exhibited at the American Art Union in 1849, many Americans could have recognized themselves in the picture. Jacksonian Americans, most of them fashionably attired, listen to the exciting news of the war that would extend the domain of the United States to the Pacific Ocean. But none of the eight white men in the view, the woman straining to hear from the window at the right, or the black man and girl in the foreground is the focus of Woodville's painting. Rather, it is the newspaper.[1]

Great advances in industrial technology and entrepreneurship gave birth in the 1840s to the "penny press," inexpensive, mass-produced newspapers. James Gordon Bennett, editor of one of the first penny-press newspapers, the New York *Herald*, used steam-powered oceangoing vessels to obtain news from around the world and steam-driven rotary presses to print twenty-five thousand sheets an hour. He introduced sensationalized police and crime reporting and daily money market and stock reports to a mass audience. Capitalizing on the public's growing taste for images, Bennett also brought the pictorial equivalent of today's "on the scene" report—crude woodcuts based on artists' renderings of events in the American war with Mexico—to the readers of the penny press.[2]

But Bennett's was not the only pictorial innovation of the day, for technological changes had come to printmaking as well. Alois Senefelder had revolutionized the industry in 1798 when he invented the process of lithography, by which a drawing could be reproduced so faithfully that artists spoke of the copies as multiple originals. The lithographic plate was easier to make than engraving or etching plates, for the artist drew directly onto a smooth, carefully prepared stone. Printers could make thousands more copies by lithography than by the centuries-old, laborious techniques of engraving and etching. Images of high quality could be produced quickly, routinely, and inexpensively.[3]

Lithography had become commercially viable in the United States in the 1820s. Beginning his apprenticeship in the lithographic business in 1828, Nathaniel Currier led a small band of artists, craftsmen, and salesmen who set their sights on creating and then satisfying the public's desire for pictures. His impact on the industry was apparent by 1840, when his best-selling lithograph of a steamboat disaster, published as a special edition of the New York *Sun*, established the idea of "rush stock"—inexpensive and timely lithographs printed to take advantage of a current event. Currier published at least seventy such prints of the Mexican War. They sold so well that he sometimes had to prepare two different stones of the same image to keep pace. His competitors copied his innovations, and other publishers distributed their prints through his network. Large-format, colored lithographs became virtually synonymous with Currier and his partner in later years, James Ives.[4]

Both the penny press and the fledgling lithographic industry were ready to respond when America's first foreign war began among the chaparral of the lower Rio Grande Valley in far south Texas on April 25, 1846. The first modern war correspondents, including artists, rushed to the scene and dispatched what the editor of the *Herald* called "daguerreotype reports," attempting to claim some of the authenticity and accuracy associated with the new photographic process for these eyewitness accounts. Their news-gathering and transportation networks were so efficient that President James K. Polk often gained his information from the newspapers rather than from his official dispatches. Before the *Herald* be-

Richard Caton Woodville. *War News from Mexico*, detail of plate 64.

64. Richard Caton Woodville. *War News from Mexico.* 1848. 27 x 24¾" (67.5 x 61.9 cm.). National Academy of Design, New York.

Facing page:
65. Emil Klauprecht (?) after Angelo Paldi. *Battle of Resaca de la Palma, May 9th 1846. Battle of Palo Alto, May 8th 1846.* 1847. Lithograph. 14⅞ x 19¼" (37.7 x 49.0 cm.). Prints and Photographs Division, Library of Congress, Washington, D. C.

gan running crude woodcuts, and before artists' drawings became available, the lithographers might also have used these early written reports as guides for their first prints.[5]

Most important events of the Mexican War are commemorated in oversize, colored lithographs. All the critical moments in General Zachary Taylor's campaign through northern Mexico are documented, as are Commodore Matthew C. Perry's attack on Veracruz and his expeditions up the Tuxpan and Tabasco rivers, Colonel Stephen Watts Kearney's rush to the Pacific, and General Winfield Scott's dramatic and relentless march from Veracruz into Mexico City. The majority of prints are hastily drawn, stereotypical battle or ceremonial scenes intended as commemorative souvenirs or memorials of brave warriors. Some depict improbable heroism, while others show camp scenes or the battle's aftermath. Most were probably copied from stock European prints or sprang from the fertile imagination of the craftsmen who worked for publishers James Baillie, Peter C. Duval, or Nathaniel Currier. Previously published images of Mexico or a *Herald* woodcut may also have served as guides for these images, which frequently bear no name other than that of the lithographer.[6] While they provide insight into the culture that created and cherished them, few historians would confuse these imaginative depictions with actual portrayals of the events themselves.

But other prints are carefully designed summaries of the conflicts based on eyewitness drawings that depict recognizable leaders, believable armies, and complex battle tactics, all evoking an immediate sense of authenticity in viewers. They are, in other words, the work of talented artists and are part of a distinguished tradition of military art and history painting. Publishers, thrilled with their new ability to communicate the immediacy of the war to the public, however, did not always see these pictures as a part of that tradition or choose to emphasize their often heroic nature. Most of these prints were smaller than twenty by thirty inches, minuscule by comparison with the great canvases history painters produced at the time. Publishers instead emphasized their timeliness, and some claimed overall authenticity, great accuracy in detail and spirit, for them. Reporters who had been on the scene verified them, and reviewers lauded them for their "faithfulness" and "strict adherence to nature." Even the grief-stricken Henry Clay of Kentucky wrote to thank one of the lithographers for the "rich and beautiful specimen of the Lithographic art" that depicted the battle of Buena Vista, at which his son had been killed.[7]

Little pictorial material other than the fanciful concoctions of Currier and his cohorts and the *Herald* woodcuts was produced until artists began to return from Mexico in 1846 and 1847. Then, dozens of prints based on eyewitness sketches were printed before the war concluded in 1848; more than one hundred were ultimately published. Indeed, artists and soldier-artists had been among the first American troops on the scene: Captain Daniel Powers Whiting commanded Company K of the Seventh Infantry in General Taylor's "Army of Observation" that arrived at Corpus Christi, Texas, on August 28, 1845; Sergeant Angelo Paldi was an Italian-born principal musician serving in the Fifth United States Infantry at the battles of Palo Alto and Resaca de la Palma; Private Stephen G. Hill was a member of the Ohio Volunteers at Monterrey; the young and untutored Samuel Chamberlain was among the fresh recruits who marched out of San Antonio with General John E. Wool's First Regiment of U.S. Dragoons bound for Mexico in September 1846. Two other painters "of known and acknowledged artistic ability, M. Chatilon of Paris, and M. Deville, the scene painter of New Orleans Theatre," might have followed the troops into Mexico with the intent of "giving to the world an accurate picture" of what happened at Palo Alto and Resaca de la Palma. And William G. Brown, a well-known artist, was welcomed into Taylor's camp to paint portraits of officers as well as a large canvas of Taylor and his officers. A sculptor named Garbeille even showed up at Monterrey to make a bust of Taylor.[8]

Private Hill's pictures of Monterrey were among the first eyewitness prints to appear because he was discharged after being wounded. He returned to Cincinnati, where he immediately made lithographs. Thomas Bangs Thorpe and William Seaton Henry included engravings after firsthand sketches in their books, *"Our Army" on the Rio Grande* (1846) and *Campaign Sketches*

of the War with Mexico (1847), and the German-language literary journal *Fliegende Blätter*, published in Cincinnati, printed lithographs based on Angelo Paldi's renderings of the battles of Palo Alto and Resaca de la Palma (plate 65). But the five prints of Daniel Powers Whiting's *Army Portfolio* marked a significant improvement over these first views, both in the quality of the original paintings as well as in the resulting lithographs.[9]

Born in 1808, Whiting was a West Point graduate who had received training in topographical drawing and had previously served in the Seminole War in Florida. He had finished his view of Taylor's Corpus Christi campsite by October 1845. By the time he reached Monterrey, on September 23, 1846, his work had come to the general's attention. Taylor excused him from all other duties and supplied him with a horse so that he could "go out into the hills" and do three more views. Whiting's brother-in-law, Napoleon J. T. Dana, also a member of the Seventh, predicted that Whiting would realize ten thousand dollars from his venture if he finished it.

Whiting sent his painting of Taylor's encampment to

BATTLE OF RESACA DE LA PALMA,
MAY 9TH 1846.

BATTLE OF PALO ALTO,
MAY 8TH 1846.

lithographer Edward Weber in Baltimore, but he was unhappy with the results.[10] The writer for *Niles' National Register* described the encampment as a "thousand spotless white tents, along the shelly margin of the shore of Corpus Christi Bay." Surviving copies of the image Charles Fenderich drew on stone for Weber appear to be similar to *Birds-eye View of the Camp of the Army of Occupation* (plate 66) as redrawn by Charles Parsons and printed by George and William Endicott. But the two versions in fact differ: the Fenderich/Weber version has more ships in the harbor and more clouds in the sky. Another view, also drawn on the stone by Fenderich but printed by Endicott, suggests why Whiting might have been displeased. Fenderich inserted three out-of-scale and out-of-place figures, a soldier (standing at left on the roof of the building in the foreground) dressed in a uniform more suitable for a veteran of the Napoleonic conflict than of the Mexican War and a pastoral group at the lower right, also on the roof of the building, sitting idly on what appear to be boulders! Fenderich may well have been attempting to add the classicism of traditional history painting to Whiting's more topographical painting.

Whiting's three other views—*Monterey, from Independence Hill, Heights of Monterey,* and *Valley Towards Saltillo*—also depict the Monterrey area. He offered the portfolio of tinted and colored prints to the public in June 1847. Family tradition holds that Whiting planned to include battles beyond Monterrey but gave up the idea when a steamboat carrying his other drawings sank en route to New York.[11] The *Army Portfolio* received enthusiastic reviews. "We had the pleasure of examining several of the original pictures as they passed through this city on their way to Washington," the New Orleans *Picayune* reported, "and can bear testimony to the spirit and fidelity with which they have been copied upon the stone. . . . All attest to Capt. Whiting's strict adherence to nature."[12] The *Knickerbocker* called it "exceedingly well lithographed."[13]

Major Joseph Horace Eaton, Taylor's aide-de-camp, provided sketches (including a portrait of Taylor) for several publications, among them Henry's *Campaign Sketches*, but his best work was a complex drawing of the crucial *Battle of Buena Vista* (plate 67), which turned into an American victory when the Mexican army left the field. The topography is generally correct, and the troop movements can easily be followed. Eaton even provided a detailed descriptive key on a separate sheet of paper. The *National Intelligencer* complimented Eaton on a work of "scenic art," while the *Literary World* concluded that the picture "conveys a more vivid and distinct impression to the mind of the beholder, than could be given in any verbal description."[14]

Following on the heels of Whiting's and Eaton's prints

Facing page:
66. Charles Parsons after Daniel Powers
Whiting. *Birds-eye View of the Camp of
the Army of Occupation, Commanded by
Genl. Taylor. Near Corpus Christi, Texas,
(from the North) Oct. 1845.* 1847. Hand-
colored lithograph. 12⅜ x 19⅜" (31.4 x
49.2 cm.). In Daniel Powers Whiting,
Army Portfolio. Amon Carter Museum,
Fort Worth, Texas.

67. Frances Flora Bond (Fanny) Palmer
after Joseph Horace Eaton. *Battle of
Buena Vista. View of the Battle-Ground
of the "Angostura" Fought Near Buena
Vista, Mexico February 23rd. 1847.
(Looking S. West.).* 1847. Hand-colored
lithograph. 19¼ x 29½" (48.9 x 74.9 cm.).
Amon Carter Museum, Fort Worth, Texas.

68. Gustavus Pfau after Henry Walke. *The U.S. Naval Battery during the Bombardment of Vera Cruz on the 24 and 25 of March 1847*. 1848. Hand-colored lithograph. 15⅛ x 22%₆" (38.4 x 57.3 cm.). In Henry Walke, *Naval Portfolio*. Amon Carter Museum, Fort Worth, Texas.

came Lieutenant Henry Walke's *Naval Portfolio*. The navy had been active in the defense of Texas, in transporting Taylor's army to Corpus Christi and in capturing Tampico and establishing a blockade of Mexico, but it had received virtually no attention until President Polk ordered the capture of Veracruz. Staying out of range of the cannon at San Juan de Ulloa, General Winfield Scott and Commodore David Conner carried out a landing on Collado beach, southeast of the city. Lieutenant Charles C. Barton, on the sloop-of-war *St. Mary's*, and Midshipman James M. Ladd, on board the *Spitfire*, provided sketches to Peter S. Duval of Philadelphia and to Currier, who published the first lithographs of naval action. But the prints that gained the most attention for the navy were the eight produced from Lieutenant Walke's paintings.[15]

Born to one of the most influential families in Virginia on December 24, 1809, Walke entered the United States Navy as a midshipman in 1827. As executive officer of the bomb-brig *Vesuvius*, he participated in the capture of Veracruz in March 1847, as well as in Commodore Perry's capture of the Mexican ports of Tuxpan and Villahermosa. The *Naval Portfolio* consists of eight tinted and hand-colored lithographs: one of the capture of Tuxpan, five of the Tabasco campaign, and two of the seige of Veracruz.[16]

The army and navy cooperated in taking Veracruz. Perry loaned naval guns, officers, and crew, which established themselves due south of the city, with the army batteries between them and the coastline. The shelling commenced when General Juan Morales re-

fused to surrender the city, the action Walke depicted in his *U.S. Naval Battery during the Bombardment of Vera Cruz* (plate 68). The fortifications and emplacements for battery number five were designed by Captain Robert E. Lee of the Army Corps of Engineers; the print shows the individual sandbags from which the breastworks were constructed. A fairly accurate view of the Veracruz skyline appears on the horizon. A comparison of the print with the original watercolor (in the collection of the U.S. Naval Academy Museum) shows that Gustavus Pfau, the lithographic artist, changed some small details of the image and inserted several neoclassical elements common to European and American history paintings of the day. In the left foreground of his painting of the bombardment of Veracruz, for example, Walke had shown four seamen carrying a wounded companion head-first off the hill. In the print, Pfau changed the grouping to three figures so that they hold the wounded man in a more classical and heroic pose. Walke's hand is, nevertheless, still apparent in the finished work.[17]

A number of artists who were already in Mexico when the war broke out also produced prints. John Phillips, a British artist, probably intended to produce a portfolio on Mexico to follow that of his countryman, Daniel Thomas Egerton's *Views in Mexico*, published in London in 1840. But when the war began, he incorporated aspects of the conflict into a number of images in his now timely *Mexico Illustrated in Twenty-Six Views* (London, 1848).[18] Little is known of Phillips or of his coauthor, Alfred Rider, but most of the pictures were probably made before the war. Some of them, such as his view of Puebla, were probably copied after Carl Nebel's earlier print of the city in his *Voyage pittoresque et archéologique dans la partie la plus interessante du Mexique*.[19]

Phillips's view *Matamoros* seems to show no evidence of the American occupation. Even the flags on the ships in the river are red, white, and green, the colors of Mexico. But a close examination of the print in the Amon Carter Museum collection reveals that the lithograph of the flag underneath the coloring appears to be the stars and stripes of the United States. Phillips might have made the print with an American audience in mind and then colored some of the prints differently as part of an effort to appeal to a non-American market, a fairly common adaptation for printmakers.[20] Several of Phillips's prints show Mexican troops—the soldiers in *Pass in the Sierra Madre—Near Monterey* (plate 69), for example, wear shakos—suggesting that he might have endured some risk to make his sketches: Americans had been ordered out of the country when the war began, and the British were often confused with Americans in Mexico.[21]

Two other artists who were in Mexico when the war began painted scenes from it. James Walker, an Englishman living in Mexico City, went into hiding when Americans were ordered to evacuate the city. He eventually made his way to the American lines, where he served as an interpreter and accompanied the troops from Puebla back into the capital. Carl Nebel was a German artist who had spent a number of years in Mexico and had published *Voyage pittoresque*, a stunning portfolio of people and views, in 1836. He was back in

Mexico in 1840 and might have remained there until the war ended.[22]

Walker witnessed a number of battles and sketched several of them firsthand. Four of his small oil sketches are in the West Point Museum, and a dozen others documenting the march from Puebla to Mexico City belong to U.S. Army Center of Military History (plate 70). Perhaps he was intending to make a print portfolio himself. His most famous painting, however, is *The Storming of Chapultepec*, which was chromolithographed by the New York firm of Sarony and Major and widely distributed. As with the battle itself, Walker's depiction was controversial because of uncertainty about who played the most critical roles in the battle. He began with the intention of showing "the assault and storming of Chapultepec on the 13th of last September, on the southeast side, by Maj. General Quitman's division." When word of the painting reached General Scott, he apparently asked Captain Benjamin S. Roberts to assist Walker with some of the details. Roberts later wrote that he had visited with Walker and arranged to purchase the painting, which "is in the hands of the Lithographers [in Mexico]" who expected soon to strike off the first copies, one of which Roberts planned to send to his wife. Walker apparently then undertook a second painting at the insistence of General Gideon J. Pillow, who claimed that the picture should show "the side of [the hill] occupied by his division," but he was diverted from the task so that he might produce another painting of Quitman's attack, which was purchased by Captain T. M. Davis, aide-de-camp to Generals John A. Quitman

69. After John Phillips. *Pass in the Sierra Madre—Near Monterey*. 1848. Hand-colored lithograph. 10⁷⁄₁₆ x 15½" (26.5 x 39.4 cm.). Plate 25 in John Phillips and Alfred Rider, *Mexico Illustrated in Twenty-Six Views* (London: E. Atchley, Library of Fine Arts, 1848). Amon Carter Museum, Fort Worth, Texas.

70. James Walker. *Scenes from the
Mexican War.* ca. 1848. 47½ x 86" (118.7
x 215.0 cm.). U.S. Army Center of
Military History, Washington, D.C.

and James T. Shields. The *Daily American Star* was lavish in its praise of the painting, concluding that it represents "faithfully one of the most gallant actions of the many that has distinguished this campaign, [and] as an historical production it is invaluable."[23]

The following month, a reporter for the *North American* noted that Walker had, indeed, begun a second picture showing the forces under General Pillow. "The view is taken from the battery commanded by Capt. Huger and takes in the grove at the foot of Chapultepec, the city of Mexico and the mountains in the rear," he wrote. "The forces under Gen's. Pillow and Worth [are] approaching from this side and we can easily distinguish the different corps, while Gen. Quitman's troops, with the storming party under Maj. Twiggs, are seen hotly engaged on the far right. In front many of our soldiers are seen advancing up the heights while the fire of musketry from the battlements looks very much as it did on the morning of the 13th of September." The editor concluded, "The picture is a very handsome one and we believe a faithful transcript of the prominent scene it represents."[24]

Nebel produced the best of the portfolios on the war in collaboration with George Wilkins Kendall, the editor and correspondent for the New Orleans *Picayune*. Kendall knew Mexico because he had been there several years before as a prisoner with the Texans captured in the Santa Fe expedition. He was with Taylor at the battle of Monterrey, perhaps, as one writer suggested, to gain some measure of revenge for his treatment at the hands of the Mexicans. Kendall was also with Scott during the southern campaign and as he entered Mexico City. Not only did Kendall agree to publish the folio of prints on the war with Nebel, but his stories, printed first in the New Orleans *Picayune* and then reprinted in newspapers throughout the nation, probably inspired dozens of artists to create their own heroic scenes of battle. Kendall thus might have been responsible for many more than the dozen prints issued under his and Nebel's names.[25]

Nebel's portfolio received good press notices even before it left Europe, where the best artists of London, Paris, and Brussels carefully drew and colored the prints at a rate of only one per day. The Paris correspondent for the *Herald* referred to the set as "one of the most superb works of art ever achieved in Paris," the plates "colored in the highest style of art." He concluded, "The fidelity of the landscapes, and the truthfulness of every point introduced into the pictures, cannot but be at once acknowledged and appreciated by the best *connoisseur*." Mentioning that Kendall had paid extra fees in order to ensure the best quality, the correspondent speculated that such a publication would be impossible in New York, even in ten years, simply because such talented craftsmen did not exist there. When the book finally reached the United States, Kendall advertised it in the *Picayune* for thirty-eight to forty dollars, depending upon the binding. The text and plates, suitable for framing, were sold separately for thirty-four dollars.[26]

There are a dozen prints in the portfolio, beginning with the *Battle of Palo Alto*, the first battle of the war, and concluding with *Genl. Scott's Entrance into Mexico* (plate 72). Kendall claimed that he had "personally examined the ground on which all [the battles] save that of Buena Vista were fought" and that Nebel had drawn most of the illustrations "on the spot," but there is no evidence that Nebel actually saw any of the battles. *Battle of Palo Alto* shows mountains in the background, but the site is in fact quite flat. Still, because artists were expected to render pleasing images of nature, Nebel probably added the scenery he felt the composition required.[27]

It is also true that Nebel did not need to visit each battle site to achieve an accurate rendering. Kendall helped him a great deal, but Nebel also had good models to work from in every instance, except for the two prints of the battle at Molina del Rey. Kendall was both reporter and participant in those conflicts, which occurred on the outskirts of Mexico City. The site was close enough that Nebel could easily have visited it. For the other battle scenes, Nebel might have used copies of the more than a dozen prints produced by Mexican lithographers, probably to sell to the occupying Americans. *View of Cerro Gordo, with Gen. Twiggs' Division Storming the Main Heights, 18th April*, for example, compares well with Nebel's print.[28]

Scott's Entrance into Mexico is an even better case in point. Nebel's picture shows the main façade of the eighteenth-century cathedral at center, the national palace with an American flag flying overhead at right, and General Scott accompanied by a body of dragoons with drawn sabers in the foreground. It is a dramatic view, clearly enhanced by Kendall's eyewitness description. It is possible also that Nebel was in the city at the time and witnessed the event. Yet the picture is, in fact, based largely on his depiction of this same view of the plaza, *Plaza Mayor de México* (plate 71), published fifteen years earlier in his *Voyage pittoresque*.

Perhaps because these images are so closely related to topographical maps and do communicate a good impression of the tactics and progress of the battles, reporters and reviewers alike heralded them as "accurate." "A half hour's study of Capt. Whiting's sketches will elucidate better than a volume of written description the movements of Gen. Worth's column in the great days of September," a reviewer for the New Orleans *Picayune* wrote, "and no other sketch impresses the mind palpably with the powers of resistance to assaults which a Mexican town presents in its mode of construction."[29] Historians, too, have suggested that these prints might be a rewarding source for students of both history and

71. Carl Nebel. *Plaza Mayor de México.* 1836. In Nebel, *Voyage pittoresque et archéologique dans la partie la plus interessante du Mexique.* Benson Latin-American Collection, University of Texas at Austin.

art.[30] But their accuracy, particularly when they are placed beside photographs of similar scenes, is open to question. The few surviving daguerreotypes of the Mexican War or the hundreds of photographs of Civil War scenes made only a decade and a half later bring to light the possibility that these prints do not present the same narrative as other sources. After Walker's *Storming of Chapultepec* was praised in the pages of the *North American*, the editors noted in a later issue that "several have complained of our notice of Mr. Walker's picture. Will these good people understand that we described a *picture—not a battle.*"[31]

James Walker must have wondered whether it was possible to paint a "correct" version of the attack on Chapultepec after being visited by Captains Roberts and Davis and having received conflicting communications from General Pillow. As he began work on his large canvas, he intended to show General Quitman in a prominent role in the attack on Chapultepec Castle. Pillow objected and offered to purchase the painting for one hundred dollars if Walker would finish it according to "the truth of history." Walker's solution was to do two or more paintings, each one, of course, depicting what the purchaser wanted to see.[32]

The most accurate paintings and prints are generally topographical in nature and compare well with maps and diagrams of the campaigns. T. M. Davis in fact used a map prepared by the Army Corps of Engineers to verify the details of Walker's work and declared it "showed with mathematical accuracy the disposition of the whole of the forces in any way engaged in storming Chapultepec."[33] Significant structures and landforms, military units, and even specific heroes of the battle, which the artist has usually highlighted in some manner, can usually be identified. But, like toy soldiers, the troops are always in step, and artists typically reduced their number significantly so as to diminish the confusion in the picture and to display the tactics clearly. There are anomalies and inconsistencies even among these prints generally esteemed for their accurate detail. In Eaton's *Battle of Buena Vista*, for example, there are no casualties on the ground, despite the fact that he pictured one of the bloodiest days of the conflict.[34]

Some writers warned of such problems. At least one soldier denounced the "tall yarn[s]" and "downright lies" that his compatriots wrote home. A reporter in Saltillo wrote that he had his "risibles considerably provoked . . . by some pictures in the 'Brother Jonathan' newspaper printed in New York, pretending to give scenes in Mexico".

> One represents Gen. Taylor mounted on a fierce, prancing steed, in full military suit, with towering plume, huge epaulettes. . . . Those who for the last five or more years have seen Gen. T, every day, and never mounted on any other but "that same old white horse," with that same old long coat on, and glazed cap, and common soldier's light blue overalls, will be forcibly struck with the faithfulness of this picture.

72. Adolphe-Jean-Baptiste Bayot after
Carl Nebel. *Genl. Scott's Entrance into
Mexico.* 1851. Hand-colored lithograph.
11⅛ x 17" (28.3 x 43.2 cm.). Plate 12 in
George Wilkins Kendall, *The War
between the United States and Mexico
Illustrated* (1851). Amon Carter Museum,
Fort Worth, Texas.

Another represents the Mexican rabble leaving Mata-moros. The artist had expended uncommon ingenuity in giving the women every variety of bonnets and head pieces, taking his idea apparently from a group of Swiss emigrants just landed at the Wharf. Now our American readers will perceive how faithful the representation is when we state, that except one or two worn by American women, we have not seen a bonnet of any kind in Mexico![35]

But from the vantage points of reporters and reviewers, these deficiencies were not visible. Perhaps the new techniques and technologies made possible such an overwhelming amount of information, some parts of it seeming to validate others, that the ubiquitous mass of news simply became convincing. Or perhaps audiences were so aware of the shortcomings of the images that they were oblivious to them and focused instead on at-tributes, which were much more unusual.

Regardless of such details, Mexican viewers might well have perceived all these prints as biased, for they all represented the American perspective. The position of the artist, with the exception of Phillips, was always on the side of the American troops, and, while these prints might occasionally record isolated incidents of Mexican bravery or tactical skill, they inevitably show Americans prevailing. Artists neither had the opportuni-ty nor were so naive as to produce scenes of Mexican heroism for sale to an American audience.[36]

Perhaps anticipating such questions, Kendall ex-plained in the preface to his book that the "general con-figuration of the ground, fidelity of the landscape, and correctness of the works and buildings introduced . . . may be strictly relied upon." Because the artist could not possibly encompass the entire battle scene, he contin-ued, he must choose "what he deemed the more inter-esting as well as exciting points of each combat." Kendall also admitted that the artist was sometimes tempted to sacrifice accuracy for effect or composition, but he assured readers that Nebel had taken particular care to avoid such compromises.[37]

The battle prints of the Mexican War contain enough perspective and detail that they were commonly com-pared to maps and first-person accounts of the engage-ments. But Nebel and the other artists also employed pictorial devices of the European and American schools of landscape painting to communicate powerful mes-sages of success and destiny. Most of the Mexican War prints, for example, employ the elevated, Olympian per-spective to produce the grand vista so well known in the works of Thomas Cole, Frederic Church, and other Hudson River School painters. The perspective of Eaton's *Battle of Buena Vista*, for example, suggests a comprehensive understanding, if not control, of the sit-uation. Then the viewer's eye catches the road that leads from the left center foreground, between the ravines and the mesas, to the mountain pass in the far

distance. It is apparent that Mexico and ultimate victory lie beyond the mountains. Nebel's more painterly ren-dering is an even stronger suggestion of American suc-cess, of destiny beyond the picture frame. *Battle of Palo Alto* shows a glimpse of the road as it leads through the Mexican forces and into a pass in the imaginary moun-tains that Nebel added to the scene; in *Capture of Mon-terey*, the city itself seems to be only a small obstacle in the valley, as the road leads onto the mountains in the distance and the capital beyond.[38]

Other pictures of the Mexican War years can be read in similar symbolic terms. Emanuel Leutze's *Storming of the Teocalli by Cortez and His Troops* (plate 73) is a dra-matic example, ostensibly a rendering of one of the more vivid episodes from William H. Prescott's im-mensely popular *History of the Conquest of Mexico*, pub-lished in 1843. Just as Prescott described Hernán Cortez's conquest of the Aztec empire, Leutze proposed five years later to depict the "final struggle of the two races—the decisive death-grapple of the savage and the civi-lized man."[39] Prescott characterized the Aztecs as a "fierce and brutal race," and Leutze pictured them as sav-ages practicing child sacrifice as they defend a forebod-ing and primitive-looking sacred pyramid, the *teocalli*.[40] An American audience already familiar with stories of savagery on the American frontier would have no diffi-culty in agreeing that progress had been served in the conquest of the Aztecs. Some attentive viewers might even have noticed a similarity between the imposing *teo-calli* and Frederick Catherwood's views of Mayan tem-ples and, perhaps, between the *teocalli* and Chapultepec castle as shown in Walker's and Nebel's prints.[41]

But Leutze did not depict the Indians as wholly bad: they are a handsome, heroic, and classically attired people victimized by superior technology. In the hands of the Protestant Leutze, the Spaniards, although repre-sentatives of a Christian nation, are worse than the Aztecs. Their black dress would have invoked images in the mind of a nineteenth-century viewer of the "black legend," which described the Spanish conquest and occupation of the New World as brutal and cruel. Leutze offered proof: they rob the dead, massacre women and children, and force their Catholic religion upon their victims. Protestant Americans would have sympathized with the dying Indian, shown in the low-er left corner of the picture, who rejects the last rites. Anyone mindful of the American victory over Mexico (the direct descendant of Spain) and the 1848 revolu-tions in Leutze's native Germany would have realized that the artist expected liberal democracy, American-style, to spread over all the world.[42]

That message may also be expressed in Woodville's two paintings related to the war, *War News from Mexico* and *Old '76 and Young '48* (plate 60), although Woodville did not see American-style democracy to be

73. Emanuel Leutze. *The Storming of the Teocalli by Cortez and His Troops.* 1848. 84¾ x 98¾" (211.9 x 246.9 cm.). Wadsworth Atheneum, Hartford, Connecticut; the Ella Gallup Sumner and Mary Catlin Sumner Collection.

as noble and selfless as Leutze apparently did. The most complimentary way to read *Old '76 and Young '48* is to see it as Woodville's effort to link the ideals of the American Revolution, in the patriarch, with those of the Mexican War, in the wholesome young man; expansionists would have understood and articulated this connection. But those opposed to expansion might have seen disillusionment in the face of the old man and have taken that expression as a subtle but uncomplimentary comparison between Revolutionary hero George Washington and Mexican War conqueror Zachary Taylor, whose reputation as a war hero helped assure his election as president in 1848.

War News from Mexico depicts a group of men, all of whom seem to have great interest in the latest news. They may have some economic stake in the outcome of the war as well, an idea suggested by the sign announcing a horse sale on the back wall. This might be the kind of enthusiasm that a war to acquire territory would encourage. Woodville shows both an everyday

scene of the sort generally attributed to genre painting and an historic moment. Yet this episode lacks the usual allegorical heroism, gallantry, and anthropomorphism associated with history paintings. The work perhaps reflects Woodville's visible contemplation of the great problem that slavery—as represented by the blacks in the picture—portends for the nation.[43] Questions of accuracy and authenticity, then, must be asked within a larger context that tied these depictions of events to deeper meanings. And these meanings must be considered from at least two points of view: those the artist intended and those subconscious, unintended ones that, though they made sense to viewers, were so well understood, so commonsensical, that they passed virtually unnoticed, much as the women and blacks fail to command attention in Woodville's painting. It is these meanings, ironically, that often claim the most interest today, and that inform us about the real contexts that inspired paintings of American history.

115

Painting the Civil War as History, 1861–1910

BRUCE W. CHAMBERS

When we look at the images generated by the American Civil War, our inclination is to think of history painting as *battle* painting—images of grand charges, spirited defenses, heroic deeds of valor. This inclination has been fortified over the past 130 years by the many illustrated histories of the war (including television documentaries) whose natural pictorial emphasis has been on the military events—the battles, campaigns, and soldier life—on which the text or script focuses.

In large part, this bias is due to changes in the definition of history painting that took place well after the war's conclusion. Painters who were active during the war produced surprisingly few battle paintings; they left such subjects largely to the artist-reporters who worked for the popular illustrated newspapers. With a few notable exceptions, it was not until the 1880s that painters began to show any sustained interest in recording the pivotal military events of the war.

There were several reasons for this postwar shift of emphasis. The growing scientific temper of the last three decades of the century encouraged a more documentary approach to the writing of history. Combined with the desire of many surviving veterans of the war to have their roles in the conflict accurately portrayed, this interest in documentation inspired a plethora of publications on the war—official war records, regimental histories, personal memoirs and biographies, albums of photographs, and overviews of the entire conflict, the last of which were often profusely illustrated.[1] The monumental *Battles and Leaders of the Civil War*, first published in serial form in *The Century Magazine* between November 1884 and November 1887 and subsequently reissued as a four-volume set of books, contained scores of maps and hundreds of illustrations.

Battles and Leaders attempted to trace the course of the war—every campaign and battle, on land, sea, and river—through the personal testimony of officers from both sides.[2]

Earlier, illustrated histories of the war, such as Benson John Lossing's 1865 *Pictorial Field Book of the Civil War*, had also represented an interest in documenting the conflict. But it was often acknowledged that such records were not likely to gain favor with the public. Lossing wrote:

> The task of making a record of the events of the late Civil War in our Republic is not a pleasant one for an American citizen. It would be more consonant with his wishes to bury in oblivion all knowledge of those events which compose the materials of a sorrowful story of a strife among his brethren, of terrible energy and woeful operations. But . . . it has become a part of the history of the inhabitants of the earth. What remains . . . is to see that the stylus of history shall make a *truthful* record. I have confined my labors chiefly to *the recording of facts*.[3] [Emphasis added.]

The reaction to those few works that attempted to present the conflict faithfully at the time demonstrated the general wish to avoid such realism. Peter F. Rothermel's *Battle of Gettysburg—Pickett's Charge* (plate 104), commissioned by the Pennsylvania state legislature in 1866, was intended to serve as a truthful pictorial account of that pivotal battle. Rothermel's painting, completed in 1870, was the largest single framed canvas in American art, some sixteen-and-a-half by thirty-two feet.[4] Not only was it a clear indication of a tendency to gargantuanism in Civil War art (the descendants of which were the panoramas and cycloramas of the 1880s); it also represented the wish to represent fairly everyone involved.[5] Each of the key figures in the paint-

74. James Hope. *Battle of Antietam,
September 17, 1862, 7th Maine Attacking
over the Sunken Road through the Piper
Cornfield.* ca. 1862. 19 x 26" (47.5 x 65.0
cm.). Private collection.

ing is a portrait made, if not from life, then from photographs. Rothermel had talked and corresponded "directly with veterans of the battle who could give at first hand, and when memories were still comparatively fresh, their impressions of what had happened. He spent countless hours in obtaining and studying the testimony of these men, and in going over the battleground."[6]

Among all the painstaking detailing of persons, actions, and costume, Rothermel attempted to convey both an overall theme ("the last attack of Lee at Gettysburg was repulsed, and the highest wave of the rebellion reached its limit, ever after to recede"[7]) and a symbolic subplot—what Edward Coddington has termed "the 'valor of the rank and file of the Union army,'" personified in the figure of a "stalwart Union soldier, stripped of a coat and accoutrements and standing one foot upon the wall and the other upon a dead Rebel, beating back the enemy with the butt of his musket."[8] Yet the work's heroic message was lost in its emphasis on detail, and it greatly disappointed the critics.[9]

Such straightforward depictions of the conflict probably failed because, as Lossing noted, most Americans were reluctant to rake the embers of passion in the years immediately following the war. But with each passing decade, there were fewer and fewer people for whom the experience of the war still held much emotional immediacy, and a growing number of Americans had little or no knowledge of the conflict. As *The Century* editors put it in 1884, the main purpose of *Battles and Leaders of the Civil War* was "interesting veterans in their own memories and . . . instructing the generation which has grown up since the War for the Union." As the years went by, it seemed increasingly important to be not only factual but also to be both analytical and comprehensive. It was this retrospective desire for greater objectivity that helped produce the emphasis on an accurate pictorial record—the who, what, when, and where of each campaign and battle—an emphasis that we today define as Civil War history painting.

During and immediately after the war, however, the nature and role of most history paintings had been quite different. For most of its tradition, the genre had traditionally aimed not simply to document but, more important, to explain and comment on the events it portrayed. Poetic license was the rule, not the exception, because to explain the tacit cultural meanings of important events meant that artists had to rearrange their subjects, emphasize the salient personalities and facts, and eliminate others deemed less important to the point. The history painter's job was to crystallize the complexities of history into unambiguous moral paradigms.

If the artist could better construct this paradigm of events by introducing symbolic elements—for instance, popular personifications of ideas, like Liberty with her cap and staff—or by referring to familiar stories and images from the ancient or Christian past, he was encouraged to do so by an American public that was well versed in the Bible and the classics and familiar through travel or, more often, books with the best-known monuments of Europe. In art, as in literature, the use of such devices enabled artists to build layers of traditional meaning into their subjects without elaborating detail—and to depend on the viewer's knowledge to fill in the gaps. Allegory, the art of constructing these layers of meaning, was a branch, perhaps then even the most important branch, of history painting.

We instantly recognize William D. Washington's 1863 *Jackson Entering the City of Winchester* (plate 75) as a history painting in this older tradition. Washington, a Richmond artist born but a few miles from Winchester in Clarke County, Virginia, had studied under Emanuel Leutze, for most Americans the exemplar of the history painter. His subject depicts one of the crucial events—for the South—early in the war.

On May 25, 1862, General Thomas J. ("Stonewall") Jackson rushed his troops to Winchester, where they routed General Nathaniel Banks's federal army and sent it fleeing back across the Potomac River into Maryland. Jackson knew his victory at Winchester was vital to the Confederate cause, because it prevented Lincoln from reinforcing General George McClellan in his drive on Richmond. In Washington's painting, Jackson enters the city in triumph, doffing his cap to a rejoicing populace. Like many other Civil War paintings, it is an *adventus* scene in the tradition of Caesar entering Rome or Christ entering Jerusalem. But now it is the main street of a small southern town that tapers into the distance behind the equestrian hero.

As Washington depicted him, Stonewall Jackson was the people's champion. An old man returns his salute; a mother looks at him with heartfelt adoration. Among Jackson's troops are a number of soldier-citizens who have fought hard for their town's liberation; one lies dead, mourned by his wife; another, his wound being nursed, reaches out to the general in gratitude. The wounded man's gesture deliberately echoes one of the best-known history paintings ever executed by an American (though not of an American subject), John Singleton Copley's *The Death of Major Peirson, 6 January, 1781* (plate 23). Like Jackson, Peirson had valiantly defended his home, the Isle of Jersey, from an invasion of foreign troops. Unlike Jackson, Peirson was killed at the moment of victory; in Copley's painting, a wounded soldier reaches out to the dying hero. Even though Washington showed Jackson very much alive, it is possible that the general had died by the time the artist finished the painting in 1863: Jackson had been the victim of his own soldiers' volley at Chancellorsville in May of that year. The painting may

75. William D. Washington. *Jackson
Entering the City of Winchester.*
ca. 1863–65. 48⅛ x 60⅛" (120.3 x 150.3 cm.).
The Valentine Museum, Richmond,
Virginia.

76. Alexander Gardner. *Home of a Rebel Sharpshooter, Gettysburg, July 1863.* July 6, 1863. Photograph. George Eastman House, Rochester, New York.

thus have served a double purpose, to celebrate the victory at Winchester and to memorialize one of the Confederacy's greatest leaders.

Mid-nineteenth-century American culture was immersed in an ancient western European tradition of symbolic speech, structured according to an art of rhetoric in which every schoolchild was educated. Even photography, that newest and, to our eyes, most truth-saying of all forms of picturing, was not immune to interpretive intervention, often through the conscious intent of its practitioners. The best-known wartime example of such intervention is Alexander Gardner's *Home of a Rebel Sharpshooter, Gettysburg, July 1863* (plate 76), taken after the Battle of Gettysburg on July 6, 1863.

Photographs of battlefield dead were not only a novelty of the Civil War; they were a public sensation, the first "visible proofs" of the horror and cost of war. Yet even with such a solemn subject, the photographer could not resist tinkering for dramatic impact. William A. Frassanito has compared this image with other Gettysburg photographs taken by Gardner and his partner, Timothy O'Sullivan, and has found that the team moved the body of this particular soldier some forty yards to the spot in Devil's Den where it was then photographed to such telling effect. Frassanito further observed:

To complete their composition, the cameramen propped a rifle (definitely not the type used by sharpshooters) against the wall and placed a knapsack under the soldier's head. . . . According to Gardner's *Sketch Book*, this soldier, described as a sharpshooter, was wounded at the stone wall by a shell fragment, whereupon the dying boy evidently laid himself down to stoically await his end. The lengthy caption continues by telling how Gardner returned to the spot four months later to find the body, then a skeleton, and the rusted rifle, both undisturbed—an obvious case of fiction.[10]

Though a fiction, the photograph of the dead sharpshooter was addressed to an audience that expected not unalloyed fact but the softening cushion of sentiment and story. *Ut photographica poesis.*

Professional artists who served as soldiers on both sides of the conflict, such as George Caleb Bingham, James Hope, and Conrad Wise Chapman, also would have had a strong motive for accurately portraying the events in which they had participated. Yet, as artists trained in the grand tradition of history painting, even when they intended their portrayals to have the same immediacy as their experience, they almost always went beyond mere recording of events.

George Caleb Bingham's *Martial Law,* or *Order No. 11* (plate 77) borrows from the art of rhetoric, one of whose branches was the study of dramatic expression. The "sciences" of facial physiognomy and phrenology claimed to be able to decipher human types, emotions, and motives from surface details. Popular literature constantly reminded Americans of the importance of appearance and demeanor and instructed them in the art of reading such outward expressions as signals of character.

In Bingham's painting, the expression on the face of Brigadier General Thomas Ewing was that of a recognizable physical and dramatic type, the sharp, glowering face of a villain. Bingham, though a strong Union supporter and, briefly, a soldier, had seen his beloved Missouri torn apart by both northern and southern guerrilla raids across the Kansas-Missouri border. Following William C. Quantrill's raid on Lawrence, Kansas, on August 18, 1863, Ewing issued a military order by which he hoped to rid the border counties of southern activists and thus calm the flames of rebellion.

This edict, General Order No. 11, called for the eviction from their homes of all persons living in three and a half of Missouri's border counties. Bingham was outraged; he realized that the order would turn many who had been sympathetic to the Union against it. *Order No. 11* was part of a sustained campaign on Bingham's part to discredit Ewing.[11] He also felt that northern guerrillas—among them, notably, Kansas Senator Jim Lane—would take the opportunity Ewing so nicely presented them to rob and destroy the properties, goods, and crops

the evicted citizens were forced to leave behind. This is, of course, exactly what happened. Avenging Kansans so thoroughly destroyed the farms and homesteads of the affected counties that for many generations thereafter the region was known simply as "The Burnt District."

Bingham's painting neatly draws upon a fiction for its effect. It portrays a moment that probably never occurred, as Ewing confronts one of the families that his order has dispossessed. In the background, immediately behind the white-haired father and directly facing the viewer, is Senator Lane, whose Union forces loot and destroy even as Ewing, his hand threateningly poised above his sword, orders the family out. Bingham depicted the dying mother and dead son at the feet of the Missouri patriarch as pietà compositions drawn from familiar Italian Renaissance prototypes, while he borrowed the poses of the fleeing black slave and his son at the far right edge of the scene directly from Masaccio's *The Expulsion of Adam and Eve.*[12] By such references, Bingham placed the issue of civil liberty—the inalienable rights of American citizens—solidly within the matrix of Christian values. Accused of painting a pro-Confederate and proslavery picture, Bingham denied the charge. The painting, he asserted, was meant "to keep alive popular indignation [at the arbitrary exercise of military power]. . . . May the American people never forget that hatred of tyranny is but another name for the love of Liberty, and that when it perishes, free institu-

77. George Caleb Bingham. *Martial Law [Order No. 11].* 1865–68. 55½ x 77½" (138.8 x 193.8 cm.). Cincinnati Art Museum, Cincinnati, Ohio; the Edwin and Virginia Irwin Memorial.

78. James Henry Beard. *The Night before the Battle*. 1865. 30½ x 44" (76.2 x 110.0 cm.). Memorial Art Gallery of the University of Rochester, Rochester, New York.

79. David Gilmour Blythe.
Old Virginia Home. 1864.
20 x 28" (50.0 x 70.0 cm.).
The Art Institute of
Chicago.

tions must perish with it."[13] *Order No. 11* was a new type of American history painting, one that neither glorified war nor papered over its consequences.

Artists contemporary with the war often produced critical, ironic, and often melancholy interpretations of events, the direct result of participation in a civil conflict in which both American sides claimed victories and suffered losses. Among the most memorable of such paintings are James Henry Beard's *Night before the Battle* (plate 78) and David Gilmour Blythe's *Old Virginia Home* (plate 79). Like Bingham, both Beard and Blythe worked in the old Midwest, Beard in Cincinnati and Blythe in Pittsburgh. Both artists inclined to satirical genre and knew each other's work; Beard had turned to at least one of Blythe's paintings for inspiration.[14] Perhaps because both artists were self-taught and were not based in one of the large metropolitan centers of the Northeast, they were able to work more freely within the traditions of history painting. Or it may have been that, as they both had immediate experience of the war—Beard served for a time in the Union army, while Blythe accompanied the Thirteenth Pennsylvania Regiment into northern Virginia in 1861—they could speak more powerfully than most of the war's devastation.[15]

Beard's subject is every combatant's fear before battle, the haunting proximity of death. It is night along some fortified defensive line. Soldiers have been playing cards to relieve the boredom and anxiety of siege duty; others have been writing letters home. All now lie asleep, exhausted from their previous day's exposure to random artillery rounds and sniper fire. Beard mirrored in the poses of the sleeping soldiers familiar compositions from the past, specifically those of Christ's disciples who, asked to watch while Jesus prayed to be relieved of his impending crucifixion, slumbered instead. On the parapet a watchful figure mans a cannon; stark white in the moonlight, it is Death itself, waiting for dawn (and, with it, the renewal of combat)—waiting to welcome fresh victims.

In Blythe's *Old Virginia Home*, a black man, his shackles broken, flees from a ruined plantation house. A battle rages in the distance, through whose smoke a Union flag is visible, raised above the fray. Out of the storm clouds sweeping across the sky, apocalyptic horsemen emerge, the marshal of War and the raven of Famine among them. The name on the shattered barrel in the right foreground is that of Henry A. Wise, governor of Virginia between 1856 and 1860 and a Confederate general—as well as one of the commonwealth's most outspoken secessionists and defenders of slavery. Twice during Wise's life his home was destroyed by fire, once by an unknown incendiary. Given Blythe's extreme pro-Union sentiments and outspoken opposition to extremists on both sides of the political divide, it would have been like him to draw a parallel between the incendiarism that destroyed Wise's own home, and Wise's "incendiarism" in fanning the flames of secession in Virginia. Although the painting alludes both to even-

80. James Hamilton. *Old Ironsides*. 1863. 60½ x 48" (151.2 x 120.0
cm.). The Pennsylvania Academy of the Fine Arts, Philadelphia; gift
of Caroline Gibson Taitt.

81. Jervis McEntee. *The Fire of Leaves*. 1862. 20 x 36" (50.0 x 90.0 cm.). Private collection.

tual Union victory and to the emancipation of the slaves, with typical ambivalence Blythe set both themes in the midst of a picture of ongoing hell.[16]

For the nineteenth-century landscape painter, the season, weather, time of day, degree of wildness or cultivation and of barrenness or fertility all were symbolic. James Hope's 1862 *Battle of Antietam, September 17, 1862, 7th Maine Attacking over the Sunken Road through the Piper Cornfield* (plate 74),[17] for example, contrasts the sunny, agrarian landscape of western Maryland with the war's harvest of death. One of the most common romantic landscape metaphors for battle or conflict was the storm, which could be threatening arrival, raging in full fury, or sweeping past, leaving peace in its wake.[18] In James Hamilton's *Old Ironsides* (plate 80), a storm is at its height. Bolts of lightning streak across the sky. A ship of the line is foundering amidst the crashing waves, its American flag torn to ribbons by the gale. On the back of the painting, Hamilton inscribed a set of verses from Oliver Wendell Holmes's poem "Old Ironsides":

> O' better that her shattered hulk,
> Should sink beneath the wave;
> Her thunders shook the mighty deep,
> And there should be her grave;
> Nail to the mast her holy flag,
> Set every threadbare sail,
> And give her to the god of storms —
> The lightning and the gale.[19]

Holmes had written his poem to save "Old Ironsides," the USS *Constitution* of storied fame. Given her nickname by sailors who saw shots bounce off her hull during her battle with the British frigate *Guerrière* in 1812,

the *Constitution* had since lain neglected and in disrepair. Holmes argued that it would be far more fitting to scuttle the heroic ship at sea than to allow her to rot; his poem inspired a successful campaign to preserve the battleship for posterity. But Hamilton depicted "Old Ironsides" neither being left to waste nor being deliberately scuttled but rather being destroyed by a great tumult. Insofar as "Old Ironsides" *is* the *Constitution*, it would have been an easy and logical step to read Hamilton's meaning: the country's constitution had been left to the mercy of the storm. This theme recurred throughout the war but most notably in 1863, a presidential election year when debate raged in the North as well as in the South over the constitutional issues of states' rights, emancipation, conscription, and the confiscation of property.

Jervis McEntee, who had just launched his long career as a Hudson River landscape painter when the war broke out, painted at least one symbolically freighted image at a time when victory for the North was still very much in doubt. *The Fire of Leaves* (plate 81) is, on the surface, a picture of two little boys huddled around a fire of leaves in the middle of a gloomy forest. It is dusk in late autumn. From the center of the composition two paths diverge, but wilderness swallows both. The boys have only each other's company and the warmth of the fire they have built together to ward off the growing cold, only the fire's flickering light to brighten the darkness. On the ground next to one of the boys is a blue cap; next to his companion, a gray one. McEntee's message is clear: if either side was to survive the dying of the light, a new spirit of brotherhood must be kindled.[20]

Southern painters, many of whom were also combatants, also turned to the traditional symbolism of land-

82. Conrad Wise Chapman. *Fort Sumter Interior, Sunrise, December 9, 1863.* 1864. 11½ x 15½" (28.8 x 38.8 cm.). The Museum of the Confederacy, Richmond, Virginia.

83. Unidentified printmaker after Henry Mosler. *Leaving for War.* ca. 1873. Chromolithograph. Eleanor S. Brockenbrough Library, The Museum of the Confederacy, Richmond, Virginia.

scape imagery to comment on the war. Conrad Wise Chapman enlisted in the Confederate Army after training under his father, John Gadsby Chapman, in Rome. Severely wounded at Shiloh, he was transferred in 1863 to the Confederate Corps of Engineers under General P. T. Beauregard in Charleston, whose harbor fortifications Chapman mapped and sketched.[21] His *Fort Sumter Interior, Sunrise, December 9, 1863* (plate 82) shows the fort still proudly occupied by Confederate troops, huddled around campfires or gazing out to sea from crumpled ramparts. But it is the sky itself that is the main actor in the drama. Filled with dawn's soft hues, it possesses a romantic, atmospheric luminosity exactly like that found in the works of Fitz Hugh Lane and other New England Luminist painters and like the radiant haze of color that envelops German Romantic artist Caspar David Friedrich's scenes of Gothic ruins. The contrast of a divine radiance with the sad remains of man's past glories sets up a tension between mortal history and the eternity under which that history is subsumed. In the work of a painter who was unabashedly allied with the Confederacy, the transcendent, ever-recurring dawn lends hope, even when the cause is in ruins.[22]

Icons of the Lost Cause proliferated after the Civil War, particularly in the form of prints furnished to southern homes by northern publishers. The tone of these works, however, was set by wartime paintings by such southern artists as Chapman and Washington, whose *Burial of Latane* (1864) took a minor event in the war—the burial of a Virginia cavalry captain—and turned it into a celebration of southern honor and piety.[23]

An entirely different image of the Lost Cause is Henry Mosler's painting of that title, completed in 1868. Mosler, who had first studied art with James Henry Beard in Cincinnati, covered the Union Army in the West as an artist-reporter for *Harper's Weekly* in 1862–1863. In 1864 he traveled to Düsseldorf, Germany, to continue his studies. Among his first commissions on his return to the United States in 1866 was *The Lost Cause*, together with its now-missing pendant, *Leaving for War*, which was reproduced in a chromolithograph printed in about 1873 (plate 83).

The pair of works is a perfect example of historical genre painting. The soldier is an ordinary yeoman farmer who, out of a sense of duty to his state, leaves his family and mountain farm to join battle with the Yankees. He is clearly no owner of plantation or slaves, nor part of the cavalier aristocracy; it was exactly men of such humble origins that supplied the Confederacy with most of its manpower. He comes home from the war only to find his farm deserted and overgrown, his cabin in ruins, and his family gone.

Mosler's *Lost Cause* is typical of a group of post–Civil War images that emphasized the wholesale destruction of a formerly prosperous and settled land, victim of a new kind of total warfare practiced most noticeably by

Sherman and his men, but also by northern and southern marauders and foragers. Mosler's painting so closely resembles a now-lost work by Jervis McEntee that Mosler could have used it as a model. As described by the art critic Henry Tuckerman, McEntee's landscape was "a small picture,—the body of which was an overgrown thicket, a neglected field where stood a dilapidated farmhouse, through whose bare rafters gleamed, under a dark, wintry sky, the cold amber light from a belt of sunset along the far horizon; the chill tone, the deserted feeling, the utter dreariness of this little scene emphasized its name as the type of desolation; it was called *Virginia in 1863.*"[24]

Throughout the war, these "types of desolation" surfaced in photographs and prints as well as in paintings. Like Thomas Cole's *Desolation*, a melancholy scene of the end of civilization from his *Course of Empire* series (1833–1836), these images speak to what must have been the most perplexing development of the war for both sides—the descent of a democratic, educated citizenry into numbing paroxysms of destruction and, with that, the radical overturning of the pastoral ideal.

The war also strained families and all other community ties to the limit. No painting speaks with more feeling—or on a more heroic scale—to the often-torn sympathies of the war's participants than Constant Mayer's *Recognition* (plate 84). Also exhibited under the title *North and South—An Episode of the War*, the painting was described in 1866:

A large Historical Work—the Story of a Battle-field. An effective and touching episode of the late fearful struggle in our own country. One brother finds another dying, as night is gathering over the battle-field. They have joined different sides in the contest, and the dramatic power of the situation, with its tearful sublimity, is as forcibly as it is simply expressed. Such a painting as this must always stir our feelings with a throb of sympathy, while it melts us to pity and tenderness.[25]

Pietàs of brotherhood such as Mayer's, with their sentimental appeal, stood in contrast to other works of the era that were instructed by recent artistic developments in Europe. Although Winslow Homer did not travel to Paris until a year after the war's conclusion (in part to see to the exhibition of his *Prisoners from the Front* at the Universal Exposition of 1867), by the end of the war he was already working toward the more powerful Realist style recently introduced in France by the works of Courbet, Legros, Breton, and Manet. Realists consciously eschewed the moral didacticism of allegory and substituted instead a commitment to honesty and sincerity in the depiction of what William H. Gerdts has described as "the here, the now, and the visible."[26]

Homer's *Near Andersonville*, painted in 1865–1866 (plate 85), embodies the Realists' precepts about painting. A young black woman stands at the door of her cabin in full sunlight. Her expression is solemn, her thoughts turned inward. For a long time, the correct title of this painting was unknown; it had been named,

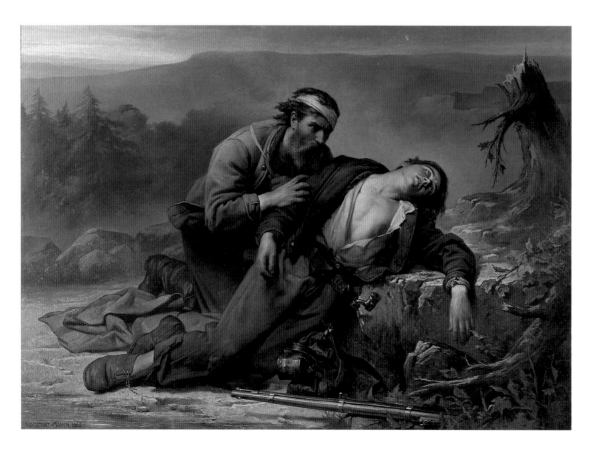

84. Constant Mayer. *Recognition.* 1865. 70 x 94' (175.0 x 235.0 cm.). The Warner Collection of the Gulf States Paper Corporation, Tuscaloosa, Alabama.

85. Winslow Homer. *Near Andersonville*. 1865. 23 x 18" (57.5 x 45.0 cm.). The Newark Museum, Newark, New Jersey; gift of Mrs. Hannah Corbin Carter, Horace K. Corbin, Jr., Robert S. Corbin, William D. Corbin, and Mrs. Clementine Corbin Day in memory of their parents, Hannah Stockton and Horace Kellogg Corbin.

simply and descriptively, *At the Cabin Door*. But that Homer had titled the painting *Near Andersonville* is clear from a review in the New York *Evening Post* in April 1866: "[Homer's] picture entitled 'Near Andersonville,' depicting a Negro woman standing at the door of her cabin, gazing at Union prisoners as they pass, is full of significance."[27] In the left background of the painting, two Union soldiers are visible, as are their Confederate captors with their flag.

At the end of the war, in April 1865, northerners discovered with unconcealed shock the abuses and starvation that had taken place at the Confederate prisoner-of-war camp at Andersonville, Georgia, as thousands of sick, emaciated soldiers—barely recognizable as human—were freed from their confinement. Even more than the images of battlefield dead and of the devastation of the land, the pitiful sight of these prisoners moved the public to realize the war's cost, not only in casualties but, perhaps more basically, in an essential human compassion.[28] As Marc Simpson has pointed out, "By entitling a work *Near Andersonville*, Homer would have necessarily conjured up the blackest villainies of the war. But as if to say that his brush was inadequate to the true horror of the site, he alludes to rather than describes the fate that awaits the two Union prisoners. Instead, he focuses attention on the noble but enslaved black woman, for whom slavery is the spiritual parallel to the harrowing ordeal of Andersonville."[29]

Homer's painting does not entirely reject allegory; it relies, however, on a more subtle kind of symbolic ref-

erence, one that does not rest on the more obvious and sometimes hackneyed elements of the history painting tradition. Although the Civil War had encouraged allegorical interpretation, a growing bias toward realism was becoming more and more dominant in Civil War imagery by the 1870s and beyond. Mark Thistlethwaite has observed that an increasing reliance on photography for visual information had much to do with this growing popular demand for improved accuracy of representation.[30] So, too, did the pictorial journalism of the popular press.[31] The Civil War had catalyzed these tendencies for the public; the immediacy of feelings on both sides and the proximity of events joined with the skills of an increasingly canny media to create—and to fill—a strong demand for images of the conflict.

Julian Scott's *Death of General Sedgwick* (plate 86) is one such grand canvas of this later period. Scott, who was one of the better draftsmen and painters of the last third of the nineteenth century, painted military subjects almost exclusively, which may explain why he has never received his just due as an artist.[32] Born in Johnson, Vermont, in 1846, Scott lied about his age in 1861 in order to enlist as a fifer in the Third Vermont Volunteer Infantry. In early 1862 he found himself on the peninsula between the James and York rivers as part of McClellan's fruitless, and seemingly endless, campaign to take Richmond. In April of that year he was part of an effort to feel out the enemy on Warwick Creek, at Yorktown.

After crossing the creek around noon on April 16, four companies from the Third Vermont encountered a

131

large force of Confederates. Their repeated signals for reinforcements went unanswered, but they held the rebel soldiers off for almost an hour before retreating. Although as a fifer Scott was officially a noncombatant, he waded back into the creek under fire to help rescue the wounded. According to Robert Titterton, Scott later told a correspondent for the *New York Tribune,* "Why, sir, it was just like sap-boiling, in that stream, the bullets fell so thick." For his valor, the young artist was subsequently awarded the Medal of Honor.[33]

The Death of General Sedgwick records one of the best-known incidents of the war, when General John ("Uncle John") Sedgwick, the much-beloved commander of the Sixth Corps of the Army of the Potomac, chided his troops for flinching and dodging at the sound of sniper fire near Spotsylvania Court House, Virginia, in May 1864. "What! What! men, dodging this way for single bullets!" Sedgwick is said to have called out jestingly to his men. "What will you do when they open fire along the whole line? I am ashamed of you. They couldn't hit an elephant at this distance!"[34] At the moment he stopped speaking, another sniper's bullet whirred out of the trees, and Sedgwick fell, mortally wounded in the face.

Scott chose to depict the moment when Sedgwick's officers realize that their commander cannot be revived. The officers who surrounded Sedgwick that day are accurately portrayed, down to their specific rank and corps badges. Colonel Tompkins, chief of the Sixth Corps artillery, is seen—as he had been seen—trying to get the attention of the brigade surgeon, while Major Whittier attempts vainly to discern the general's heartbeat and pulse. In the circle around the central group, the artist captured the poses and shocked expressions of other officers and ordinary soldiers, among them a young drummer boy—a character who appears frequently in Scott's work and seems to stand in as an observer for the artist himself. Unlike many late-century Civil War paintings, which sacrifice coherence to detail or, alternatively, tend to an artificial theatricality, Scott's composition is notable both for its credibility and the fitting gravity of its mood.

By the turn of the century, interest in the war had started a long, slow process of waning, which, despite such cinematic landmarks as *Gone with the Wind,* continued until the war's centennial in the 1960s began what has today become a dramatic revival of attention. Public demand for information on the old war had been sated by 1900, arguments over who did what to whom died with the deaths of their protagonists, and new wars had appeared on the horizon to capture the attention of the chroniclers and reporters.[35]

The mood of the country was changing as well. Partly in reaction to the increasing professionalization of historical scholarship, ordinary Americans began to explore the past on their own. A taste for a more informal, "storytelling" kind of history developed. For many people, this meant the refraction of history through a softer, more romantic lens. The sweeping overview was replaced by a meandering chain of anecdotes, the comprehensive analysis by a rambling assortment of picturesque objects.

Typical of this new mood in both scale and subject is Howard Pyle's *"She Drew Bridle Listening —There Was No Sound."* Designed specifically to illustrate "Special Messenger," a short story in a 1905 issue of *Harper's* by Robert W. Chambers, Pyle's painting is an image that, independent of its literary context, almost no one today would associate immediately with the Civil War.[36] A young woman sits on her horse in the midst of a dark forest. On her face is an expression of apprehension; in her hand a pistol. In Chambers's story, the woman was a Union spy carrying vital information about the Confederates' position to Meade's headquarters outside Gettysburg. Because it is essential that she not be discovered or betrayed, she rides at night and hides in barns in the daytime. On the third day of her journey, the woman leaves the wagon road for a cowpath to avoid the Confederates' pursuit. It is sundown before she stops. Chambers described the scene in suggestive terms:

> She drew bridle, listening, her dark eyes fixed on the setting sun. There was no sound save the breathing of her horse, the far sweet trailing song of a spotted sparrow, the undertones of some hidden rill welling up through matted tangles of vine and fern and long wild grasses. Presently she slipped off one gauntlet, fumbled in her corsage, drew out a crumpled paper, and spread it flat. It was a map. With one finger she traced her road, bending in her saddle, her eyebrows gathering in perplexity. Back and forth moved the finger, now hovering here and there in hesitation, now lifted to her lips in silent uncertainty. Twice she turned her head, intensely alert, but there was no sound save the cawing of crows winging across the deepening crimson in the west.

It must have been refreshing to Pyle's audience to see, finally, a heroine amidst all the carnage and manly death that had for so long dominated Civil War imagery. Just as important, Pyle's painting provides not a literal depiction of events but an impressionistic "slice of life." It exemplifies what in 1880 the critic William C. Brownell termed "modern realism," which "consists in stimulating the imagination instead of satisfying the sensibility."[37]

The contrast between Pyle's work and the long succession of battle subjects that had dominated the walls and pages of the 1870s and 1880s is readily apparent. Though more modern in its indirectness, it reverts in a way to the mood of paintings of the Civil War itself, which placed their primacy on emotion, rather than on descriptive fact.

86. Julian Scott. *Death of General
Sedgwick.* 1889. 92 x 118" (230.0 x 295.0
cm.). Drake House Museum, Plainfield,
New Jersey.

Picturing Lincoln

BARRY SCHWARTZ

Every nation, as Robert Bellah has observed, is "a community of memory" that retains its past by retelling the same "constitutive narrative" and recalling with variable precision the people who embody its ideals.[1] In the American community of memory, two Abraham Lincolns have played an important role. The first is the rail-splitter, the rude man from the prairie and the river bottoms, the storytelling folk hero of common touch and homely virtue. The second Lincoln is the savior of the union, liberator of the slave, martyred hero of godly virtue. The first Lincoln ascended from the masses but never left them; the second Lincoln transcended the masses and guided them from a distance.

American history painters represented both Lincolns. Painters in the "grand style" concentrated on grand events; their goal was to dignify Lincoln, as Benjamin West would have put it, "by transmitting to posterity his noble actions, his mental powers, to be viewed in those invaluable lessons of religion, love of country and morality."[2] Such paintings present idealized versions of Lincoln's political accomplishments and moral character.[3] By contrast, the realist or "genre" history painters depicted Lincoln doing ordinary things in familiar scenes. Whether they portrayed Lincoln in a private, mundane role or in a public role dealing with mundane matters, genre history painters humanized him. Grand-style and genrefied paintings thus formulate contrasting relations between reputation and social distance. The former elevate Lincoln's reputation by revealing how his superior talents and moral virtues separate him from ordinary people; the latter enhance his reputation by emphasizing common traits with which ordinary people can identify.

Most nineteenth-century paintings of Lincoln followed the grand style. Between Lincoln's death in 1865 and the dedication of his national memorial in 1922, however, the United States evolved from a rural republic into an industrial democracy. Influenced by this transformation, twentieth-century artists increasingly saw Lincoln as the epitome of the common man, and they produced genrefied representations of him in greater numbers than ever before. Yet they could not put aside completely the nineteenth-century artist's appreciation of Lincoln's epic qualities. These two approaches to painting Lincoln, then, make the public's visual understanding of him clearer. The first relates the genrefication of Lincoln's image to the concerns and needs of a new and more egalitarian generation. The second approach attends to the enduring perception of Lincoln's epic greatness and to its maintenance in the face of social change.

The Making of an Epic Hero: Nineteenth-Century Images of Lincoln

When painters and printmakers first turned to him, Abraham Lincoln was "one of the two or three most unpopular living presidents in American history."[4] His election provoked the secession of southern states and led to a war that many would have liked to avoid. Lincoln fought that war too timidly for some, too stubbornly for others; and, after sending hundreds of thousands of men to their deaths, he wanted to treat the enemy as if there had been no war at all. In November 1864, after pivotal victories on the battlefield changed the minds of thousands who thought the war unwinnable, Lincoln won reelection with 54 percent of the northern vote. Yet even with military successes behind him, many believed

Dennis Malone Carter. *Lincoln Greeting the Heroes of War,* detail of plate 96.

135

87. David Gilmour Blythe. *Abraham Lincoln Writing the Emancipation Proclamation*. 1863. 21¾ x 27½" (55.2 x 69.8 cm.). The Carnegie Museum of Art, Pittsburgh; gift of Mr. and Mrs. John F. Walton.

that Lincoln's reelection reflected the public's dislike of challenger George McClellan rather than its endorsement of the president himself.[5]

Five months later, the assassin's bullet dramatically elevated Lincoln's prestige, but the widely held belief—based largely on impressive and prolonged funeral rites—that his death caused people to appreciate his greatness and realize how much they loved him cannot be sustained by evidence. Horace Greeley, for example, surmised in his editorial several days after Lincoln's death "that Mr. Lincoln's reputation will stand higher with posterity than with the mass of his contemporaries." Likewise, the Reverend George Briggs declared in his funeral eulogy that Lincoln would be "hailed in the coming time . . . with a truer, deeper homage than he wins today." George Templeton Strong also believed Lincoln was lacking in too many ways to earn the respect of his own generation, but "his name will be of high account fifty years hence."[6]

Contemporary critics considered Lincoln a boorish country lawyer whose background disqualified him for any public office. They ridiculed his accent, dress, physical ungainliness, and demeanor; they could not understand how he became president. When political

allies turned against him, they used the same language. "He does not act, or talk, or feel like the ruler of a great empire in a great crisis," Richard Henry Dana observed. "He likes rather to talk and tell stories with all sorts of persons . . . than to give his mind to the noble and manly duties of his great post."[7] The rail-splitter image that made Lincoln attractive as a presidential candidate was evidently all too convincing; it undermined his dignity as president.

Clearly, then, contemporary opinion of Lincoln was not uniformly positive. History painters who admired Lincoln or accepted commissions from his supporters could not alter this opinion, but they countered it forcefully. Depicting him in the grand style, pro-Lincoln artists believed their efforts would be of no social significance if they did not inform and shape rather than articulate public opinion. History painters thus contrived a counterimage to the rail-splitting common man, one that ennobled Lincoln and depicted him as a president of grand and stately mien. After Lincoln's Emancipation Proclamation and his assassination dramatically altered the course of American history, they converged on an epic portrayal of Lincoln that Americans would eventually come to know best and embrace.

Emancipation

Lincoln's popularity was at its lowest point when he signed the Emancipation Proclamation in September 1862. "No event in the history of this country since the Declaration of Independence itself . . ." the *Illinois State Journal* proclaimed shortly afterward, "excited so profound attention."[8] Scores of prints immediately marked the occasion. They portrayed Lincoln at his desk writing the proclamation, signing it, or acknowledging the gratitude of black people. Other prints—more than two dozen, many bordered by approving allegorical figures—reproduced the proclamation's text. The extraordinary outpouring of "emancipation prints" met the demand of Lincoln's large antislavery constituency, but it never reflected widespread support for emancipation itself. Announced before the November 1862 elections, Lincoln's abolition policy evoked fears of a northward migration of blacks and caused heavy losses for his Republican party.

Even Lincoln's admirers acknowledged the public's ambivalence toward the proclamation, an admission that sometimes weakened their statements on his behalf. Painter David Gilmour Blythe, a staunch opponent of slavery, thought his *Abraham Lincoln Writing the Emancipation Proclamation* (plate 87) would help promote the president's cause. He was wrong. Unlike his

earlier painting, *Lincoln Crushing the Dragon of Rebellion* (plate 88), which dramatically marks Lincoln's struggle against the Confederacy and its New York City supporters, Blythe's *Emancipation Proclamation* is ambiguous. Unconventional in design and execution, it succeeds best in magnifying the qualities of conventional history painting. Blythe's emancipator, with pen in hand, composes his proclamation. But the great man is half-dressed, wearing a rumpled shirt with cuffs rolled up, baggy pants, one slipper off, another on. The painting's moral lesson is vague. Lincoln sits among petitions against emancipation as well as for emancipation. Many objects in the picture, including the maul, window-curtain flag, and masonic emblems, possess no clear meaning. Even the Bible and U.S. Constitution, resting on Lincoln's lap and presumably representing his main sources of inspiration, give inconsistent guidance; they were invoked by both sides to justify or to condemn slavery. The painting is so densely symbolic, so intellectually complex, that only the most sophisticated viewer could decipher it. When lithographed and put on the market, few bought the prints.

Yet, the people that favored emancipation were determined to sanctify Lincoln's measure. They sought painters to articulate the proclamation's merit, not its controversial reception. Lincoln supporters in Philadel-

88. David Gilmour Blythe. *Lincoln Crushing the Dragon of Rebellion.* 1862. 18 x 22" (45.7 x 55.9 cm.). Museum of Fine Arts, Boston; bequest of Martha C. Karolik for the Karolik Collection of American Paintings, 1815–1865.

89. William Marsh. *Abraham Lincoln*. 1860. Photograph. Gilman Paper Company Collection, New York.

phia therefore commissioned Edward Dalton Marchant to celebrate the proclamation's signing with a commemorative portrait. Lincoln liked the idea so much that he allowed Marchant to reside in the White House while he worked on the painting and arranged for Marchant's son, also an artist, to take leave from military duty to assist his father.

Assuming the portrait would be permanently exhibited at Independence Hall, Marchant conceived his work within the state portrait tradition (plate 90). Twice the size of Blythe's portrayal, Marchant's shows Lincoln in front of the oversized columns, drapes, chair of authority, and covered table that represent the majesty of the state. With quill pen in one hand, he secures with his other the proclamation he has just signed. Immediately behind him is a pedestal supporting the figure of Liberty and a broken chain symbolizing emancipation. Mar-

chant enshrines Lincoln by enveloping him in the trappings that had framed every presidential portrait since those of George Washington.

Marchant's painting must have satisfied its patrons, for it expresses with great dignity their feelings about both Lincoln and the prospect of slavery's demise. The public appeal of Marchant's style, however, was relatively limited. Neither Marchant's emancipation painting nor comparable paintings in the state portrait tradition by William Travers (1865), Solomon Nunes Carvalho (1865), and William Cogswell (1869) attained the popularity of Francis Bicknell Carpenter's group portrait, completed in 1864 (plate 91).[9]

An ardent opponent of slavery, Carpenter proposed to Lincoln a life-size painting of the president reading the proclamation to his entire cabinet. A less ambitious work, Carpenter maintained, would be unworthy of "this new

138

90. Edward Dalton Marchant. *Abraham Lincoln*. 1863. 55 x 45" (139.7 x 114.3 cm.). The Union League of Philadelphia.

epoch in the history of liberty."[10] Impressed by the young artist's political vision and by his letter of introduction from Illinois congressman and friend Owen Lovejoy, Lincoln approved the plan and made Carpenter artist-in-residence, as he had Marchant six months earlier.

The completed painting, Carpenter stated, contains "no imaginary curtain or column, gorgeous furniture or allegorical statue"—a critical reference, probably, to Marchant's rival painting. The subject itself—"the salvation of the Republic—the Freedom of a Race"—would engage any audience "without the aid of conventional trappings."[11] In fact, though, Carpenter merely replaced one set of trappings—the state portrait's—for another— what Mark Thistlethwaite has termed history painting's "civil heroic tradition," exemplified by John Trumbull's *Declaration of Independence* (plate 42) and Benjamin West's *The American Commissioners; or, Signing the*

Treaty of Paris (plate 92).[12] An expression of collective will, the act of signing unifies the paintings' content. Trumbull's colonial delegates and West's peace commissioners are small companies of men whose center of influence is indiscernible. Thomas Pritchard Rossiter modified this pattern in *Signing the Constitution of the United States* (plate 93) by elevating George Washington above the many other delegates on the scene and surrounding him with an aura of light. The scale of Carpenter's painting is smaller, the contrast between his main and peripheral subjects less vivid than Rossiter's, but his composition is similar. Carpenter set Lincoln apart from his seven cabinet officers and arranged the entire scene around him.

For Lincoln's admirers, the *First Reading of the Emancipation Proclamation by Abraham Lincoln* was more than a history painting; it was "The Great National Pic-

139

91. Francis Bicknell Carpenter. *First
Reading of the Emancipation
Proclamation of President Lincoln.* 1864.
110 x 180" (279.4 x 457.2 cm.). U.S.
Capitol, Washington, D.C.

ture"—an emblem of their vision of America. Authenticity made this emblem powerful. Many cabinet scenes, including Alonzo Chappel's *Lincoln Reading the Emancipation Proclamation to His Cabinet* (1862), were imaginary and hastily produced. Carpenter's scene was based on meticulous research.[13]

Carpenter's close attention to the cabinet's seating arrangement revealed its members' ideological division. The radical members of the cabinet are to Lincoln's right; the more conservative members to his left. The artist enhanced this "curious mingling of fact and allegory" by selecting from the actual meeting room certain "accessories." The *New York Tribune*, opposed to slavery, lies at the lower left near War Secretary Edwin M. Stanton's feet. A portrait of Simon Cameron, Stanton's predecessor and the first cabinet member to avow a radical emancipation policy, appears at the extreme left, above Stanton's head. Andrew Jackson's portrait, in contrast, is located in the center behind white-bearded Navy Secretary Gideon Welles. Jackson's determination to uphold national union brings him into the picture, but his friendliness toward slavery places him on the side of the conservatives. Occupying the symbolic chair of authority (unembellished, but the only one with armrests—a traditional symbol of authority in the hierarchy of seating furniture), Lincoln positions himself between the radicals and conservatives and mediates their claims. The docu-

ment he has just signed is a compromise that resolves competing interests: it will preserve slavery if the rebellion ceases, destroy slavery if the rebellion continues.[14]

Consecration

Just as emancipation enshrined Lincoln as a symbol of freedom, Gettysburg linked him to patriotic sacrifice and heroic death. Six months after Lincoln signed the Emancipation Proclamation, Union forces won the battle of Gettysburg; soon afterward, by invitation offered only on second thought by a local committee, Lincoln consecrated the dead at the dedication ceremony for the new Gettysburg Cemetery. The occasion failed to capture artistic attention: not a single painting or print of the event or even decorative copy of Lincoln's speech appeared during the war. By 1876, however, growing public interest in the Gettysburg Address became evident in many centennial observances, which moved Albion Harris Bicknell to design a life-size representation of Lincoln at Gettysburg (plate 94).

The stiffness of Bicknell's painting betrays the fact that his likenesses were based on photographs taken separately and having no previous relationship to one another. Although rendered authentically enough, his subjects resemble a waxwork collection. The whole, in

92. Benjamin West. *The American Commissioners; or, Signing the Treaty of Paris.* 1783. 28⅜ x 36¹⁵⁄₁₆" (71.0 x 92.2 cm.). The Henry Francis du Pont Winterthur Museum, Winterthur, Delaware.

93. Thomas Pritchard Rossiter. *Signing
the Constitution of the United States.*
1867. 24¼ x 48¾" (60.6 x 121.9 cm.).
Fraunces Tavern Museum, New York.

94. Albion Harris Bicknell. *Lincoln at
Gettysburg.* 1879. 108 x 216" (274.3 x
548.6 cm.). Malden Public Library,
Malden, Massachusetts.

95. Emanuel Leutze. *Abraham Lincoln.* 1865. 69 x 50" (175.26 x 127 cm.). Union League Club, New York.

this sense, is less than the sum of its parts. In another sense, the rigid cast of the painting adds to its intended solemnity. Lincoln dominates the scene at center-foreground, standing beside a drape-covered table. His right hand grasps his address; his left, gracefully bent, touches the bottom of his lapel. The platform is decorated with a colorful carpet and floral bouquet. Lush trees in the left and right background frame the cemetery's horizon. Arrayed behind Lincoln are twenty of the war's most visible men—military officers, state governors, senators, vice presidents, and journalists.

Although most of them were not actually present with Lincoln at Gettysburg, and many known to have been on the platform are excluded from the picture, Bicknell's scene is not altogether fictional. Completed as southern influence reasserted itself and Reconstruction ended in 1879, the painting re-creates symbolically the coalition that fought the war. The pictured assemblage (whose members were identified by a key accompanying the printed reproductions) is weighted in favor of antislavery opinion—epitomized not only by the pres-

ence of antislavery radicals Henry Wilson, Salmon Chase, and Benjamin Butler, but also by black journalist and political leader Frederick Douglass (with whom few politicians, including Lincoln, would have dared to share a public platform in 1863).

Bicknell's composition, like Carpenter's, portrays the enactment of a ritual and embodies its expression of national solidarity. As anthropologist David Kertzer has observed, rituals such as proclamation signings and memorial orations "provide a mechanism for people to express their allegiance to an organization or to a movement without requiring common belief. . . . Solidarity is produced by people acting together, not by people thinking together."[15] Just so, Carpenter and Bicknell depict men whose presence together dramatizes common identification with the nation and mutes conflicting beliefs about how it should be preserved. Lincoln, the object around and through which this unity becomes manifest, thus achieves a symbolic status that transcends his individual actions and powers.[16]

Bicknell's painting shares the formality and disregard

96. Dennis Malone Carter. *Lincoln Greeting the Heroes of War.* ca 1865. 34 x 47" (85.0 x 117.5 cm.). The Hendershott Collection

for Lincoln's "human side" that characterize Marchant's and Carpenter's depictions—as well as, for that matter, almost all popular history painting executed in the late 1860s. But, if any president seemed human and informal, it was Lincoln. He was the people's president, his plebeian background the distinguishing mark of his public identity. That artists preferred images of him in the grand style of history painting, then, is traceable not to Lincoln's personal qualities but to the prolonged Civil War over which he presided. War is one of the traditional subjects of the grand style. As wartime painters felt their own energies and political passions aroused, however, they attributed to Lincoln powers and virtues that exceeded what he in fact possessed.[17] The idealistic cast of their grand-style portrayals of Lincoln was thus accentuated.

Victory

The paintings of Marchant, Carpenter, and Bicknell describe events that occurred early in 1863 when the North's military fortunes and Lincoln's popularity were at low ebb. Nevertheless, they enhance Lincoln by representing the dignity of his office, the importance of his deeds, and the vast diversity of the nation he sought to unify. Emanuel Leutze's 1865 portrait of Lincoln (plate 95) reaffirmed and magnified these qualities. Commemorating the second inauguration in March 1865, Leutze de-

picted a dominating, stately Lincoln standing in front of the Capitol with his hand on the Bible and U.S. Constitution. In the remote background, a large and diversified crowd listens to the great leader's address.

George P. A. Healy and Dennis Malone Carter depicted events that occurred in April 1865, the last month of the conflict. But because they were painted well after the war was over, their works add new qualities to Lincoln's historic identity. Healy superimposed the image of Lincoln as conqueror upon the image of Lincoln as emancipator and consoler. Completed in 1868, his painting (plate 97) is a composite of separate portraits, the oldest of which represented Lincoln during his first year in office. The presidential virtue Healy wished to stress was not sternness but magnanimity, as his choice of title—*The Peacemakers,* as opposed to "The Victors" or "Conquerors of the Rebellion"—indicates. Healy depicted Lincoln in the midst of a shipboard conference at City Point, Virginia. General Ulysses S. Grant sits on Lincoln's right, General William T. Sherman before him, and Admiral David Porter on his left. A profound serenity radiates from Lincoln's face and permeates the scene. With legs crossed and head resting in hand, he calmly looks at Sherman as the general leans forward to make his point. Lincoln is shown as he prepares to command his officers to give the enemy the mildest possible surrender terms.[18]

When Sherman set these terms before Joseph Johnston and his North Carolina army, Republican leaders publicly rebuked him because of their burning resentment toward the South and their objection to Lincoln's magnanimous proposal.[19] But sympathetic viewers knew little about this detail and probably would have cared even less. They saw what they wanted to remember—the victorious commander's kindness to his enemy—a trait that by 1868, notwithstanding the retributive aspects of Reconstruction, had already begun to lose the negative associations it had in 1865.

Yet even in 1865 there were indications that Lincoln's "gentle conqueror" image would enhance his reputation. Local reactions to his entering Richmond is a case in point. "Never in the history of the world," according to Lincoln's secretaries John Nicolay and John Hay, "did the head of a mighty nation and the conqueror of a great rebellion enter the captured chief city of the insurgents with such humbleness and simplicity."[20] Carter's *Lincoln's Drive through Richmond* (plate 98) sets this scene on canvas. Carter began this painting after completing another representation of Union triumph: *Lincoln Greeting the Heroes of War* (plate 96), in which Victory introduces Lincoln, the commander-in-chief, to Grant and Sherman. In *Drive through Richmond*, however, Lincoln is the war's hero, and he alone dominates the viewer's attention. Lincoln is accompanied by Admiral Porter and a military escort, but he looks more like Christ entering Jerusalem than Caesar entering Rome. Light emanates from his figure, bathing even the admirers who approach him. The picture vibrates with the excitement and movement of the crowd. Hats are tossed in the air. The older bid the young, as do parents their children, to look upon the great man. A baby is held up to Lincoln by her father, as if to be blessed. The painting shows no aged people, and its foreground is composed almost entirely of children. A new era is evidently in the making. Still, the old endures: two unsmiling women at the right, loyal to the defeated Confederacy, with eyes ahead and backs to Lincoln, afford the sinister contrast. They distinguish themselves from the joyful assemblage by leaving it.

Carter was in New York when Richmond fell and probably learned about Lincoln's visit from eyewitness correspondents. His painting seems to reproduce the *Boston Journal*'s account:

> No written page or illuminated canvas can give the reality of the event—the enthusiastic bearing of the people—the blacks and poor whites who have suffered untold horrors during the war, their demonstrations of pleasure, the shouting, dancing, the thanksgivings to God, the mention of the name of Jesus—as if President Lincoln were next to the Son of God in their affections—the jubilant cries, the countenances beaming with unspeakable joy, the tossing up of caps, the swinging of arms of a motley crowd—some in rags, some barefoot . . . yet of stately bearing.[21]

Two thirds of these spectators, the correspondent estimated, were blacks; one third, whites.[22] Carter reversed these percentages in his painting, possibly after learning from the *New York Times* that were it not for the army's ordering white people "to remain within their homes quietly for a few days, without doubt there would have been a large addition to the numbers present."[23] Carter

97. George P. A. Healy. *The Peacemakers*. 1868. 47⅛ x 62⅜" (119.7 x 159.1 cm.). The White House Historical Association, Washington, D. C.; photograph by the National Geographic Society

98. Dennis Malone Carter. *Lincoln's Drive through Richmond.* 1866. 45 x 68" (114.3 x 172.7 cm.). Chicago Historical Society.

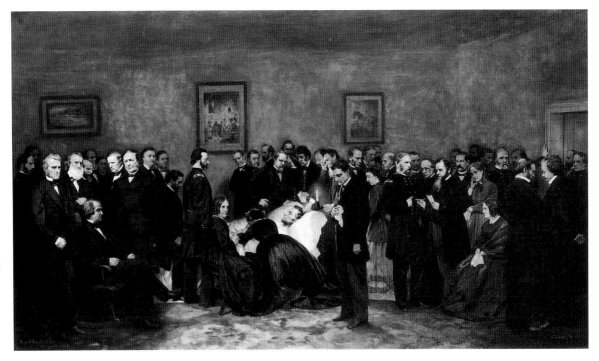

99. John Bachelder and Alonzo Chappel. *The Last Hours of Abraham Lincoln.* 1865–1868. 25⅜ x 43½" (64.0 x 108.7 cm.). McLellan Lincoln Collection, John Hay Library, Brown University, Providence, Rhode Island.

may have described Richmond's reception of Lincoln as it would have been if all citizens were allowed to express their true feelings. However, he may have meant his painting to be a moral lesson rather than a counterfactual statement, an account of Richmond's reception of Lincoln as he thought it should have been—or would have been if that city's residents were inspired by the correct moral sentiments (comparable, in all probability, to his own).

The liberation of white as well as black southerners enlarged Lincoln's historical role. Paradoxically, however, the spectacle of white Richmond celebrating Lincoln's arrival must have confirmed the widespread northern belief that his peace terms were too lenient, a cruel insult to the hundreds of thousands of men who died at his command. The white Confederate sympathizer who shot Lincoln to death confounded the irony.

Martyrdom

Lincoln's assassination led to great rites of national mourning and enhanced his stature.[24] National mourning is not the spontaneous expression of personal emotions; it is a duty imposed by the community. History painters had therefore always portrayed the death of a leader as a public rather than private event. Their intention, as sociologist Emile Durkheim would have put it, was to remind viewers "of the blow which has fallen upon society and diminished it."[25] In West's *Death of General Wolfe* (plate 17), officers and men dutifully mourn their dying leader in the very heat of battle, while Copley's *Death of the Earl of Chatham* (plate 22) shows

members of a startled House of Lords surrounding their fallen colleague in stately sorrow. Presidential deathbed scenes, on the other hand, include family members as well as official representatives and show more clearly the distinction between personal and obligatory grief. Given the trauma of assassination, the Lincoln paintings exemplify this genre in dramatic terms.

Alonzo Chappel's *Last Hours of Abraham Lincoln* (plate 99) is the most prominent painting of the Lincoln death vigil. The scene is a room in the Peterson house, located across the street from Ford's Theater. New York publisher John Bachelder had commissioned Chappel to paint a view of the deathbed scene that placed more emphasis on symbolic than historiographic accuracy. The room in which Lincoln died measured ten by fifteen feet and could comfortably accommodate only a few people, but Bachelder wished to bring together in one painting everyone who had visited Lincoln after he had been shot. This artistic license changes the painting's essential quality: it transforms a simple bedroom into a room of state and creates a ritual atmosphere that gives great dignity to Lincoln's last hours. Even the eight physicians are dispersed among the assemblage, paying respects to Lincoln rather than treating him.

Chappel's rendering of the scene's ritual character conformed to protocol specifying who is to be at the side of an injured or dying president. Navy Secretary Welles knew how the rules applied to him: they compelled him "to attend the President immediately."[26] Stanton, according to Welles's diary, felt the same way, as apparently did the six other cabinet secretaries and assistants and the fifteen military officers who also appear in the painting.

The Last Hours, advertised as the "Golgotha of American History," is probably among the most ambitious deathbed paintings ever produced. As soon as Lincoln's remains were taken from Washington, Bachelder contacted everyone who visited Lincoln on his deathbed at the Peterson house (including Robert Todd Lincoln) and photographed them in the position they would occupy in the painting. Bachelder then arranged the forty-seven figures (seven less than the actual number of people who came to see the dying president) and had Chappel set them to canvas.[27] By 1869 the job was done, and prints (accompanied by a key to identify the painting's subjects) were advertised.

Lincoln is placed exactly at the center of the painting. The candle behind his head cannot account for the shadowless illumination of his face and pillow. Lincoln is the source of his own illumination, and in the expanding glow the tension between devastating private grief and obligatory public mourning resolves itself. Robert, the president's son, with handkerchief in his right hand and head lowered, stands in the foreground while his mother Mary lays her head upon her dying husband's breast. Family friend Senator Charles Sumner stands behind Lincoln, just to the right of his head, at the painting's center. Four women are present, each placed in the front row of visitors. Clara Harris, the New York senator's daughter who accompanied the Lincolns to the theater, stands alone just behind Robert. (Her escort and fiancé, Major Henry R. Rathbone, is in the company of his colleagues on the other side of the room.) The wife of Senator James Dixon sits at the bed beside her friend Mary, while Mrs. Dixon's sister and niece attend with handkerchiefs in their hands at the right. Thus, three of the four women are linked directly or indirectly to the president's wife; the fourth, Miss Harris, separated from her escort, must share with the other women a private rather than public role. A kind of symbolic division of labor emerges: men mourn the president; women, the husband and father.

Public interest, however, supersedes private calamity. Already, Secretary Stanton is attending to state affairs: he stands at right with pad and pencil giving orders to General Auger, the District of Columbia commander. Vice President Andrew Johnson appears on the left, the chair on which he is seated an obvious reference to the powers he is about to assume. Reverend Dr. Gurley, congressional chaplain (pictured behind Robert) and Judge Cartter, Chief Justice of the District of Columbia, in the extreme right foreground, stand by.[28] Everyone is self-possessed, but the sheer density of the scene gives the impression of selfless solidarity. *The Last Hours of Abraham Lincoln* is a symbolic drama in which scores of people known to differ with each other on every conceivable issue close ranks around their dying leader. In the portrayal of death, as in the portrayals of the Emancipation Proclamation and the Gettysburg Address, the history painting's ritual dimensions and formal style define its objective—not factual recording but epic dedication and apotheosis.

History paintings did not cause Lincoln's apotheosis, but they helped greatly to convey it. General Sherman and Admiral Farragut, not Edward Marchant and Francis Carpenter, assured his 1864 reelection. General Grant, not Dennis Carter, enabled him to enter Richmond victoriously. History painters could not necessarily persuade Lincoln's critics that his presidency was a success, but they could articulate his supporters' desire for success. They could produce visual interpretations of Lincoln that made success seem natural, even attributable, to him, and in so doing their works helped make him a national emblem.

Rediscovering the Man of the People

Although many of Lincoln's contemporaries were happy to see him removed from the political scene, assassination greatly increased his stature. The reputation of no pre–Civil War American public figure, in fact, had been elevated so far in so short a time. In the last third of the nineteenth century, Lincoln's reputation became even more secure. In the early years of the twentieth century, however, it surged and surpassed Washington's.[29] The 1909 centennial of Lincoln's birth precipitated this development, but its deeper causes lay in changes wrought by the industrial revolution.

By the 1890s, as historian Henry Steele Commager observed, industrial development, population growth, and the rise of cities led the American people to a watershed—a widespread realization of the obsolescence of many political and economic traditions. During the ensuing Progressive Era (1900–1920), economic and political reforms extended the rights of common people.[30] Correspondingly, Lincoln's commonness, infrequently celebrated in nineteenth-century visual art but central to the period's idea of the man, took on an almost militant meaning. In 1860 Lincoln's campaign managers invoked symbols of his humble background, including the log cabin and ax, in their effort to persuade people to identify with and vote for him. Fifty years later, Progressive reformers seized upon these same symbols in their struggle to redistribute political and economic power. Lincoln centennial speakers pointed out that "The Great Commoner" would oppose child labor and the exploitation of adult labor. They claimed he would recognize that "socialism is the new slavery" but would say the same about "corporations that break the laws with insolence and impunity." Lincoln was a natural "labor leader" who recognized both the legitimacy of property and the essential rights of the working man.

In the end, it was less important to know what Progressive measures Lincoln would have supported than to know what traits of character, what virtues, that support would reveal. Hence the endless public reminiscences of Lincoln's simplicity and unpretentiousness, his merciful attitude toward condemned soldiers, his magnanimity toward defeated political and military opponents, his accessibility and responsiveness to people without influence and power, his profound sympathy for the casualties of war and their aggrieved families. Each reminiscence depicts the blurring of hierarchical distinction; each depicts the common man in interaction and close moral affinity with the state. Lincoln's character and life on the one hand, Progressive Era political and economic reforms on the other, were thus seen to be infused with the same egalitarian principle, such that the invocation of one invariably brought to mind the other. New Lincoln paintings effectively visualized the connection.

The Reconstruction of Abraham Lincoln

Before the twentieth century, artistic conceptions lagged behind the widely held, popular conceptions of Lincoln's commonness. It was not that nineteenth-century painters who wished to represent Lincoln's ordinary side lacked imaginative models. In 1860 David Gilmour Blythe produced *Abraham Lincoln, Rail Splitter*, showing the president-elect standing with an ax and maul over a split log, his jug and lawbook lying nearby, his baggy pants held up by a single strap. In 1865, after Lincoln's death, printmakers brought out a series of Lincoln family scenes, revealing a part of his private life never depicted before. Later, in 1868, Eastman Johnson completed his *Boyhood of Lincoln* (plate 100), showing the nation's savior as a youngster seated with book in hand before a glowing fire. Johnson's depiction, in the words of art historian Patricia Hills, "brought history painting in America to the intimate and humanizing scale of genre."[31] The trauma of war and its aftermath, however, eclipsed this imagery and made the grand style more appropriate.

When early twentieth-century illustrators again emphasized Lincoln's humanity, the public was receptive. Howard Pyle's 1907 *Harper's Monthly* depiction of Lincoln seated at his presidential desk, deep in thought and peeling an apple, represents the best of many genrefied magazine and book portrayals.[32] But nothing captured Lincoln's common side more effectively than Jean Leon Gerome Ferris's history paintings. In a reform-conscious environment, Ferris brought to democracy's egalitarian dimension an iconic vividness it had never before possessed. He brought the ideal of equality down to eye level. A keen sense of the order of face-to-face encounters and a gift for finding the power relations of society

in the subtle gestures of everyday life are evident in each of Ferris's works. Combining sociological perceptiveness and artistic talent, his work suited the era's taste for both strong leadership and equality. Ferris's aim was not to elevate Lincoln's commonness but to humanize his greatness.

Lincoln and the Contrabands, 1863 (plate 101), although lacking in factual foundation, is typical of Ferris's work. Runaway slaves designated "contraband of war" and entitled to state protection encounter the president. The purpose of the meeting is unclear, but the petitioners are evidently in transit (a valise lies in the lower foreground): some are disheartened (including the woman with head in hand sitting behind the guard); others are eager to talk (especially the elderly man whom the guard restrains). Lincoln has been promenading in the company of two finely dressed ladies, but he allows himself to be interrupted. A young mother with children sustains his attention while his companions wait. The older child fearfully grasps his mother's apron, but the president wants to get close. He removes his hat out of respect, stands beside the poor woman, and affectionately places his left hand on her younger child's shoulder. Physical closeness, Ferris is saying, affirms equality in God's sight. *The Contrabands* thus differs from nineteenth-century sculptors' and printmakers' images of liberated bondsmen bowing and scraping to Lincoln in gratitude. Ferris's counterparts are polite, not slavish.

Lincoln's Last Official Act, 1865 (plate 102) extends the president's kindness from former slaves to condemned soldiers. As the popular media printed countless anecdotes about the tenderhearted president saving young men from firing squads, the believing public must have welcomed Ferris's painting. Lincoln was in fact inclined toward leniency, but he approved most of the hundreds of death sentences imposed on Union deserters during the war. Having no time to investigate details, he was likely to revoke a death warrant only as a political favor or when a case was brought to his attention by a political friend.

Ferris, however, shows Lincoln petitioned by a condemned man's wife. No account of Lincoln's last day in office mentions this meeting, but the painting condenses similar scenes known to have taken place previously. With head in handkerchiefed hand, Ferris's petitioner inclines in gratitude toward the president, who holds an order that will prevent her husband's execution. He does his good deed at an inconvenient time. The desk is covered with papers, the floor strewn with office debris. Behind the guard at his office door await others with pressing business. Still, the president finds time to convert a young wife's grief to joy.

The politically resonant aspect of the painting is its subjects' physical proximity. A powerless petitioner sits

100. Eastman Johnson. *Boyhood of Lincoln.* 1868. 46 x 37" (116.8 x 94 cm.).
The University of Michigan Museum of Art, Ann Arbor; bequest of Henry C. Lewis.

101. Jean Leon Gerome Ferris. *Lincoln and the Contrabands, 1863.* ca. 1921. 24 x 35" (61.0 x 88.9 cm.). Archives of 76, Cleveland, Ohio.

on the president's own chair (presumably by his invitation) and rests her arms on his desk. Her mobile left hand pivots on the elbow, seeking the president, wanting to touch him. Lincoln leans compliantly toward the grateful woman and places his hand upon her head, more aware of her anguish than of her husband's offense. This is not only a ruler but also a friend. *Lincoln's Last Official Act* is the epitome of early twentieth-century history painting—affirming hierarchy by reducing it to genre.

Continuities in the Making of an Epic Hero

A stronger dose of egalitarianism was required to democratize Lincoln's pictorial image than was needed to democratize his biographical and poetic images. The human side of Lincoln was not widely articulated in visual art until the Progressive Era, when the nation's democratic ideals and expectations reached a critical threshold of development. Yet, the same national crisis that promoted grand-style history painting in the early 1860s was present, on a lesser but still intense scale, in the early twentieth century. Out of the excitement of the Spanish-American War and the suffering of World War I, the United States emerged as a global force needing a grandly styled Lincoln to symbolize its expanding power as well as a genrefied Lincoln to symbolize its expanding democracy.

Ferris had recognized this dual need in *Lincoln at In-dependence Hall, 1861*, which he completed along with *The Rail Splitter* in 1908. The Independence Hall painting shows Lincoln delivering a Washington's Birthday speech in Philadelphia, where he had stopped on his way from Springfield to assume the presidency. In the address, Lincoln publicly defied a plot to kill him the next night as he passed through Baltimore. Rather than surrender the principle of equality for all citizens, he declared, "I would rather be assassinated on this spot." Ferris showed Lincoln having finished the speech. Lincoln steps to the flag and grasps its cord in his right hand; just before he raises it, he points dramatically with his left hand toward the sky. The flag itself is a curtain that sets Lincoln in front of· the platform's other occupants, and the minutely drawn audience exaggerates his prominence.

An equally ennobling Lincoln painting, designed in an attenuated grand style, is Robert Marshall Root's *Lincoln-Douglas Debate at Charleston* (plate 103). The content of the debate, from a late twentieth-century standpoint, was anything but ennobling. It began on the issue of race, with each candidate trying to assure the audience of his contempt for black people.[33] Slavery, Lincoln explained, was wrong, but that did not mean social equality was right. He had never been in favor "of making voters or jurors of negroes, nor of qualifying them to hold office, nor to intermarry with white people."[34] In Root's painting, Lincoln strikes a Bicknell-type epic pose as he speaks. He stands at the picture's center, his right hand resting on a table (as in a state portrait), his left gesticulating to emphasize his belief in white supremacy. On Lincoln's right side sits his opponent, Douglas; behind Lincoln sit local and state dignitaries whose likenesses Root copied from photographs. Root's grand style is violated, however, by his conspicuous incorporation of spectators, including distracted mothers and children—an unmistakable mark of genrefication.[35] But the occasion, not Lincoln himself, is genrefied. Lincoln remains a man above the people rather than a man of the people.

A Cumulative Vision

The traits most celebrated in great leaders reflect the main premises of their culture. The dual premises of American culture have always placed limits on the kind of man that could be made of Lincoln. Great and powerful nations cannot be represented by common, weak leaders. Democratic nations cannot be represented by remote, elitist leaders. The Lincoln image has for these reasons pulled in two opposite directions: toward stateliness, authority, and dignity on the one hand, and toward plainness, familiarity, and homeliness on the other. These two sides of the Lincoln image express two fundamental cultural themes—the egalitarian theme, rooted in the Jefferson-Jackson traditions, and the hierarchical theme, rooted in the Federalist and antebellum Whig traditions.[36] Lincoln personified both themes, the egalitarian and the hierarchical, from the very moment he was elected to the presidency, but these themes have informed his pictorial images unevenly. Lincoln images of the Civil War era were made largely of hierarchical stuff; images of the Progressive Era were more egalitarian and elaborately humanized. The pictorial past is thus constantly restructured in order to legitimize present interests and articulate present values.

In one sense, painters' depictions of Lincoln differed little from their depictions of other public men before his time. No one mistook George Washington for Lincoln, but state portrait and history painters followed similar conventions in their depictions of both leaders. In another sense, however, Lincoln was a unique subject. Washington was already an epic, godlike hero when American artists took him as their subject. As the years passed, the artists' problem was to show Washington to be like ordinary men. In contrast, Lincoln began as an ordinary man, and the task for artists of his own and later time was to make him godlike. And it was always a difficult task. To make Lincoln an epic hero during his own lifetime, painters worked against, not with, public opinion; to make him a folk hero in more recent times, painters risked obscuring his epic achievements.

Continuities in the artists' image of Lincoln center on his greatness, while the public image of Lincoln has always emphasized common traits. During the early twentieth century, the depictions of Lincoln' epic qualities became unnatural and forced—almost as if artists doubted their authenticity. No other historical figure presented artists with such a problem. Ferris made many paintings of George Washington enacting domestic roles in order to reduce the remoteness associated with his great stature. Lincoln, on the other hand, already seemed earthy and plain. Concerned that humanizing Lincoln would diminish him, Ferris preferred to show him acting within a presidential role. When Ferris treated him in the grand style (*Lincoln at Independence Hall*), he grossly exaggerated Lincoln's physical stature relative to his audience's. Root's portrait showing Lincoln's dignified oratorical pose also appears inflated, at least beside Bicknell's similar composition.

Lincoln's uniqueness as a problematic subject of art mirrors his singularity as a man and a president. No other historical figure brings into such balance the common and sublime, the low and high, the egalitarian and hierarchical ideals of American culture. History painters did not create this dualism, but they have played a major role in preserving it. To have maintained it for so long, despite rapid and pervasive changes in social structure and artistic taste, may be their most notable contribution to the Lincoln legacy.

102. Jean Leon Gerome Ferris. *Lincoln's Last Official Act, 1865.* ca. 1912. 35 x 28" (88.9 x 71.1 cm.). Archives of 76, Cleveland, Ohio.

103. Robert Marshall Root. *The Lincoln-
Douglas Debate at Charleston.* 1918. 20 x
60" (50.8 x 152.4 cm.). Illinois State
Historical Library, Springfield.

Paintings for the People

American Popular History Painting, 1875–1930

BARBARA J. MITNICK

In 1876 Americans celebrated their country's one hundredth birthday at the International Centennial Exposition staged in Philadelphia's Fairmount Park. No longer viewing themselves as citizens of a fledgling nation devoid of tradition, Americans now had their own heroes, cultural institutions, and political history. Like the concept of progress itself, the centennial fair looked forward and backward. In Machinery Hall, the giant Corliss engine, which furnished power to all of the exhibits, symbolized the advance of American technology, but the exhibition of landscapes and other conservative paintings by American artists in Memorial Hall reminded fairgoers of an earlier agrarian age, perhaps in an attempt to counteract the problems of the new urban and industrial era.[1] While Centennial visitors contemplated the engine, they could also witness the reenactment of the 1775 battle of Lexington, the first engagement of the Revolutionary War, on the grounds of Fairmount Park. As they marveled at the newest scientific achievements, they could also watch women in colonial costume bustle about a "New England Kitchen" preparing Yankee beans and brown bread, a nostalgic reminder of the "good old days" of the eighteenth century even for people who had never used such a kitchen or eaten these traditional foods.

The nation was entering a period known today as the American Renaissance. Some Americans in this maturing society began to travel to and study the art and architecture of the fifteenth-century Renaissance, and, in a similar spirit of rebirth, to create an American version of European art and culture. Others endorsed and participated in the development of a uniquely national art inspired by the past. Thus the "Colonial Revival" began in earnest. Americans collected eighteenth-century relics; manufacturers produced decorative arts recalling early

models; composers wrote patriotic music; architects designed enlarged replicas of colonial and Federal homes.[2] Encouraged by this nostalgic and patriotic sentiment, artists began to produce popular images related to early American history that the public and critics alike received warmly. Indeed, such imagery had grown so successful by 1895 that one magazine writer declared, "This is an art of which we cannot have too much, for nothing strengthens national life, so nourishes patriotism, as the revival in the popular imagination of those historical periods which were full of heroism and romance and splendor of deeds, as well as beauty and dress and grace of manners."[3]

This attitude toward history painting represented a change from the critical distaste for such art immediately after the Civil War. For one writer, history painting had come to be "the representation of the destructive and aggrandizing action in war of great nations."[4] A critic for the *Art Journal* was similarly offended by Peter F. Rothermel's *Battle of Gettysburg* (plate 104), exhibited at the Centennial:

> Our space forbids us to dwell much on ill taste, to say nothing of the bad art, of such pictures as the "Battle of Gettysburg" which, even if it were a fine picture which it is not would be an unsuitable reminder, at this Centennial time, of discords that are past and troubles which will scarcely be renewed. Could a large group of good Allstons, or Benjamin West's pictures or of many artists we might name, have occupied these big spaces on the walls, their beauty and dignity would have dominated the collection and given it a positive character that it now lacks.[5]

For some Americans, scarcely more than a decade removed from the war, all history painting had become synonymous with ghastly scenes of battle. Horrific de-

N. C. Wyeth. *In a Dream I Meet General Washington,* detail of plate 120.

104. Peter F. Rothermel. *Battle of Gettysburg—Pickett's Charge.* 1867–70. 194 x 377" (485.0 x 942.5 cm.). Pennsylvania State Museum, Harrisburg.

105. Jean Leon Gerome Ferris. *Writing the Declaration of Independence, 1776.* ca. 1921. 30 x 24" (75.0 x 60.0 cm.). Archives of 76, Cleveland, Ohio.

pictions of blood and carnage carried little currency with an audience interested in sentiment and reunification rather than the harsh realities of life and war.

Based on the supposition that significant production and collection of historical works virtually ended after the Civil War, modern scholars of history painting have generally tended to ignore the post-Centennial period.[6] However, recent scholarship has established that late nineteenth-century popular history painters tended to focus their attention on nostalgic depictions while generally eschewing horrific battle scenes and other distasteful subjects. Thus history painting survived in a changed form intended to appeal to a wider audience—not only to public patrons, as was the case early in the nineteenth century, nor just to collectors and readers of history books, who at midcentury were able to visualize written accounts by examining historical illustrations that accompanied them. By the late nineteenth century, history painting also reached ordinary Americans, who could buy mass-produced calendars, posters, and magazines created by the newly invented four-color printing process.

Postwar history painters not only made their work available in different forms, they also offered a different view of the past. In the early years of the nation, artists commonly depicted historic events in an idealized and heroic manner according to the conventions of grand narrative painting. John Trumbull's *Declaration of Independence, July 4, 1776* (plate 42), which he replicated several times during the early nineteenth century, depicts Thomas Jefferson presenting the document to John Hancock, president of the Continental Congress. John Adams, Roger Sherman, Robert Livingston, and Benjamin Franklin stand in formal, statesmanlike poses around Jefferson; no evidence of the human effort necessary to produce the Declaration is visible.[7] Trumbull's figures, lined up in heroic mission, are the icons of our early history. But when the history painter Jean Leon Gerome Ferris depicted the same subject more than one hundred years later in *Writing the Declaration of Independence, 1776* (plate 105), the setting was an ordinary room. Evidence of the struggle to create the Declaration appears in the numerous torn papers on the floor as well as in the concentration evident on the faces of Franklin, Adams, and Jefferson.[8] The human side of historic subject matter had informed history painting. The meaningful symbolism is no longer the ceremonial presentation of the document but the workaday world of its creators.

The modern viewer tends to accept both versions of the subject as simple alternatives, different stages of the same event, which, indeed, they could have been. Having had the benefit of earlier nineteenth-century sources, Ferris could have produced a version of the iconic Trumbull painting, yet he chose not to. Conversely, artists of Trumbull's time were not likely to have envisioned the event in the terms Ferris chose, for it would then have been unseemly to identify such behind-the-scenes activity as an apt subject for history painting.

159

106. Junius Brutus Stearns. *The Marriage of George Washington to Martha Custis.* 1849. 44½ x 61½" (111.2 x 153.7 cm.). Virginia Museum of Fine Arts, Richmond; gift of Col. and Mrs. Edgar W. Garbisch.

This major alteration in the focus of the genre came about partly as a result of changes in the nature of patronage for art in the United States. As Americans sought to build a new nation during the first few decades of the nineteenth century, the national government recognized the need for monumental works executed in the grand style that featured important Americans standing in heroic poses above and apart from ordinary people. Similarly intent on creating a sense of nationalism, the writers of historical and biographical narratives that were published during this period also presented their subjects in lofty terms.[9] But there was little or no American demand for such traditional European forms of history painting as allegory, religion, mythology, and literature, and there were few private collectors interested in large-scale heroic subjects. "You had better learn to make shoes or dig potatoes," John Trumbull is reported to have told an aspiring young history painter, "than become a painter in this country."[10] Some adapted their talent to portrait painting; others sold engraved reproductions of their historical works. Still others, such as Benjamin West and John Singleton Copley, sought both training and markets for their work in Europe.[11]

The circumstances that helped assure Andrew Jackson's election to the presidency in 1828 signaled change both in the attitude toward and the audience for history painting. The first six presidents of the United States had been wealthy, well educated, and elected to the post by an electoral college distantly representing the people. Jackson, born on the frontier and self-made, was sent to the highest office by a direct appeal to the mass of voters rather than through a specific political organization. His inauguration was even attended by ordinary citizens.[12] The nation, it seemed to many, was becoming the democracy envisioned by the Founding Fathers, where citizens could aspire to enjoy "life, liberty and the pursuit of happiness" regardless of their origins. It is not surprising, then, that within this context American artists began to see possibilities in genre painting, which dealt with the lives and events of ordinary Americans.[13] A significant example is Tompkins H. Matteson's *Spirit of 1776* (plate 53), exhibited at New York's National Academy of Design in 1845, which incorporated patriotic imagery within an everyday environment.[14]

During the late eighteenth century and for the first few decades of the nineteenth, George Washington was depicted as almost superhuman, devoid of emotion. By midcentury, as technological progress and territorial expansion created an unsettled national atmosphere and both home and family came to be viewed as safe, tranquil havens, Washington the military hero became the father not only of the country but also of the collective American family. Mount Vernon, his home, became America's home, and a major drive was begun in the

107. Auguste Regnier after Junius Brutus Stearns. *Life of George Washington: The Citizen.* 1854. Hand-colored lithograph. Virginia Museum of Fine Arts, Richmond.

1850s to restore it to its former glory.[15] The restoration came on the heels of the celebration of the centennial of Washington's birth in 1832 and the dedication of the Washington Monument in 1848, events that further inspired American artists and writers to focus on the leader's human side.

Junius Brutus Stearns appears to have been the first artist to create a series related to events in Washington's life. In *The Marriage of George Washington to Martha Custis* (plate 106), Stearns depicted a scene virtually unknown in American art to that time. Early nineteenth-century biographers of Washington barely mentioned his marriage, undoubtedly because they believed that any description of such a mundane event would compromise their iconic presentation of the great leader.[16] Stearns, however, saw such a humanized subject as crucial to an understanding of Washington's true nature.

Patrons and collectors responded enthusiastically to such images of the nation's heroes, and, by 1835, American taste for history and historical genre was growing perceptibly: such paintings began to appear on exhibition, and lithographers began to make prints of well-received works for a wider audience. M. Knoedler, undoubtedly with Stearns's permission, published a lithograph of the marriage of Washington titled *The Citizen* (plate 107).[17] The view showed Washington engaged in a ritual common to most Americans, and, in lithograph

form, this humanized persona of the first president became eminently accessible. While Stearns could claim to have presented a "real" event in Washington's life, he nonetheless cast it in an idealized, sentimental light, an attitude that clearly informed the work of artists later in the century.

In *Washington as a Farmer at Mount Vernon* (plate 108), completed in 1851 and subsequently exhibited at the National Academy of Design in 1854, Stearns also appears to have been motivated more by historical veracity than by a need to keep Washington on his proverbial pedestal.[18] But for Stearns, veracity meant depicting a scene from Washington's life, not necessarily its context. Indeed, Stearns included no reference to the enslavement of the African Americans depicted in the painting, despite the growing intensity of the contemporary antislavery movement.

By midcentury biographers had also begun to probe for details of Washington's career as a farmer, an occupation most Americans of the period shared. In 1845 Horatio Hastings Weld even placed the great leader's agricultural interests on a level with his military accomplishments:

> Washington on his farm at Mount Vernon, performing his duties as a virtuous and useful citizen, is not less worthy of contemplation than Washington leading his country to independence, and showing her how to enjoy it after-

108. Junius Brutus Stearns. *Washington as a Farmer at Mount Vernon.* 1851. 37½ x 54" (93.8 x 135.0 cm.). Virginia Museum of Fine Arts, Richmond; gift of Col. and Mrs. Edgar W. Garbisch.

wards. The former example is indeed more extensively useful, because it comes home to the business and bosoms of ordinary men, and is within the reach of their imagination.[19]

But grand-style traditions still dominated the approach of history painters interested in Washington's military career. In 1851 Emanuel Leutze brought his monumental *Washington Crossing the Delaware* (plate 30) from Düsseldorf, Germany, to the United States, where it was exhibited to great acclaim at Goupil's Gallery in New York and subsequently in the Capitol Rotunda in Washington, D.C.[20] The positive response of the crowds as well as the critics indicated that a grand-style conception of Washington leading his troops was alive and well in 1851.

That such heroic depictions continued to find an audience in the United States is indicated by New York art dealer William Schaus's 1853 commission of Tompkins Matteson to paint *Signing the Compact on Board the Mayflower* (plate 109), intended to commemorate "the first and accordingly the most important civil and constitutional document to be drawn in America."[21] Inspired by the commercial success of engravings after Trumbull's *Declaration of Independence*, Schaus believed he could accomplish the same result with a large folio mezzotint engraving of Matteson's work. Schaus's approach represents a change in patronage by midcentury: whereas government had been virtually the only support for the work of those few American painters interested in historical events earlier in the century, Schaus anticipated a sizable profit in commissioning paintings by history painters of the day and subsequently publishing them as prints for wide distribution.

The midcentury proliferation of illustrated books also affected the nature of history painting. The tendencies to humanize heroic subjects and to depict them in the grand style appeared to merge in the book illustrations of such artists as Felix Octavius Carr Darley and Alonzo Chappel. These printed works were an important transition to the enormous numbers of late nineteenth-century reproductions of history paintings in various media.[22]

Chappel's education in historical painting seems to have relied mainly on exhibitions of such works in New York, primarily at the National Academy of Design, the American Art-Union, and the Düsseldorf Gallery.[23] Although his opportunity for success in the field came through commissions for book illustrations, it appears that Chappel intended to exhibit his paintings: several were created in color at a time when it was not possible to print in color. Exhibition records document that his paintings were included in shows at the National Academy of Design and the Brooklyn Art Association.[24]

Chappel's first commission was to illustrate John Frederick Schroeder's *Life and Times of Washington*, a two-volume biography published in 1857.[25] Included

109. Tompkins H. Matteson. *Signing the Compact on Board the Mayflower.* 1853. 36 x 48" (90.0 x 120.0 cm.). Private collection.

Facing page top:
110. Alonzo Chappel. *Washington's Farewell to His Officers.* ca. 1857. 10 x 13½" (25.0 x 33.8 cm.). Chicago Historical Society.

Facing page bottom:
111. Nathaniel Currier. *Washington's Farewell to His Officers.* 1848. Lithograph. Museum of the City of New York.

was *Washington's Farewell to His Officers* (plate 110), which depicts the famous parting at New York's Fraunces Tavern in 1783. The composition appears to have been the first to follow faithfully nineteenth-century accounts of the event by several of Washington's biographers—including Schroeder. The formal embrace of Washington and General Henry Knox is the focal point and heeds Schroeder's account of the same year: "Washington, incapable of utterance, grasped [Knox's] hand, and embraced him."[26] The war is over; the soldiers are parting emotionally from their leader. Earlier illustrations of the event had presented Washington in straightforward and heroic pose, formally taking leave of his men; Nathaniel Currier's 1848 lithograph was little more than a formal group portrait of the attending officers (plate 111).

The melding of genre and aspects of the grand style in history painting might have continued unabated had it not been for the Civil War. Unlike Rothermel's *Battle of Gettysburg*, much history painting after 1865 avoided the depiction of battle and other grim subjects. But even as sentimentality predominated, such critics as Henry Tuckerman, writing in 1867, stressed the need for truth in historical representation. Others disagreed about the degree to which sentiment could be taken as artistic "truth." As Mary E. Nealy stated in 1876, "The standard of the true artist is taste and feeling; his object, to give refined pleasure."[27] By the late nineteenth century, history painters seem to have become accepted as interpreters of history, generally choosing to present the positive character of earlier events and characters in accord with popular sentiment about the American past.

By the 1870s, a group of painters began to depict an American history filled with characters looking more attractive than they ever could have appeared during earlier and more difficult times.[28] Some works were historical genre, historic events taking place in the everyday world. Others were genrefied history, showing recognizable historic figures engaged in purely ordinary activity unaccompanied by reference to their historic greatness. By 1870, too, calendar, book, magazine, and other publishers sought these works, as did a growing number of private collectors. Painters tended to produce historical works in sizes more easily exhibited in private homes than had often been the case earlier in the century.

These postwar artists did not form a "school" of painting but were connected by generation, training, and a penchant for historical research. Most were born in the 1850s and 1860s and came into their maturity after the centennial, but history painters born after the centennial continued the tradition well into the twentieth century. Their works combined technical skill, historical understanding, and a philosophical viewpoint informed by the nationalistic optimism and inspiration of the Colo-

nial Revival. Vanguard art movements such as Impressionism, tonalism, and the emerging modernism of the early twentieth century were taking place all around them, but these painters were generally unaffected. Their works instead reflected an interest in the accuracy of period detail (encouraged by earlier critics and artists), the influence of the genre tradition, and the patriotism of the period. And they satisfied the desires of a wide array of patrons.

Despite the popularity of these sentimental scenes of history, modern critics have tended to classify them as "mere" illustration, a form of artistic expression traditionally considered to be beneath painting. "It is a curious conceit of recent artistic criticism to belittle illustration and illustrators," one commentator has observed. "Even when someone is credited with being a successful illustrator, he is somehow thereby deprived of the elevated status of artist."[29] Though many of these postwar artists were successful illustrators, most also created paintings for exhibition. That their paintings were so plainly appealing that publishers replicated them for a mass market does not by itself diminish the quality of their art. These works familiarized a vast public with American historical characters and events. And, in a nation whose demography was rapidly changing with the arrival of large numbers of immigrants, they had new didactic value.[30]

One of the most significant artists to make the transition from illustration to "fine art" was Howard Pyle (1853–1911), who regularly produced illustrations for popular magazines as well as for books generally featuring imaginary heroes and romance.[31] *Attack on the Chew House* (plate 112), for example, illustrated Henry Cabot Lodge's "The Story of the Revolution" in *Scribner's* and revealed Pyle's interest in careful research. The painting shows the fog that plagued Washington's 1777 engagement with General William Howe's forces around the home of Judge Benjamin Chew in Germantown, Pennsylvania, a condition Pyle's research determined had helped prevent an American victory. Still, in his Wilmington, Delaware, art school and in summer classes at Chadds Ford, Pennsylvania, Pyle trained his students to emphasize imagination rather than pure technical facility. His influence endured long after his premature death in 1911 in the works of the numerous artists he trained and in book illustrations that affected generations of younger readers.[32]

Unlike Pyle, Jean Leon Gerome Ferris (1863–1930) came from a family extensively involved in the production of art. His father, Stephen James Ferris, was a well-known Philadelphia portrait painter and etcher; two of his uncles, Edward and Thomas Moran, were history painters working in the traditional grand style. By contrast, Edward Moran's sons and Ferris's cousins, Jean Leon Moran and Edward Percy Moran, were more inter-

112. Howard Pyle. *Attack on the Chew House (The Battle of Germantown)*. 1898. 23¼ x 35¼" (58.1 x 88.1 cm.). Delaware Art Museum, Wilmington; Howard Pyle Collection.

113. Percy Moran. *Washington Entering New York*. N.d. 30 x 40" (75.0 x 100.0 cm.). Private collection.

ested in historical genre. Percy Moran's *Washington Entering New York* (plate 113), depicting the general's triumphant entry into the city after the British evacuation of 1783, reveals a continuing interest in the life of Washington.[33]

Ferris's training at the Pennsylvania Academy of the Fine Arts primarily under Christian Schussele may have played a role in stimulating his interest in historical genre, as did his later private study with Jean Léon Gérôme in Paris.[34] Indeed, it seems to have been Gérôme who had the most influence on Ferris's choice of subject matter, for as Ferris later wrote in his unpublished autobiography, "His axiom was that one would paint best that with which he is most familiar, and he strongly discouraged the habit of so many American artists to blindly imitate European methods and subjects."[35]

Ferris was a regular visitor to Independence Hall, and, by the time he reached his maturity, he was arguably as much an historian as a painter. To accompany many of his works, he prepared detailed explanations of the subject matter. For *The First Thanksgiving, 1621* (plate 114), for example, Ferris's statement explained what contemporary historical accounts had revealed about the foods probably served on the occasion and the clothing worn.[36] His knowledge of early American history was sufficiently detailed that he was able to build accurate models of coaches and ordnance for use as props in many of his paintings.

By 1895 Ferris had achieved a measure of fame as a historical painter. His work was chosen to illustrate "Artists as Historians," an article by critic Clarence Cook published in the January 1895 *Monthly Illustrator*. "The artist must be archaeologist, scientific man, traveller, man of the world, and not only go everywhere and see everything," Cook wrote, "but report what he sees and learns, and is honor bound to tell the truth." The artist must also observe "the minutist accuracy in dress and scenery," he declared. In his estimation, Ferris satisfied these strict requirements.[37]

Like his uncle Edward Moran, Ferris envisioned creating a series of works that visually conveyed an historical narrative, in this case the history of his country. His dream, according to his autobiography, was to keep the series together, an aspiration that required either an unusually supportive patron or an alternative method of making a living.[38] As he continued to add paintings to the series, Ferris began to sell reproduction rights and create works on commission.

Painted not in chronological order of the events but rather as the subjects "suggested themselves," the series was exhibited to throngs of visitors at Independence Hall beginning in 1916. Wilfred Jordan, then curator at Independence Hall, declared that Ferris's paintings provided "a more comprehensive idea of early America and the great events of the history of this nation than can be acquired through a year of study in the class room from textbooks."[39] Yet the paintings fit squarely into the sentimental taste of the Colonial Revival: *The First Thanksgiving, 1621* makes no allusion to the enormous loss of life that preceded the feast, and works depicting Washington show him in domestic or ceremonial scenes rather than in battle.

While he studied in Paris, Ferris rented rooms with Edwin Willard Deming (1860–1942), who, despite having received much the same professional training as Ferris, took a different subject as his life's work. At the turn of the twentieth century, Deming was regarded as an expert on the American Indian and a dedicated painter of native American life.[40]

Deming was born in Ashland, Ohio, but moved with his family shortly after his birth to a tract of land at the original Sac and Fox reservation near Geneseo, Illinois. He played frequently with Indian children, often hunting and fishing with them on the Rock River. A Mississippi River cruise to St. Paul, Minnesota, in his eighteenth year and a later visit to the territory of the Ponca, Pawnee, and other tribes deepened his interest in native American life.

In 1882 Deming rejected the career in law that his family had envisioned for him and traveled to New York, where he studied at the Art Students' League and supported himself in part by providing sketches for *Harper's Weekly;* he also painted portraits, theater cur-

tains, and cycloramas.[41] His association with Ferris may have encouraged his interest in historical subject matter. In January 1885 he wrote to his family from Paris, "I have been thinking about painting Indian subjects as there are a great many incidents in . . . history . . . that would make splendid subjects for a picture. Wish I could get one for a model this summer." Deming seems to have viewed the exotic Algerians in Paris much as he perceived native Americans. "The Luni Indians and their costumes and surroundings are very much like the Algerians . . ." he wrote, "and I like them very much. They are so suny [*sic*] and there is such a field for a fellow in such subjects."[42]

In 1885, after Deming returned to New York, he began to receive commissions to create illustrations for *Harper's Weekly* and *The Youth's Companion,* and by early 1886 he was able to raise enough money to visit the Apache reservation in Arizona. He maintained a schedule of winter work in New York and summer trips to live among the Indian tribes even after his marriage in 1892.[43] An avid reader and book collector, Deming developed a vast knowledge of Indian costume and ritual. History painting permitted him to join his historical interests and his artistic inclinations—and to express his conviction that American Indians, the first occupants of the land, had been wronged and misunderstood.

Deming created *Bird Woman Sacajawea Meeting*

114. Jean Leon Gerome Ferris. *The First Thanksgiving, 1621.* ca. 1915. 25 x 35" (62.5 x 87.5 cm.). Archives of 76, Cleveland, Ohio.

Lewis and Clark on the Upper Missouri (plate 115) undoubtedly in response to the 1904 St. Louis centennial celebration of the 1804–1806 travels of Meriwether Lewis and William Clark, the first government-sponsored expedition to the Pacific. Deming's extensive library included the *Original Journals of the Lewis and Clark Expedition 1804-1806*, published in 1904.[44] His painting depicts the young Shoshone "bird woman" Sacajawea, whom the Hidatsa Indians had kidnapped. Sacajawea accompanied her husband, the French Canadian interpreter Toussaint Charbonneau, on the expedition and served Lewis and Clark as a guide through her native Shoshone region. Deming emphasized the significance of her role by making her the focal point of the work; she stands with Lewis and Clark as an equal partner in the exploration.[45]

Deming was also drawn to more traditional historical subjects. Like many history painters of his generation, he was intrigued by the career of George Washington, as he demonstrated particularly in *George Washington Selecting the Site of Fort Duquesne*, which depicts the general's role in the French and Indian Wars. He also painted a trilogy of large-scale works on the early history of New York—*Verrazzano Leaving New York Harbor*, *Peter Minuit Buying Manhattan Island*, and *Jonas Bronck Trading with the Indians at Spuyten Duyvil Creek*.[46]

Perhaps no artist better exemplifies the fusion of historian and painter than John Ward Dunsmore (1856–1945). Descended from a Revolutionary War veteran, Dunsmore was an active member of the Sons of the Revolution, and historical research was for him a continuous and lifelong undertaking. He believed history painting must be based on meticulous research and must depict events accurately because it had a role to play in arousing patriotic feeling in coming generations and the foreign-born. Dunsmore was especially interested in original sources, such as the letters and diaries of Revolutionary War soldiers, which he believed provided intimate insights into character, time, and place. He traveled frequently to Mount Vernon, spent many Christmases at Valley Forge, and visited Independence Hall and Yorktown, the site of the British surrender in 1781.

After finishing his research for each picture, Dunsmore's method was to engage living models resembling his historical figures as closely as' possible. He amassed numerous eighteenth-century costumes and relics so that his models could wear authentic costumes and stand among appropriate backdrops; his aim was to paint events as if "from life." He once wrote, "The researches necessary in some cases consume from three

115. Edwin Deming. *Bird Woman Sacajawea Meeting Lewis and Clark on the Upper Missouri*. ca. 1906. 27 x 34" (67.5 x 85.0 cm.). Private collection.

Facing page top:
116. John Ward Dunsmore. *Betsy Ross and the First Stars and Stripes, 1777*. 1920. 24 x 34" (60.0 x 85.0 cm.). Fraunces Tavern Museum, New York.

Facing page bottom:
117. John Ward Dunsmore. *The Marriage of Nellie Custis at Mt. Vernon: Washington's Last Birthday, 1799*. 1909. 24 x 34" (60.0 x 85.0 cm.). Fraunces Tavern Museum, New York.

DEC. 26, 1776
JAN. 2, 1777

THE DEFENDER OF THE MOTHERS WILL ALSO PROTECT THE DAUGHTERS

N.C. WYETH

Facing page:
118. N. C. Wyeth. *Washington's Reception by the Ladies of Trenton on His Way to Assume the Presidency of the United States, April 21, 1789.* ca. 1930. 204½ x 144" (511.2 x 360.0 cm.). CoreStates New Jersey National Bank, Trenton, New Jersey; photo by Fiorella/Gamma Liaison.

119. Nathaniel Currier. *Washington's Reception by the Ladies, On Passing the Bridge at Trenton, N. J., April 1789, On His Way to New York to be Inaugurated First President of the United States.* 1845. Lithograph. Prints and Photographs Division, Library of Congress, Washington, D.C.

to six months before a stroke is laid upon the canvas. Then preliminary sketches and studies with models, and all the paraphernalia needed, conspire to make the work very costly."[47]

Dunsmore's background and talent suited him to the task of creating works that embodied the principles he felt history painting in general should serve. He decided to paint a series on the American Revolution at an early age, but thirty years passed before he was able to embark on the project. In 1875 Dunsmore traveled to Paris to study with Thomas Couture, also a painter of historical subjects. Only after fifteen years spent painting genre and portraits, teaching art, and serving as the first director of the Detroit Museum of Art was he finally able to turn to his first love—the early history of the United States.

Revolutionary War images, many involving Washington, became a large part of Dunsmore's repertoire. He painted Washington on the occasion of his possibly apocryphal visit to the home of Betsy Ross to commission the first American flag (plate 116) and at the reception at Mount Vernon where he first received notice of his election to the presidency. Like other history painters, Dunsmore was also interested in the private lives of American heroes. *The Marriage of Nellie Custis at Mt. Vernon* (plate 117) shows this domestic event taking place in the accurately rendered hallway of Mount Vernon.[48]

Newell Convers Wyeth (1882–1945) carried on the sentimental tradition of history painting in an era even more noted for rapid social change and artistic controversy. Born in Needham, Massachusetts, Wyeth developed an early interest in art with the encouragement of his family. After attending several Boston art schools, he found his style and subject in the studio and classes of Howard Pyle. Pyle's dictum, "One must live in the picture," survived in Wyeth's memory and work.[49]

Wyeth's illustration *Bronco Buster* was accepted by the Curtis Publishing Company in 1903 and subsequently used on the February 21 cover of its major publication, *The Saturday Evening Post*. In the same year, he provided illustrations for such other publications as *Success* and *Leslie's Popular Monthly*. In 1904, when Curtis commissioned him to illustrate a story about America's West, Wyeth felt he must visit the region in order to provide more authentic scenes. Howard Pyle reportedly helped convince the publishers of the *Post* and of *Scribner's* to finance the excursion.[50]

Wyeth was commissioned repeatedly to illustrate classical and contemporary literature; his history paintings illustrated such popular books as *The Long Roll* (1911) by Mary Johnston, Thomas Bonaventure Lawler's *Essentials of American History* (1918), a 1920 edition of Longfellow's *The Courtship of Miles Standish*, and *Poems of American Patriotism* (1922).[51] But he also worked on a monumental scale, producing murals, lunettes, and triptychs for hotels, banks, and public buildings. In 1920 Wyeth painted two lunette murals depicting Civil War scenes—*The Battle of Wilson's Creek* and *The Battle of Westport*—for the Missouri State Capitol at Jefferson.

In 1930, when the First Mechanics National Bank of Trenton, New Jersey, opened on a site known as "Corner Historic," Wyeth was commissioned to create a mural to remind Trentonians of their early history.[52] Wyeth chose to depict Washington as a newly elected president passing through Trenton on his way to his New York inauguration in 1789 (plate 118). Believing that the Nathaniel Currier version of the event, *Washington's Reception by the Ladies, On Passing the Bridge at Trenton, N.J., April 1789, On His Way to New York to be Inaugurated First President of the United States* (plate 119) was inaccurate, Wyeth studied written accounts of the event in the Trenton Public Library archives. On the basis of an April 23, 1789, letter and a May 1789 issue of *The Columbian Magazine*, Wyeth eliminated from his mural the flags, bunting, shields, and other embellishments commonly featured in earlier views of the familiar historical subject and restored the sunflower and twin dates of the battles of Trenton engraved on the arch above Washington.

During the installation of this mural, Wyeth almost fell from the top of the scaffolding, thirty feet above a marble floor. According to him, the episode triggered a recurrent dream that haunted the artist until he painted it on canvas. *In a Dream I Meet General Washington* (plate 120) shows Wyeth perched on scaffolding in the midst of Brandywine's historic battlefield. Washington, approaching on his white horse, narrates the Battle of the Brandywine as the event itself—complete with troops, artillery, smoke, and even General Lafayette—unfolds in the background. "Why do you fight this battle again?" Wyeth asks Washington in his dream. "It was all over 150 years ago." "Well," answered Washington, "we all wanted to show those gentlemen down in Washington what kind of a ruckus we kicked up here in '77."[53]

Wyeth's enormous popularity documents that the events of the Revolutionary War generation still had emotive power for American audiences more than 150 years removed from the event. The reliance of artists such as Wyeth on historical research filled their works with accurate period detail, but the romantic associations of the Revolutionary "ruckus" inspired them to depict events that showed the past in an unambiguously glorious light. Their paintings presented to a vastly enlarged group of Americans a version of history that was in many ways even more iconic and idealized than the grand-style works of Trumbull and West, and in fact even more sentimental than the charming genre scenes of midcentury. It was history as Americans, amid the flag-waving nostalgia of the Colonial Revival, might have liked it to be.

174

120. N. C. Wyeth. *In a Dream I Meet General Washington.* 1930. 72⅜ x 79" (180.9 x 197.5 cm.). Collection of The Brandywine River Museum, Chadds Ford, Pennsylvania; purchased with funds given in memory of George T. Weymouth.

A Fall from Grace

The Critical Reception of History Painting, 1875–1925

MARK THISTLETHWAITE

From the mid-eighteenth century to the mid-nineteenth, American artists and art writers accepted and perpetuated history painting's traditionally elevated status. Especially from the 1830s through the 1850s, painters created a large body of works representing scenes from American history. Critical enthusiasm for history painting was, however, tempered by an ambivalence that acknowledged its importance and the significance it could play in securing a national identity and also lamented the brevity and unpicturesque nature of the American past, as well as the technical deficiencies American artists exhibited in creating successful multifigural, narrative compositions.

Although the middle decades of the nineteenth century witnessed the production of an impressive quantity of history paintings, the advocacy for and critical estimation of the genre dropped significantly by the last quarter of the century. Several factors contributed to this situation, including the failure of history painters to find in the Civil War a fruitful and inspiring subject; the proliferation of photography as an alternative means of recording contemporary history; the identification of history painting with illustration; the strong interest among many artists, critics, and patrons in representations of the present rather than the past; and the modernist sensibility that emphasized innovative technique and personal expression over subject matter. Historical imagery—particularly in murals and illustrations in popular books and magazines—continued to render, reinforce, and even critique earlier perceptions of American history. But many artists and most art critics came to regard the theory and practice of history painting in its traditional sense—the domain of the serious painter and, because of its important themes, the "best" type of painting—as representing an outmoded taste in a nation increasingly and consciously modern.[1]

Between 1875 and 1925 the nation experienced intense and seemingly endless changes. Change, indeed, became the norm and the expectation. The multiple labels and traits assigned the period—the Gilded Age, the Brown Decades, the Confident Years, the American Renaissance, the Progressive Era, the Quest for Unity, the Search for Order—testify to its vigorous and often confusing pluralism and eclecticism. Popular literature continually declared the age to be one of transition and perpetual change. Americans were depicted as the "hurrying race" "rapidly casting off traditions and beliefs," and American writers celebrated "our restless, nervous, but virile energy, our instinct and sense for the vivid in anything, our vivacity and touch-and-go of manner, whether in an individual's movement, carriage, conversation, gestures, or in a painter's brush-work."[2] For an era that embraced the social implications of Darwinism—the United States was frequently understood to have become through "constant struggle . . . a powerful organism, fitted to survive in the battle of life"—the field of American art displayed the fruits of benign and inevitable evolution. Indeed, commentators repeatedly claimed that "Americans have made more rapid progress in art than anyone in the world's history."[3] The event that more than any other both signaled this progress and spurred a new sense of artistic achievement was the Centennial Exposition in Philadelphia in 1876. Late nineteenth-century writers continually cited the exhibition of art at the Centennial as the birth, or rebirth, of American artistic interest.[4]

The art department of the Centennial contained several paintings of American history—about twenty out of

Thomas Hart Benton. *New York History*
(*Today*), detail of plate 132.

177

a total of approximately six hundred oil paintings. Although relatively small in number, this body of historical imagery was the largest that had been seen in a single exhibition in fifteen years. Still, the *National Repository* reported that American artists achieved "all their triumphs in landscape painting. . . . In historic painting or in high ideal art Americans have as yet achieved few triumphs. We attribute this largely to the total lack in this country of great galleries and museums, where the young artist can find grand inspiring suggestions in these higher departments of work."[5]

In truth, Americans had failed to embrace history painting as easily and as comfortably as they did portraiture, landscape, and genre painting, nor was it as easy to undertake. Looking back in 1905, Samuel Isham asserted bluntly: "In fact, historical painting was almost impossible in America. . . . There were no suitable studios, no models, no costumes, no means of supplying the backgrounds or hundreds of accessories needed."[6] Another writer remarked on the eve of the Centennial's opening: "Historical painting has not found in America the encouragement accorded to other branches of art, partly, perhaps, because we have never had a really great historical painter, and partly because the genius of the age does not favor it."[7] Other reviews of the exposition's art exhibition take the same tenor, and few critics actually discussed the specific images of American history on view. Brief commentaries did appear on Julian Scott's Civil War scenes, George Maynard's *1776*, George H. Boughton's *Pilgrims Going to Church* (plate 121), and Imogene Robinson Morrell's *Miles Standish and the Indians*.

The painting that received the most press, and nearly all of it negative, was Peter F. Rothermel's huge representation of the battle of Gettysburg, which covered an entire end of the American gallery in Memorial Hall (plate 104). Even critics who reviewed Rothermel's composition favorably felt compelled to acknowledge how negatively most people responded to the painting. In his *Illustrated Register* of the Centennial, Frank Norton wrote, "This picture has been the object of considerable severe and not a little hostile criticism on the part of the Press . . . [yet] it is not by any means a discreditable battle-piece. The composition is not exaggerated or unnatural, and the figures are full of vitality, where there is much in the composition of the work to attract favorable criticism."[8] Most other critiques were more caustic. "The picture is bad in every sense. . . ." *Appleton's Journal* argued. "Rothermel seems in this painting to have taken fiendish delight in bringing forward, almost to the feet of the spectator, multitudes of the bodies, bloody and wounded, of dead men; and when the eye, sickened with the confusion and turmoil of the fight in the distance, drops upon the near images, it is caught and horrified by the sight of so much death, which would be

appalling if it were not painted so weakly. . . . It is the life and not the death of battle with which art can legitimately concern itself."[9]

This concern with technique and a decorous subject manifests itself repeatedly in critical commentary. Prior to the Civil War, critics often overlooked history painters' flaws in light of their ambition and patriotism.[10] But they were far less tolerant in the postwar years. New York critics, who often displayed a seemingly innate animosity toward Philadelphia art throughout the nineteenth century, treated the work of Rothermel, that city's most important history painter, especially harshly. John Sears characterized the *Battle of Gettysburg* as a "fearful and wonderful production, about the size and shape of a drop-curtain and of the same order of merit." Sears suggested that Rothermel should have withdrawn the work so as not to wound the sensibilities of his compatriots, particularly southerners.[11] The critic Clarence Cook expressed his outrage over the work in a long letter to the *New-York Tribune*.

> The picture is not a picture of heroism. It is a picture of blood and fury, of men—of brother-men, of fellow-citizens—murdering one another in the heat of hate; of dead men with blue faces and swollen hands—horrors piled on horrors for a central show-piece at the Centennial feast of peace and goodwill! . . . [The painting] will make us the laughingstock of every foreign critic. But we might stand being laughed at, if the picture were one in sympathy with the time and place; one that would prove bound to bind our people closer together, instead of being, as it will prove to be, one that will sow ill-will, add discord, and reopen wounds once closed.[12]

Works that seemed to focus excessively on their subjects were disparaged as idealism gained ground over realism after 1876. As Cook wrote a month later, "It is delightful to see stories beautifully and truthfully painted, but the greatest pictures of the world are those that feed our souls and our senses with something far higher than any anecdote or any history."[13]

The criticism of Rothermel's *Battle of Gettysburg* also suggests why the Civil War did not lead to increased activity in history painting, a situation that apparently surprised contemporaries. The editor of the *North American Review* wrote in 1877:

> It is impossible to account for the small demand which the war created for scenes and episodes from the great struggle which for years was foremost in the minds of the people. . . . This may be accounted for by lack of public encouragement, or by the more charitable supposition that artists and the public were willing that the recollections of our civil war should drop into oblivion.
>
> If this be so, it is well that painters should have led the way in this patriotic feeling, and done nothing to commemorate a struggle which all are now willing to forget.[14]

121. George H. Boughton. *Pilgrims Going to Church.* 1867. 28¼ x 51½" (70.6 x 128.7 cm.). New-York Historical Society, New York.

122. Timothy O'Sullivan. *A Harvest of Death, Gettysburg.* Negative 1863. Albumen silver print 1865 by Alexander Gardner. In Alexander Gardner, *Gardner's Photographic Sketch Book of the Civil War* (1866). The Amon Carter Museum, Fort Worth, Texas.

Unlike the Revolutionary War, which could be cast as a heroic breaking away from distant oppressors, the Civil War was more obviously a fratricidal conflict, a nation breaking apart; this partially accounts for the lack of Civil War scenes. Moreover, photography played a profound role in imaging the war for a wide audience and in a manner that appeared absolutely realistic and authoritative (plate 122). The place of photography as recorder of history appears in one writer's comments on the history paintings of John Trumbull. After complaining of the "extreme woodiness" and "rude grouping" in Trumbull's pictures, the critic opined, "It is to be hoped that the sensitive art-lover will only regard these relics as the substitute of that time for the all-pervading photographs of the present."[15]

It is curious that so few writers in this period discussed the connection between photography and history painting; perhaps this owes to photography assuming, so logically and completely in the popular imagination, the mantle of historical recorder. Keith F. Davis has recently and convincingly described photography as "the ideal picture-making tool for American society during the war."[16] Thousands upon thousands of photographs of the war were made available to Americans in photography galleries, albums, and popular illustrated newspapers and journals that frequently based their images on photographs.[17] Numerically, photographs of the

war overwhelmed painted renditions, despite the advantages that painting had over photography: vivid colors, impressive size, and compositions and subjects limited only by the imagination of the artist. Unlike a photograph, a painting could express the heat of battle; no clear photograph of an actual battle scene from the Civil War exists.[18]

Yet painting's advantages probably also worked against its success; presumably, Americans did not desire to view large, colorful, and intense compositions depicting "brothers" killing one another. For instance, the one major history painting of the Civil War that garnered praise from both northerners and southerners, Winslow Homer's *Prisoners from the Front* (plate 123), features neither the chaos nor drama of conflict but the still informality that imbues a photograph.[19] Also, like a photograph, Homer's picture offers a rather open-ended narrative and meaning that differs from the didacticism or moralizing typically associated with history painting. In *Prisoners from the Front*, as in numerous photographs of this first modern war, the viewer assumes an active role in searching out and constructing meaning rather than receiving the more obvious narrative of the typical history painting. Such personal interaction generally characterizes modernism's relationship of spectator to art object. Compared to Rothermel's *Battle of Gettysburg*, Homer's picture and much Civil War pho-

123. Winslow Homer. *Prisoners from the Front.* 1866. 24 x 38" (61.0 x 96.5 cm.). The Metropolitan Museum of Art, New York; gift of Mrs. Frank B. Porter.

tography offered the viewer a sense of what Robert Penn Warren has termed the essential American experience, both personally and nationally, of the Civil War: "inwardness."[20]

In reviewing an 1862 Mathew Brady photographic exhibition called "The Dead of Antietam," a *New York Times* writer noted:

> Mr. BRADY has done something to bring home to us the terrible reality and earnestness of war. . . . Of all objects of horror one would think that the battle-field should stand preeminent, that it should bear away the palm of repulsiveness. But, on the contrary, there is a terrible fascination about it that draws one near these pictures, and makes him loath to leave them.[21]

After observing that "these pictures have a terrible distinctness," the reviewer added, "By the aid of the magnifying glass, the very features of the slain may be distinguished."[22] In this sense, the viewer had control over photography; an individual dominates a photograph physically and chooses whether or not to examine its image more closely and for what length of time. By contrast, a history painting, particularly an immense, public one like Rothermel's, dominates the viewer, assaulting the senses and memory. This suggests another reason why so few major history paintings of the Civil War exist compared to the vast number of photographs: photography's reduced format essentially domesticated and allowed a measure of control over the horrors and tragedies of war.

Despite exhibiting a number of history paintings (including Rothermel's monumental battle scene) and being heralded as beginning a new period in American art, the Centennial did not spark the expected resurgence of the sort of history painting that had been current before the war. The Centennial did generate a colonial revival, but compared to the most impressive and popular symbol of the Exposition—the mighty Corliss engine— the traditional idea of *history* painting likely appeared old-fashioned and unworthy of revival.

After the Centennial Exposition few history paintings appeared in the annual exhibitions of the National Academy of Design and the Pennsylvania Academy of the Fine Arts or in other exhibitions of American art held at home and abroad. After 1876 history paintings typically constituted about 1 percent of the total number of works exhibited in any given annual show at the National Academy and Pennsylvania Academy. The Pan-American Exposition in Buffalo in 1901 featured even fewer: only five American historical subjects were exhibited among the approximately nine hundred oil paintings on view.[23] Critics frequently noted this paucity of history paintings. Russell Sturgis wrote of the American works at the Paris Exposition of 1878, "It is curiously characteristic of the time and the people that in the

American gallery there is not one historical picture, whether in the usual sense 'historical' or the remoter past or even representing a scene of American history. There is not one scene from the civil war, not one from American history, military or ceremonial, not one from European or other history, ancient or modern."[24]

Another reviewer did find hope for history painting in the same exhibition in the work of Arthur Bridgman. "There is abundant necessity at Washington for such a man," he wrote, ". . . so that the national capitol may be freed from the artistic frauds and impostors, foreign and domestic, that have so long infested it."[25] The public and critical opinion that the Capitol lacked significant works of art was long-standing. "There are no first-class historical paintings as yet in our Capitol," proclaimed another 1878 writer.[26]

Earlier history painters whose works were to be seen at the Capitol, such as John Trumbull and Emanuel Leutze, fared poorly in the estimation of many critics writing after 1876. An 1878 *New York Times* article expressed the contemporary lack of regard for Leutze and his work. "Leutze was a man who feared neither space nor paint. No canvas was too big for him, no color too crude. . . . His imagination was powerful and his training vigorous, but his brain was by no means subtle, and his hand anything but that of an artist."[27] A writer of 1895 asserted that no one would call the "industrious and capable Leutze" a genius.[28]

More positive were the remarks of S. G. W. Benjamin, who, in 1880, offered one of the most detailed and reasoned discussions of history painting in America. Benjamin saw Leutze as "a man who was cast in a large mould, capable of a grand enthusiasm, and aspiring to grasp soaring ideals. Although his art was often at fault, it makes us feel, notwithstanding, that in contemplating his works we are in the presence of a colossal mind which, under healthier influences, would have better achieved what he aspired to win. . . . He was Byronic in the impetus of his genius, the rugged incompleteness of his style, the magnificent fervor and rush of his fancy, the epic grandeur and energy, dash and daring, of his creations." Benjamin concluded, "While we find in Leutze the qualities we have described, it cannot be said that he sought out any new methods of expression, or that he undertook to suggest the deeper and more subtle traits of human nature; he was content to work after the manner of the school in which he studied."[29]

Leutze resurfaced in art commentary when his *Washington Crossing the Delaware* (plate 30) was acquired by the Metropolitan Museum of Art in 1897. The *New York Times* noted, "The value of a picture so famous and familiar as a national possession is of course not the same as its value as a work of art. GOETHE'S saying holds true that wonder-working pictures are generally poor paintings. This is by far the luckiest of LEUTZE'S

124. Eastman Johnson and Emanuel Leutze. *Washington Crossing the Delaware.* 1851. 40½ x 67⅛" (101.2 x 169.7 cm.). The Manoogian Foundation. (This is a copy, produced in Leutze's studio, of the painting reproduced on pages 48–49.)

compositions." To the *Times* reviewer, the painting was the typical representation of the Revolutionary period, "the standard American historical picture."[30] Samuel Isham declared that the painting "has fairly entered into the national consciousness and not unworthily. It is a good picture of its kind. . . . The picture succeeds by its story-telling rather than its artistic side."[31] Ambivalence, and certainly confusion, characterized Charles H. Caffin's description of the work in his 1907 history of American painting. Caffin wrote that *Washington Crossing the Delaware* was not "theatrical," but "simple and sincere, without heroics." Yet the caption to the book's reproduction of the painting contradicts the text by calling the image "theatrical in composition and hard in drawing. . . . Truth was sacrified to an effective tableau." These opposing descriptions metaphorically represent the ambivalent attitude toward history paintings in general.[32]

Trumbull, like Leutze, received mixed reviews as a painter of American history. One 1897 writer referred to "the technical incompetency of TRUMBULL, combined also with an undue sense of the dignity of history, hindered his well-meant delineation of Revolutionary scenes from being accepted by the people."[33] On the other hand, the painter John F. Weir claimed in 1913 that Trumbull's "historical pictures, as such, have not since been equalled in American art."[34] Benjamin considered Trumbull's *Death of General Montgomery* and *Death of General Warren at the Battle of Bunker's Hill* (plate 133) as "by far the most remarkable military paintings produced by an American artist" and as works "not surpassed by any similar works in the last century, and thus far stand alone in American historical painting."[35]

But Benjamin believed that the best history paintings had been created a century before his 1880 overview of American art was published; overall, he was not positive about the progress of history painting in the United States thereafter.

Summarily evaluating works produced between 1828 and 1878, Benjamin wrote, "Our historical painters of this period rarely created any works deserving of note or remembrance. . . . The historic art of the period has been neither prolific nor attractive, with a few exceptions." These exceptions included the works of Wordsworth Thompson and Julian Scott. In Thompson, Benjamin found "an artist who seems to realize the possibilites of American historical art" and whose *General Washington Reviewing the Continental Army* ranked in his estimation next to the works of Trumbull.[36] Julian Scott, who had served in the Union army from 1861 to 1863, built a reputation as a painter of Civil War scenes (plate 86). Benjamin determined Scott "measurably successful" in his *In the Cornfield at Antietam*, one among "a class of pictures of which we hope to have more in the future."[37]

Critical discussion during this era consistently focused on the matter of subject, which was still cited as a significant aspect of history painting even as it was viewed as less important in painting in general at the time. Another issue apparent in the overall critique is the association of genre and historical painting. From the middle decades of the century, history painting merged with genre painting, resulting in pictures that featured historical figures in incidental moments and those that depicted anonymous figures in historical settings. This surely contributed to the uncertainty with which history painting was received. Also animating the critical discussion was the issue of technique. Whereas earlier in the century critics often allowed the subject to redeem, at least partially, a work's lack of technical proficiency, later critics were much less willing to do so. After the Centennial celebration, American artists were expected to demonstrate a high level of technical skill, so that subject matter alone was insufficient to make a work of art acceptable or successful. William A. Coffin remarked in 1894, "We have shown since the local renaissance in 1876 less and less of the story-telling and literary sentiment that has destroyed the vigor of the English school, and a more general and increasing excellence in technical qualities."[38] Increasingly, as the critic for the *Boston Evening Transcript* wrote in the early 1880s, "the question is not nowadays so much the matter upon which you employ your art as with how much force and truth you can present it" and the belief that "the test of a painter is the painting of an appearance, not a story, a sentiment or an idea."[39]

Given the concern about technique, expression, definition, and subject matter, it is not entirely surprising that the 1882 history painting competition sponsored by the Pennsylvania Academy of the Fine Arts proved to be a fiasco. The Temple Competition of Historical Painting, funded by Philadelphia businessman and art collector Joseph Temple, offered a prize of three thousand dollars, as well as gold, silver, and bronze medals. Entries had to be oil paintings no larger than eight by ten feet, had to have been executed specifically for the competition by American artists, and had to depict "the most important subjects," American history of the Revolutionary period.[40] The exhibited works would form part of the academy's annual exhibition in 1883.

At the close of the competition, nearly a year after its announcement, only four paintings had been submitted and these by four young, and relatively unknown, artists: H. T. Cariss, Sarah Paxton Ball Dodson, Frank T. English, and William Trego. Such well-known artists as Peter F. Rothermel, Edwin Blashfield, and George H. Boughton chose not to submit work, nor did such lesser-known but active history painters as Gilbert Gaul, Julian Scott, Wordsworth Thompson, and Augustus Heaton. The Temple Competition jury was so unimpressed—and one imagines so disappointed—with the work submitted that it elected to withhold the first-place prize. The Temple Competition probably failed to attract artists in part because the very nature of the competition—possibly spending as much as a year on a large painting on speculation—was surely unappealing and impractical. Also, at least as important, the large-sized history paintings that the competition required must have seemed outmoded and unrelated to the dominant artistic interests of the day which favored more domestic, easel-sized compositions. Further, in the face of a bur-

geoning sense of cosmopolitanism, which found American artists and patrons increasingly traveling to and being influenced by European art, such a nationalistic endeavor, organized by the country's oldest art academy, must have appeared provincial in character. Arguably, the competition might have succeeded had it taken place later in the 1880s when mural painting—frequently historical in theme—emerged as a significant mode.

The competition might have been better received had it occurred even a year later, after the publicity surrounding the exhibition of Thomas Clarke's substantial collection of American art. At the end of 1883, 140 American paintings owned by Clarke served as a benefit exhibition to raise funds for the National Academy of Design. A *New York Times* reviewer, noting the absence of history paintings, queried, "Would it not be well for Mr. Clarke and other collectors of native painting to hold out a reasonable hope to certain artists who have shown ability in historical and religious compositions, and thus encourage them to undertake work of greater scope and deeper thought?"[41] The question reveals a continuing lack of interest among American collectors in history paintings. Clarke's collection never included many history paintings; a checklist of the works he owned from 1872 to 1899 indicates that only 22 out of 735 were probably American historical scenes.[42] The Clarke collection and the Temple Competition suggest, as one critic observed also of the National Academy of Design's 1884 annual exhibition, "Historical painting . . . has become almost a forgotten art among us."[43]

Despite its diminished presence, history painting continued to be produced and critiqued. For instance, in exhibition reviews of 1883 and 1884, Blashfield's *Minute Men*, Julian O. Davidson's historical marine scenes, Charles Yardley Turner's *Courtship of Miles Standish*, and Gaul's Civil War subject, *Silenced*, were all discussed. Thomas Hovenden's highly romanticized *The Last Moments of John Brown* (plate 125) toured a number of American cities to critical and public acclaim; a *New York Times* writer concluded, "Certainly it is the most significant and striking historical work of art ever executed in the Republic."[44] Using photographs of Brown, visiting the Charleston, West Virginia, jail where Brown was held, and even interviewing the man who had been Brown's jailer, Hovenden rendered the 1859 event—which in fact never occurred as represented—in minute and convincing detail.[45] Through the 1880s and 1890s other artists, including Carlton Chapman, John Ward Dunsmore, Jean Leon Gerome Ferris, Edwin Willard Deming, George de Forest Brush, and Jennie Brownscombe (plate 126), consistently exhibited history paintings. Still, a review of the 1887 Society of American Artists' exhibition noted, "There are no historical paintings at all," while an 1889 writer on the National Academy annual exhibition remarked, "A picture in the

125. Thomas Hovenden. *The Last Moments of John Brown.* ca. 1884.
46⅛ x 38⅛" (117.2 x 96.8 cm.). The Fine Arts Museums of
San Francisco; gift of Mr. and Mrs. John D. Rockefeller 3rd.

126. Jennie Brownscombe. *Washington Greeting Lafayette at Mount Vernon*. N.d. 30 x 40" (75.0 x 100.0 cm.). Kirby Collection of Historical Paintings, Lafayette College, Easton, Pennsylvania.

historical line by Oliver I. Lay—'The Last Days of Aaron Burr'—deserves notice for the boldness of its maker in attempting a field from which most of our modern painters shrink."[46] In 1888 one writer in fact considered George Brush "apparently the only hope for historical painting"; that a single artist was seen as representing the mode's "only" hope clearly indicates its dire straits.[47]

Characteristic of the mixed reviews history painters received is a *New York Times* notice of the National Academy of Design's 1889 spring exhibition. The reviewer critiqued an Aztec subject by Brush and Civil War subjects rendered by Gaul, Scott, Charles X. Harris, and Hovenden. The review focused on Hovenden's *In the Hands of the Enemy*, which portrays a rebel wounded at Gettysburg being tended by a Union family. Acknowledging that the painting deserved its place of prominence in the exhibition, the *Times* critic observed, "It has a value in the sentiment which is one peculiarly appropriate to the month in which we celebrate the close of the Presidential century." The figures show a "good deal of naturalness in the poses and gestures," the writer remarked, but his assessment of the work was equivocal:

> One cannot, however, find a very high level of art in this scene, though it seems to have escaped it by a hair's breadth. Its appeal to fraternity between South and North is not only obvious but strong, and yet neither in its technical qualities nor its imaginativeness does it bear the stamp of a great work. It would make a good illustration for a weekly and without question the artist is right to secure it by a copyright; for it has every element of popularity. But some people are cruel enough to demand more than that before they surrender to the claim that "In the Hands of the Enemy" is a great painting.[48]

The distinction between illustration and painting was commonplace in reviews, as was the linkage of illustration to popular appeal. A decade later, another writer stated that while the Gilbert Gaul painting *News from the Front* told a good story, it was crude in color and "would make a better illustration than picture."[49] Although such criticism certainly connotes that illustration was perceived to lack the gravity and therefore the status of painting, illustration then enjoyed tremendous growth and widespread appreciation and respect.

For artists interested in rendering historical subjects, illustration was a viable outlet. From the late 1880s through the First World War, a period often described as the golden age of American illustration, newspaper and magazine articles frequently touted its popularity. "But if we would find where in the world of art the artist is most sure of winning and keeping the heart of the people,—and of the American people, perhaps, most of all—we must turn to illustration, a field which is perhaps on a lower plane than some branches of painting,

but which requires the keenest perception of detail and the most facile handling of human nature and its surroundings."[50] William Herbert Hobbs claimed in 1901, "If painting and architecture have acquired in America a new importance, it is nevertheless in a widely different field [illustration] that American art has made its most remarkable advance. . . . The most notable growth of this department of American art has been largely confined to the last fifteen years, and it has attained its full flower only during the past decade." Hobbs praised in particular illustrators Charles S. Reinhart, Charles Dana Gibson, Edwin Austin Abbey, A. B. Frost, Frederic Remington, Elihu Vedder, F.C. Yohn, Howard Chandler Christy, Ernest Peixotto, Maxfield Parrish, Ernest Haskell, and Howard Pyle who, he declared, "belong to no school and have no one characteristic so marked as that of individuality."[51]

Critics invariably compared illustration and painting. For instance, Hobbs saw painting as aiming to please the eye and aesthetic taste, whereas illustration sought to please the intellectual faculties already addressed by the text; illustration's primary function, he stated, is to illuminate the text.[52] "We care less, as a people, for the lofty canvases of some modern Rafael," Philip Paulding wrote in 1895, "than for the more tangible and useful excellences of beautiful books and handsome periodicals."[53] As in historical fiction of the period, illustrations depicting the past focused on romanticized colonial and Revolutionary themes, views that offered an idealist escape from the brutal realities of the Civil War, not to mention from the turbulence of the contemporary moment. Paulding also argued that the works of Kenyon Cox, Reinhart, Will Low, and Elihu Vedder made it "difficult to draw a precise line between our illustrators and our ideal painters."[54] Stylistically, the sophisticated, highly competent delineations by history painters and illustrators of what a later critic called "sanguinary buccaneers and sweet colonial misses" appeared to many Americans critics to be much advanced over the works of earlier artists.[55]

Not only did painters create illustrations, but illustrators exhibited their work in galleries as well. In 1898 an exhibition of the work of more than a hundred well-known American book and magazine illustrators traveled to major American cities, including New York. The *New York Times* stated, "Howard Pyle leads all the rest with his paintings of the 'Fight on the Common, Lexington,' two of the series of twelve pictures of the 'Battle of Bunker Hill,' of which the remainder are to appear, and of 'Jefferson Writing the Declaration of Independence.'"[56] Samuel Isham also praised Pyle, calling him "the only man who seems to know thoroughly the colonial and Revolutionary epoch" and declaring that he "merit[s] a special note of thanks in that he has represented the founders of the Republic as they were,—sturdy, hard-headed folk, with strong characters and few graces, who wore the rather rigid costumes of the time with dignity and not like singers in comic opera or dancing masters."[57] Isham's remarks, published in 1905, reflect a bias against the overly refined and elegant illustrations of American history then appearing in great profusion in numerous popular books and magazines. The appearance of numerous favorable comments concerning Pyle's and other renderings of the American past evince the perceived importance of illustration in disseminating popular images of American history.

Simultaneous with the popularity of illustration was the emergence of another significant vehicle for historical imagery, mural painting. In 1903 Russell Sturgis assessed it in terms nearly identical to those William Herbert Hobbs used to evaluate illustration only slightly earlier. "It is in mural painting that the greatest advances have been made, at least in the United States," Sturgis observed. "The introduction of such art into this country is of very recent date. It was during the last fifteen years of the nineteenth century that there was produced nearly everything that can be called by that name."[58] Mural painting had indeed become established as an important and highly visible mode of art largely due to the grandiose murals appearing at the 1893 World's Columbian Exposition in Chicago and the ambitious decorative programs adorning numerous public buildings, especially the Library of Congress (1892–97). Many artists and critics saw the mural movement as an American continuation of a deeply embedded Western tradition; undoubtedly, American imperialistic ambitions of the late 1890s also conditioned the creation of grand decorative wall paintings.

Several artists regarded as major illustrators were also deemed major muralists, such as Edwin Austin Abbey, Kenyon Cox, and Maxfield Parrish. Also, like a number of illustrations, murals typically embraced the notion of the ideal. During its early years (the mid-1880s and the 1890s), American mural painting clearly focused on ideal and allegorical subjects. In a *Scribner's Magazine* listing of mural paintings created by thirty-six artists in the country before 1899, virtually all are allegorical representations; none appeared to represent American history per se. Between 1899 and 1906, however, thirty-seven artists painted numerous American historical murals—Edwin Deming's *Braddock's Defeat* and *The First Treaty between the Dutch and the Indians, in New York*, Charles Yardley Turner's *Opening of the Erie Canal* and *The Burning of the "Peggy Stewart,"* Henry Oliver Walker's *The Pilgrims on the Mayflower*, Edward Simmons's *Concord Bridge* and Edwin Blashfield's *Washington Surrendering His Commission at the Feet of Columbia* (plate 127). William Walton, writing for *Scribner's* in 1906, noted that much debate occurred over the issue of the allegorical versus the historical. By way of an example, he quoted the muralist Joseph Lauber: "The cry has been raised that too much of our work in the past has been allegorical; that we had a history which ought to be depicted on our walls. That allegory was rot, anyway, etc., etc. There is no objection to a historical painting on the walls provided it can be made to fulfill the first condition, namely, to decorate; to have that balance in composition, scale, and color that will make it *a part of the building.* Otherwise it should be an easel picture." Walton quoted other artists, such as Childe Hassam, who were less enthusiastic about historical imagery in murals. "The historical subject is the thing that is usually done—all very well, too, I admit—but I should like to see other things done."[59] Russell Sturgis likewise called for a more open approach to subject matter in mural painting. In his view, landscape was a most appropriate subject because it was "that one branch or kind of painting in which the nineteenth century excels."[60]

Like many other critics both before and after the Civil War, Sturgis cited the unpicturesque nature of American costume as a hindrance to historical scenes: "The costume of his [modern man's] own time is impossible; the costume of the time immediately past—of the century before his day—is ugly in its lines and masses and dull in color, however quaint it may appear in book illustration."[61] Will H. Low, muralist and critic, also perceived "a difficulty if he [the muralist] desires to treat a subject taken from our own history. The world, grown sadder since our earlier day, has adopted a garb of sombre hue. . . . the frock coat and trousers in which our statesmen have lived should forever banish them from decorative themes."[62] In virtually the only discussion of mural paintings that even acknowledges native Americans, Low suggested that the North American Indian might serve as a subject, "and it is often urged that with his dim historic past he is our very own, and our painters might, in depicting his life and legends, interest our people."[63]

In spite of his disinclination toward historical subjects, Russell Sturgis did recognize a number of successful historical mural paintings, especially those by Edwin Blashfield and Charles Yardley Turner, who "has used historical painting for mural decoration and done it nobly." Sturgis added, "To think that twenty-five years ago we were all pooh-poohing historical painting! The dulness [sic] of it, the lack of trustworthy record, the general air of pompous inanity—these were the thoughts that arose in the mind of a reformer in the Fine Art world of that day. And now we find that, given the life-size figure, the permanent place on the wall, the not inappropriate surroundings, historical painting in the right hands makes noble decoration." As evidence of a successful work, Sturgis described Turner's depiction of the burning of the *Peggy Stewart*, a teaship of 1774: "Here is, then, a great composition full of narrative, carefully based upon

127. Edwin Blashfield. Studies for
*Washington Surrendering His
Commission at the Feet of Columbia.*
1902. 48 x 116" (120.0 x 290.0 cm.).
Maryland Historical Society, Baltimore.

·DEC 23 1783·

ascertained facts, full of well-studied costume, full of such portraiture as was possible; and, in this way, is gained what may be truly called history embodied in art, with such patriotic thoughts as an honorable and self-devoted action in the past may rightly suggest."[64] These criteria for success suggest also that the muralist was thought to function as, in the words of Edwin Howland Blashfield, "both celebrant and recorder."[65]

Blashfield was a painter, muralist, and author whose important book on the essentially conservative and traditional genre of mural painting in America appeared in 1913, the same year that modern art exploded upon the American public at the Armory Show in New York City. For Blashfield, a "consideration of the first importance in mural painting is subject, or what I should prefer to call significance," and the most appropriate subject for him was that which dealt with American life and history. "It is then of utmost importance that our artists learn to treat decoratively the marking events of our history, past or contemporaneous, of our Puritans and Dutch, our Revolutionary heroes, our Argonauts of '49, our pioneers and colonizers and soldiers of the Civil War, our inventors and organizers, our men in the streets and in the fields of to-day."[66]

In advocating the significance of the subject, Blashfield aligned himself with other antimodernists, including Arthur Hoeber and Kenyon Cox. In a 1909 article titled "Unrest in Modern Art," Hoeber argued, "It is not the manner of doing it so much as the thing that is done; and I contend therefore that this question of style is rel-atively unimportant. The question is rather, has the artist given us the lovely thought. . . . The tendency of the times is, alas, for novelty, for the search after some new manner of conveying an impression, not of high thoughts, not of noble sentiments, but of a way of putting pigment on canvas, of rendering some substance dexterously."[67] Although Hoeber mentioned no American history paintings specifically in the article, he declared that John Millais's *Christ in the House of His Parents* (1850) exemplified the kind of seriousness he found lacking in modern painting.

Kenyon Cox, like Blashfield, created both easel paintings (plate 128) and murals and also wrote, but he was more highly regarded than Blashfield as an art critic. A conservative and idealist, Cox's most famous written work, published two years before Blashfield's 1913 book, was *The Classic Point of View*. Like Blashfield, he argued for the importance of subject matter and acknowledged that the "idea that the subject of a work of art is of no importance whatever has been taught us so thoroughly and has become so ingrained in us that it seems almost necessary to apologize for mentioning such a thing to a modern audience."[68]

Cox cited three factors that he believed had contributed to the depreciation of subject: artists had depicted trivial stories; they had rendered stories inappropriate to pictorial narration; and they had told the stories poorly. Cox claimed that it was "the unfitness of many stories for telling in the language of painting that makes so many historical pictures altogether unsatisfactory and

128. Kenyon Cox. *Tradition.* 1916. 41¾ x 65¼" (106.0 x 165.7 cm.). Cleveland Museum of Art, Cleveland, Ohio; gift of J. D. Cox.

129. E. L. Henry. *First Railroad Train on the Hudson and Mohawk Railroad.* 1892–93. 48¼ x 114⅜" (120.6 x 285.9 cm.). Albany Institute of History and Art, Albany, New York.

dismal."[69] He cited the difficulty of expressing in painting the significance and dignity of a subject such as the signing of the Emancipation Proclamation. And, although Leutze's *Washington Crossing the Delaware* (plate 30) possessed more inherent visual interest than the proclamation signing did, Cox cast a negative eye on Leutze's composition:

> But can you tell what went before this crossing or is to come after it? Can you give any notion of the real and essential meaning of the incident? And how are you to make your hero conspicuous among the crowd of other actors? You can make him stand when others are seated; you can wrap him in a blowing cloak and give him an expression of brooding intentness; and you can relieve his well-known profile against the sky and put an American flag behind him. You will have made it plain that your subject is Washington crossing a river in the winter, and perhaps the historical knowledge of your audience may be expected to supply the rest—but you will have rendered your picture immortally absurd.[70]

In mural painting, Cox acknowledged, the demand for historical imagery was natural yet problematical, because "our history is short, our modern costume formless and ugly, and American historical subjects particularly unfitted for pictorial and, especially, for decorative treatment."[71] Mural painting, for Cox, inherently opposed depicting history:

> From its association with architecture, [mural painting] is especially an art of formal and symmetrical composition, of monumental arrangements and balanced lines and masses, and such composition necessarily destroys all illusion of veracity in the depiction of an historical incident. Finally, decoration demands sumptuous and brilliant, or, at any rate, studied and beautiful, color; and too many of our historical subjects afford little opportunity for this.
>
> Thus a love for the human figure, a love for monumental and truly decorative composition, and a love for color, all tend to lead our mural painters away from the historical subject and toward an allegorical, or rather symbolic, treatment.[72]

Cox did allow the possibility that a mural could effectively combine the historical and the symbolic: Edwin Blashfield's *Washington Surrendering His Commission at the Feet of Columbia* (plate 127; also titled *Washington Laying Down His Command*) was to his mind a notably successful work. But Cox's advocacy of subject in art only marginally concerned history painting; though conservative, he by and large dismissed the historical mode.

Cox's 1911 call for the subject in art came after more than two decades of negative sentiment about the importance of subject in painting and of a corresponding enhancement of the value of a work's appearance. "The true elements of art which make it characteristic of a people, and therefore a national art, are found, not in the subject, but in the mind of the artist himself," Frank Millet wrote in 1891.[73] The critic and historian Charles H. Caffin wrote in 1908, "Whereas in the past it [painting] was pre-eminently an art of representation, to-day it should be an interpretation of expression." He then proclaimed bluntly and provocatively, "No longer is there a need for the painter to occupy himself with representation."[74] As one *Scribner's* writer put it in 1922, "Only in comparatively recent times, possibly since the third quarter of the last century, have artists recognized gen-

130. George Bellows. *Massacre at Dinant.* 1918. 49½ x 83"
(123.7 x 207.5 cm.). Greenville County Museum of Art, Greenville,
South Carolina; anonymous loan.

erally that subject is less important than the beauty that clothes it, because of certain conditions of color and atmosphere."[75]

Modernists were of course more critical about subject in painting. Willard Huntington Wright, a major critic and a vocal proponent of modernism, argued that the "impelling dictate of all great art" has been the search for composition; the human figure and other natural forms were "only auxiliaries, never the sought-for result." He continued, "Therefore it is not remarkable that, with the introduction of new methods, the illustrative side of painting should tend toward minimization. The elimination of all the superfluities from art is but a part of the striving toward defecation. . . . A picture to be a great work of art need not contain any recognizable objects."[76] These modernist declarations of independence from subject are clearly antithetical to Kenyon Cox's point of view and, fundamentally, to history painting.

History painting was ever more diminished in stature as modernism took hold in the first quarter of the twentieth century. In his 1907 book on American painting, Caffin cited Edwin Austin Abbey as "the most important survivor . . . of the vogue of the historical subject," a trend that had "given way before the increased attention paid to the manner of representation, rather than to subject; to the aim of the modern painter to study his subject at close and intimate range, for which purpose he chooses a simple one, and makes the expression of his picture grow out of the technical expression."[77]

Everyone seemed to take potshots at history painting. The modernist collector Leo Stein referred to the pictures in the Capitol Rotunda as "stupid atrocities" and found the Library of Congress to be "full of most abominable painting which ought to be redone."[78] In an "appreciation" of the recently deceased historical painter E. L. Henry, a 1920 writer praised his commitment to his art, no matter how out of step it was with current styles (plate 129). The writer's repeated references to the "quaintness" of Henry's work served, however, only to subvert any assertions of its artistic quality and integrity. Henry's painting, the writer concluded, "has nothing to do with art at all. . . . In their rare sincerity and their quaintness it is my belief that they will always be of interest and of value to our people, and will throw an ever-penetrating light into our vanished customs and past social history."[79] To many critics, history painting was a precious remembrance, but it lacked viability. Even art writers who maintained that the subject should not, or could not, be overlooked urged the rendering not of the "quaint" past but of the dynamic present. While this attitude fundamentally opposed the traditional character of history painting, it reasserted a mid-nineteenth-century idea that true history painting rendered only contemporary life and events. As the critic Christian Brinton declared in 1911, "[In] American art of to-day

we do not need feebly imaginative compositions or sanguinary buccaneers and sweet colonial misses of the past so much as an honest record of contemporary manners and customs."[80] Another writer, finding American artists overly enamored of technique—creating "arpeggios in pigment"—wondered why artists did not take advantage of "all the magnificent opportunities" of the day:

> Can our artists find nothing worthy of their brushes in the international peace movement, the cause of labor, the rise of women, racial conflicts on the Pacific Coast and in the South, the development of the Philippines, the digging of the Panama Canal, the dominance of the trust, the opening of the irrigation empire, and the problems of immigration? . . . It is no more difficult now to advocate free trade with paint than it was to defend the doctrine of the Immaculate Conception.[81]

The painter Birge Harrison suggested other contemporary themes in 1909, including the picturesqueness of steel mills, skyscrapers, and "the teeming and kaleidoscopic life of our city slums, which the inexorable law of migration has crowded with strange peoples from the far corners of the earth; peoples who are as yet unassimilated, who still wear their exotic costumes and live their strange, foreign lives in our every midst."[82] Harrison's urban subjects match those seen in the contemporary genre paintings of Robert Henri and the "Ashcan School."

The advent of modernism in America paralleled the height of immigration into the United States, and just as immigrants then were often referred to as "the riff-raff of many nations," so antimodernists came to view modern art as a foreign invasion, or "Ellis Island Art," as Royal Cortissoz called it in 1923, just a year before passage of the National Origins Act.[83] While critics like Cortissoz dismissed cubism as "neurasthenic piffle" and classified modernist artists as ignorant, dishonest, disingenuous, or insane, antimodernist sentiment did not impel artists to create history paintings.[84]

For some art writers and artists, World War I offered a subject and salvation for art. Herbert Adams, president of the National Academy of Design in 1919, claimed the war would provoke "a renascence of motive, of theme, of expression."[85] But while the war did profoundly affect the art of the poster designer and illustrator, it little influenced easel painting and, like the Civil War, sparked little interest in history painters. George Bellows, best known for his dynamic urban genre scenes, was one of few who did approach the war as subject. Bellows created a series of sixteen lithographs and five oil paintings in 1918 depicting German atrocities against the Belgians. His large *Massacre at Dinant* (plate 130) displays both the ambition and problems that characterize the series.

The picture renders a multitude of distraught figures reacting variously to the horrific event. Despite the subject's inherent tragedy, Bellows's composition fails to stir the viewer. Figures appear too stiff and exaggeratedly theatrical in their gestures and postures. The artist's attempt to render chaos takes on a highly contrived look, mainly resulting from Bellows's utilization of the principles of Dynamic Symmetry. Originated by Jay Hambidge, Dynamic Symmetry was a compositional system based upon a complex application of mathematics and ratios that offered the artist a "correct" composition. Bellows had met Hambidge in late 1917 and thereafter followed the system of Dynamic Symmetry.[86] *Massacre at Dinant* exemplifies then a fascinating attempt at history painting: the subject is contemporary; the idea of painting a large image of a massacre of innocents is traditional; and the usage of Dynamic Symmetry is both traditional, in its appeal to ancient ratios such as the "golden section," and modernist, in its expression of a faith in science. Unfortunately, this history painting's rendering of a war atrocity fails to inspire or impart a moral lesson, and, though praised for its sense of power, was criticized, as were other pictures of the series, for lacking psychological subtlety and naturalism.[87]

Walt Kuhn, one of the principal organizers of the Armory Show, was a modernist who attempted history painting. Between 1918 and 1920, Kuhn executed twenty-nine small paintings as part of his "Imaginary History of the West." Painted in a loose, expressionist style, the paintings failed to spur much critical interest. A *New York Times* writer, who considered that "much of the work is illustration," offered faint praise by deeming the paintings "delightfully fashionable in a fashion that could be worn by a nice, refined old lady who wanted to keep up with the times without sacrificing her own proprieties."[88]

Writing in 1925, the critic Thomas Craven, a proponent of American regionalist painting, clamored for a kind of contemporary history painting. Craven charged that the "trouble with painting in the modern world, and particularly in America, is that it has lost its spiritual office; it has ceased to function as a medium for communicating with intelligence and power the experiences of mankind and has degenerated into a study of physical processes." In hysterically homophobic and misanthropic fashion, Craven asserted:

> [The artist] is an effeminate creature who paints still-life, tepid landscapes, and incomprehensible abstractions purporting to express the aesthetic states of his wounded soul. No doubt the increasing effeminacy of the American environment has much to do with the shaping of his conceptions, but if he possesses no masculine virtues to begin with, let him bob his hair and design Futurist lingerie or sets for movies.

> Painting is essentially a man's art, and all great painters have been coarse, earthy and intolerable. In the entire range of art there is not a single picture entitled to a moment's consideration that has been done by a woman.[89]

For Craven, what art needed was a "reckless, unrefined Yankee . . . a man like Mark Twain or Walt Whitman, with brains, energy and original vision, who will convert the vast panorama of American life into living form." Thomas Hart Benton, "waging a terrific battle to find a background for his historical decorations," was Craven's image of *the* artist.[90]

From 1919 to 1926, Benton was absorbed in an ambitious mural series he called the *American Historical Epic*, which aimed to reject international modernism and to emphasize what Benton called "a people's history."[91] Critics said little about this work, although Lewis Mumford did praise Benton's efforts.[92] In regard to another, related Benton set of murals, *New York History* (plates 131 and 132), Mumford admired how "Mr. Benton designs pictures to take the place which is commonly occupied by conventional relief sculpture."[93] Undertaken (but never installed) for four niches on the third floor of the New York Public Library, *New York History* received mixed critical response, from being "pleasing and pungent" to demonstrating that "mannerism is the pit into which Mr. Benton has fallen."[94] Benton continued his historical interests through the 1930s as he and other American regionalists created numerous paintings and murals representing events from American history. These works, often public in location and popular in appeal, were generally poorly received by modernist critics because of their blend of narration, history, and realism.

Mural painting in particular helped prolong history painting, but the notion of the genre as a special mode occupying the most elevated place in the hierarchy of subjects nonetheless ceased to function. Indeed, the very idea of such a hierarchy collapsed under the sway of modernism. Ironically, historical societies and organizations proliferated between 1875 and 1925, as did literature—fiction and nonfiction—portraying American history; yet the world of modern art increasingly viewed the past as distant and infertile territory. The decline of history painting marked the eclipse of the tradition that every picture should tell a story, particularly a didactic and ennobling one. The belief that painting should convey and inculcate patriotic and moral lessons gave way to artistic concern for decorative, formal, and personal expressiveness. Historical scenes appeared old-fashioned to those critics who saw a dynamically expansive, industrialized, and modern America. And modernism, though never shutting it down, clearly overpowered history painting.

131–132. Thomas Hart Benton. *New York History (Colonial)* and *New York History (Today)*. 1925. 70 x 36" (175.0 x 90.0 cm.). Lyman Field and United Missouri Bank, n.a., Co-Trustees of the Thomas Hart Benton and Rita P. Benton Testamentary Trusts, Kansas City, Missouri.

On the Margins
of American History

MATTHEW BAIGELL

Marginality is a two-sided issue filled with ambiguity. Every culture or society needs its ideologies of cohesion and its binding myths, and, in America, history painting might have been expected to contribute to the unification of a populace with different political and social traditions and spread out across a large geographical area. The artist John Neagle certainly envisioned such a purpose for the genre when he defined it in 1836 as "those arts, which, without fanning the flame of political disquietude, excite a moral and religious influence over the mind, elevate the character of the people, and by their pictorial commemoration of national events inculcate or confirm that love of country which is the safeguard of our liberties."[1]

But it is reasonable to point out that, sometimes incidentally and sometimes not incidentally, some person or some group was diminished in the process of creating these works. This process of devaluation, as Joel Kovel has described it, has been an historical constant in American society. "Men have long tried to identify themselves not only as individuals but as members of social groups; and to set up viable social groups, they have thrust others out," Kovel has observed. ". . . And all these 'others' have one feature in common: they are never quite as good as the self. Some mysterious tag of devaluation is attached to the other person as his essential point of distinction from the group of selves."[2] This essay analyzes both history and genre paintings, for both reveal majoritarian assumptions about race, gender, and status. Both depicted African Americans, native Americans, women, and post–Civil War immigrants in ways that reveal the limitations the artists' culture placed upon their thought.

Most American painters of the nineteenth and early twentieth centuries belonged to the majoritarian culture, a group whose members, whatever their differences, shared similar biases that helped shape a dominant ideology. By the early nineteenth century, this majoritarian ideology—what literary historian Sacvan Bercovitch has termed "interlinked ideas, symbols, and beliefs by which a culture . . . seeks to justify and perpetuate itself; the web of rhetoric, ritual, and assumption through which society coerces, persuades, and coheres"—had begun to be articulated in art.[3] Historian Raymond Williams has defined this cultural "hegemony" as "a more or less adequate organization and interconnection of otherwise separated and even disparate meanings, values, and practices, which it specifically incorporates in a significant culture and an effective social order." Williams has argued that tradition is an important aspect of a group's hegemony, most particularly the development of "an intentionally selective version of a shaping past and a pre-shaped present, which is then powerfully operative in the process of social and cultural definition and identification."[4]

However much we might be entranced by the ideas set forth in the Constitution, the Declaration of Independence, and the Pledge of Allegiance, history painters in most instances shaped their works according to the ideological parameters of a culture that, while celebrating certain people, automatically devalued others. We read their works, these days, less to find out what happened in American history than to find out what they thought happened in American history and to ascertain the ways in which their works reflected their beliefs. The majority culture used various stereotyped behaviors associated with the marginalized—those not at the center—as so many levers of power to reinforce marginal-

John Trumbull. *The Death of General
Warren*, detail of plate 133.

201

133. John Trumbull. *The Death of General Warren at the Battle of Bunker's Hill, June 17, 1775.* 1786. 25 x 34" (62.5 x 85.0 cm.). Yale University Art Gallery, New Haven, Connecticut.

ization: African Americans liked music, native Americans were savages, pioneer women were helpless without their men. So, in a sense, history painting can be seen as a form of oppression. Members of the majority culture accepted Sir Joshua Reynolds's dictum that only acts containing "heroic action or heroic suffering" not "degraded by the vulgarism[s] of ordinary life in any country" were worth recording. Yet this Reynoldsian logic would not help them explain to native Americans why, in Benjamin West's painting *The Death of General Wolfe* (plate 17), the general's death on what had been their land exemplified heroic suffering better than would their own deaths on that ground.[5]

In the years after the Revolutionary War, most white Americans probably agreed with the language used in the prospectus for advertising the sale of prints after John Trumbull's 1786 paintings, *The Death of General Warren at the Battle of Bunker's Hill, June 17, 1775* (plate 133) and *The Death of General Montgomery in the Attack on Quebec, December 31, 1775*:

> No period in the history of man, is more interesting than that in which we have lived. The memory of scenes in which were laid the foundations of that free government, which secures our national and individual happiness, must remain ever dear to us and to our posterity.[6]

Trumbull himself stated that "to preserve and diffuse the memory of the noblest series of actions which have ever presented themselves in the history of man, is sufficient warrent of it [history painting]."[7] So he showed General Warren dying for the American cause. Warren, according to Abigail Adams, was evidently decapitated by British officers after being shot in the face, but Trumbull, emphasizing the Reynoldsian view that the history painter was to reveal the character of a person through his actions, showed an officer deflecting the bayonet from Warren's body.[8] Trumbull, then, complimented all involved in the painting's major actions—heroic death and humanitarian gesture.

But in the lower right-hand corner of the painting, Trumbull depicted a black man cringing behind a white man. The identity of this black man has not been established, although some art historians have identified him as Peter Salem.[9] Salem, a free man when he joined the army, was in fact one of the heroes of the battle. At a key moment, one of the British officers, Major John Pitcairn, mounted a redoubt and shouted, "The day is ours." Salem, in response, killed him with a rifle shot, temporarily checking the British advance.[10] Major Pitcairn's death is recorded in Trumbull's painting in the central midground where he is shown falling into the arms of two soldiers, one of whom is his son. But neither Salem nor anyone else is seen firing at Pitcairn.

We might charitably postulate that Trumbull forgot or was unaware of this part of the battle as he worked up his designs in London, but I would argue instead that his cultural system set limits on his thought. If there were black heroes in American battles, their presence and actions were not recorded. In the 1860s critics called Trumbull's historical paintings "graphic, well-designed compositions with spirited action and an elevated conception of his theories . . . devoid of exaggeration, truthful as narratives, national in motives, painting gentlemen as *gentlemen*." But the facts of the matter establish how profoundly both the comments and the painting marginalized anyone not in the majority culture.[11] As literary historian Henry Louis Gates, Jr., has observed, "The large number and variety of inherently racist images in American culture attest to a particularly American preoccupation with marginalizing black Americans by flooding the culture with an-Other Negro, a Negro who conformed to the deepest social fears and fantasies of the larger society."[12] Trumbull's black who cringes behind the white is a powerless, neutralized black who threatens nobody, who is weak, who will not take up arms and thus will not take part in a slave uprising. He is thus one of the most reassuring figures in the painting.

In Trumbull's day, many felt that black inferiority was the result of environmental factors based on climate or living conditions.[13] By the 1830s and 1840s "scientific" racism based on genetics and heredity convinced most whites that blacks were and always would be inferior beings. "The African in this country," according to the *African Repository*, the mouthpiece of the largely white American Colonization Society, "belongs by birth to the lowest station in society; and from that station he can never rise, be his talent, his enterprise, his witness what they may."[14] Statements of this sort were proffered ad infinitum, ad nauseam. One clergyman stated in 1833, "Find [blacks] where you may, whether in Philadelphia, Cincinnati, Richmond, or Charleston—in a free or slaveholding state, you find them with very few exceptions, the same degraded race. No individual effort, no system of legislation, can in this country redeem them from this condition, nor raise them to the level of the white man, nor secure to them the principles of freemen."[15]

African Americans were deemed not intelligent enough to be more than minimally educated. Neither could their social condition nor character be changed. Researchers measuring skull sizes invoked the "science" of phrenology to prove these assumptions of racial inferiority. In addition, by 1850, an American school of ethnology—represented by as respected a scientist as Louis Agassiz—had affirmed its belief in polygenesis, the theory that the races had evolved from separate human origins. Adam and Eve had sired, evidently, only the white race; blacks had been created separately as a lesser species.[16]

Knowingly or not, willingly or not, artists gave visual form to these beliefs through the middle decades of the century. Never painting blacks in their own social context, artists instead showed them only in relation to whites whose depictions suggest they reserved for themselves all power and authority.[17] One of the more pernicious beliefs reflected in numerous paintings was that of the happy black worker who, if left alone, would revert to immoral and dissolute living. "The Negro thrives under the shadow of his white master," as one writer put it, "falls readily into the position assigned him, and exists and multiplies in increased physical well being." Slavery, it was often argued, improved the health of blacks, elevated their minds and morals, and provided them with greatly improved living conditions.[18]

Junius Brutus Stearns's *Washington as a Farmer at Mount Vernon* illustrates this point of view as well as any painting (plate 108). Completed in 1851, barely a decade before the Civil War, the painting presents the proslavery position brilliantly. Washington visits his fields to discuss matters with a white overseer. In the center, robust slaves receive refreshment, while others bind and throw wheat on a wagon. In the left foreground, Washington's adopted grandchildren play. The institution of slavery, not the slaves, is heroized. Everyone seems to accept their roles in society. Nothing and no one threaten. All will sleep comfortably in their beds at night, not least the contemporary viewers of the painting.[19]

Of course, no one asked the slaves for their opinions of the situation Stearns depicted, just as no one asked for native American views of the battle on the Plains of Abraham. To have done so would have been tantamount to treating them as equals. As Kovel has suggested, dehumanization has two aspects—first, "the formation of an idea of another living person as less than a person," and, second, "an *action* upon that person so as to sustain one's dehumanized conception of them."[20] Asking is a humanizing action.

Whites also assumed, or hoped, that singing and entertaining were among the highest aspirations of black culture. Minstrel shows, with whites in blackface, helped institutionalize this aspect of accepted and expected African-American behavior. "Of all the varieties of the human race and of human condition that have ever fallen under observation," the novelist James Kirke Paulding proclaimed, "the African slave best realizes the idea of happiness . . . for he is . . . the most light-hearted, sportive, dancing, laughing being in the world."[21] Historian Houston A. Baker, Jr., commenting upon both the kind of music associated with blacks and the often nonsensical patter in minstrel shows and related entertainments, found that such performances were "designed to remind white consciousness that black men and women are *mis-speakers* bereft of humanity—carefree devils strumming and humming all day," and that the nonsense sound of minstrels is "the sound of the Negro."[22]

Today, we can recognize that such behavior on the part of African Americans was in part a defense against white racism. As sociologist Barry Adams has noted, "Inferiorized persons . . . develop repertories of behaviors employed for specific audiences, shifting from one

134. James Goodwyn Clonney. *Militia Training.* 1841. 28 x 40" (71.1 x 101.6 cm.). The Pennsylvania Academy of the Fine Arts, Philadelphia; bequest of Henry C. Carey (the Carey Collection).

behavior set to another as the occasion demands."[23] Finding themselves in a situation like that recorded in James Goodwyn Clonney's *Militia Training* (plate 134), African Americans might have assumed the entertainer's role as a defensive strategy against white racism. They cavort for the amusement of the crowd and for their own self-protection, even if they are not in immediate physical danger. They know their place, as indicated by a contemporary reviewer who remarked that the dancing Negroes had been "painted with great truth," an extravagantly clear instance of the power of the majoritarian culture to impose its construction of reality on all concerned—the artist, the subjects, the newspaper reviewer, and the general audience.[24]

In the 1860s and 1870s some artists portrayed African Americans with greater sympathy; Winslow Homer and Thomas Eakins, among others, avoided caricaturing African Americans in some of their works (plate 85).[25] But the depiction of African Americans in paintings after the Civil War remained much the same as before. In part, the continued racism reflected the growth in nationalism toward the end of the century and the belief that democracy was the product of race—of heredity—rather than of external causes.

Instances of these beliefs abound in the contemporary literature. In the book considered to contain the most influential discussion of race in the late nineteenth century, Frederick C. Hoffman stated that since the Civil War "thirty years of freedom in this country . . . have failed to accomplish the original purpose of the abolition of slavery. That is the elevation of the colored race to the moral, mental and economic level of the white race."[26] Stretching his conclusions to a global scale, Hoffman went on to assert as other learned academics and respected authors did (and continued to do) that "it is not in the conditions of life [environment], but in race and heredity that we find the explanation of the fact to be observed in all parts of the globe, in all times and among all people, namely, the superiority of one race over another, and of the Aryan race over all."[27] The Supreme Court decision in *Plessy v. Ferguson* (1896), which affirmed establishing separate but equal facilities for blacks and whites, gave federal imprimatur to racial segregation and reflected the changes in both public and private opinion since Reconstruction.

In art, as in life, native Americans fared even worse than African Americans. White relations with blacks revolved around the bedrock issue of controllable labor. Territory was the principal point of contention with native Americans. They were in the way. They blocked "progress." They had to be evicted. So, in the minds of whites, native Americans were unconnected to American culture—differently, but no less thoroughly, than African Americans were. In the paintings of most white American artists, blacks were slaves, but Indians were killers. Blacks, who were brutalized, were rarely shown being brutalized; Indians, who also were brutalized, were almost always depicted as brutalizers, as murderers of innocent women and children. History paintings did not show whites looting, pillaging, or burning Indian villages. Even if native Americans were sometimes shown as noble savages (a concept of European invention, after all), they were still marginalized.

Contest between the races, then, became a major subject for artists. Attacks on wagon trains and fights between native American and white men became standard fare through the middle and late years of the century. Even paintings of ostensibly peaceful encounters with native Americans were subliminally encoded with discriminatory values, such as Thomas Birch's *Penn's Treaty with the Indians*, in which Penn was depicted as though he were the first white man to arrive on the banks of the Delaware River when, in fact, several thousand others had preceded him. Penn, unarmed, his hand extended in friendship and peace, bravely approaches a native American. The native American, holding a tomahawk, is probably part of a hunting party that has just killed a deer. He is armed and possibly dangerous. The painting suggests that Penn is a man of such peaceful nature and grand moral stature that he subdues the native American's evident warlike nature by the sheer strength of his character and the civilization he represents.[28]

Such paintings were, in the end, less about noble deeds and personal heroism, despite the endless number of novels and stories, than about territorial expansion. The production of these paintings was predicated on the assumption that whites were entitled to the western lands and, accordingly, justice was on their side. As historian Francis Jennings has stated, "Myth contrasts civilized war with savage war by accepting the former as a rational, honorable, and often progressive activity while attributing to the latter the qualities of irrationality, ferocity, and unredeemed retrogression."[29] Native Americans were painted as aggressors and whites as defenders, when, in fact, whites were invaders. In effect, artists heroized intrusive acts, and, it should be noted, underscored how limited the Declaration of Independence's guarantees of life, liberty, and the pursuit of happiness really were.[30]

Justification for expansion fell under the rubric of Manifest Destiny, a term coined in 1845 by journalist John L. O'Sullivan. The roots of this term, however, can be traced to the first English settlements along the eastern coastline. O'Sullivan, arguing against potentially hostile actions by Mexicans (which led to the Mexican-American War) and the British (which led to the Oregon Compromise) in the middle 1840s, wrote, "It is our manifest destiny to overspread and to possess the whole of the continent which Providence has given us for the

135. Frederic Remington. *The Scream of Shrapnel at San Juan Hill, Cuba.* 1898. 35¼ x 60¾" (88.1 x 151.9 cm.). Yale University Art Gallery, New Haven, Connecticut; gift of the artist, 1900.

great experiment of liberty and federated self-government."[31] Possession of the land, which in the language of Manifest Destiny was given by God to the whites, was a right anchored in Genesis 1:28. "God blessed them [Adam and Eve] and God said to them: Be fertile and increase, fill the earth and master it; rule the fish of the sea, the birds of the sky, and all living things that creep on earth." Generations of whites, beginning with New England's John Cotton in 1630, interpreted this passage to mean that tilling the soil gave the settlers the right to possess it. In 1859, journalist Horace Greeley professed his conviction that because most native Americans did not cultivate the land, "these people must die out—there is no help for them. God has given this earth to those who will subdue it and cultivate it, and it is vain to struggle against his righteous decree."[32]

Religion coupled with racism and nationalism fueled the ideology of expansionism. "We were Anglo-Saxon Americans," one writer stated in 1846. "It was our destiny to possess and to rule this continent—we were *bound* to do it! We were a chosen people, and this was our allotted inheritance, and we must drive out all other nations before us."[33] *The Baptism of Pocahontas* (plate 46) by John Gadsby Chapman is especially interesting, even insidious, in this regard. In the Rotunda of

the Capitol Building, where it has been seen by millions of visitors, the painting portrays native Americans cooperating in the destruction of their culture. If this painting has one subtext, it is that white religion—namely, Christianity—represents civilization and that native Americans become acceptable only by becoming Christian and accepting white values and customs.

But the subject of Chapman's painting was already anachronistic in 1840, for it was predicated on a belief no longer current among Americans. As historian Roger Horsman has suggested, "There is considerable evidence to show that after 1830 neither the mass of American people nor their political leaders believed that the Indians could be melded into American society."[34] In a manner akin to the marginalization of African Americans, biology had been yoked to American expansionist thought in assigning native Americans a position of racial inferiority, particularly through the research of phrenologists and craniologists. Skull measurements "proved" their lesser moral and intellectual development; their brain matter rendered "them little susceptible of becoming civilized, humanized, and educated." Needless to say, Adam and Eve were not necessarily considered their first parents.[35]

Such artists as Frederic Remington and Alfred Jacob

136. George Catlin. *LaSalle Erecting a Cross and Taking Possession of the Land.* March 1682. 14¾ x 22⅜" (37.2 x 55.3 cm.). Paul Mellon Collection, National Gallery of Art, Washington, D.C.

Miller wrote about their dislike of native Americans.[36] Even George Catlin, despite his well-known desire to record images of Indian life (plate 136), was nevertheless a Manifest Destinarian. He considered land near the Missouri River not as the present and future home of its then-current inhabitants, but, in "a few years of rolling time," as the site of "splendid seats, cities, towers and villas," as well as "new institutions, new states, and almost empires." For the native Americans dispossessed by these developments, Catlin offered this proposal:

> And what a splendid contemplation too, when one (who has travelled these realms, and can duly appreciate them) imagines them as they might in future be seen, (by some great protecting policy of government) preserved in their pristine beauty and wildness, in a magnificent park, where the world could see for ages to come, the native Indian in his classic attire, galloping his wild horse, with sinewy bow, and shield and lance amid the fleeing herds of elks and buffaloes. What a beautiful and thrilling specimen for America to preserve and hold up to the view of her refined citizens and the world, in future ages! A nation's park, containing man and beast, in all the wild and freshness of nature's beauty![37]

In other words, native Americans would become tourist attractions in something of a human zoo.

Asher B. Durand's *Progress* (plate 54) is one of the great visual celebrations of Manifest Destiny. In 1853, when it was first exhibited, a critic wrote that "it is purely AMERICAN. It tells an American story out of American facts, portrayed with true American feeling."[38] In two sentences, the word "American" appears four times without any explanation of what it meant; clearly, the author assumed his readers knew. A late twentieth-century reader might get the following message from this painting: the native Americans, who appear at the left in the wilderness, do not subdue the land nor make it bloom. Instead, they live in a timeless, ahistorical present, lacking any sense of development or progress. As one of Durand's contemporaries pointed out, "They have ever existed . . . like a vacuum in the system of nature." Another noted, "Left to themselves, [native Americans had] not in two hundred years, advanced one step in improvement beyond the contemporaries of Raleigh and the Pilgrims. Not one scientific or literary production; not a single invention or discovery in even the practical appliances of life."[39] Certainly, in this particular social construction of reality, the whites had earned the moral right to possess the land. Through their intelligence and determination, and through God's munificence, they had made the land bloom.

During the 1880s and 1890s, as the nation grew to continental dimensions, the federal government grew increasingly interested in acquiring overseas territories to house naval bases necessary for trade with Asia. Un-

til these decades, it was assumed that newly acquired territories on the North American mainland, populated primarily by Anglo-Saxons, would be admitted as states. Now, at century's end, it seemed equally clear to many that potentially new subject populations in Hawaii and the Philippines might never be accorded citizenship but instead would be kept in a state of permanent dependency for reasons of race.[40] Elaborate justifications for Anglo-Saxon supremacy were outlined in books by Hoffman as well as by clergymen, historians, and political scientists. Paralleling the arguments contained in these books and reflecting governmental domestic and international policies, pictorial images of native Americans reached new heights of virulence, particularly in the works of Remington, Charles Russell, and Charles Schreyvogel.

The painting that perhaps best reflects this strain of American thought is Albert Bierstadt's *Landing of Columbus in San Salvador* (plate 137), in my view one of the most blatantly racist works ever painted by an important American artist. The newly landed Columbus is bathed in the symbolic sunshine of God's grace and favor. Native Americans, who remain in shadow, are actors in a white supremacist fantasy: they kneel before Columbus, somehow knowing that a superior civilization had arrived.

All these paintings of the West and the various statements of Anglo-Saxon supremacy and hegemony were predicated upon white male domination of space and of other cultures (plate 135). Women, until recently, did not figure directly in this history or in the landscape, which historian Susan Armitage has called "Hisland."[41] Her terminology is justified by the evidence of American history paintings. Men are active; women are passive. Men fight; women huddle in the wagons. Men exist in open spaces; women are often confined to the repressive and controlled spaces of the wagons. Men are armed; women are defenseless.[42] In addition, the activities of men and women seem entirely separate. Except for being in the same place at the same time—at a campfire, on the trail—men and women do not appear to share the same experiences.[43] Clearly, the artists, mostly based in the East, visualized the West according to an eastern cult of true womanhood, where women were pious, pure, submissive, and concerned with as well as fulfilled by domestic chores.[44]

From the evidence in diaries written by women on the trail, images such as Emanuel Leutze's *Indians Attacking a Wagon Train* (plate 138) have little to do with reality. Rather, as historian Lillian Schlissel has pointed out, women knew "the economics of the road . . . were as knowledgeable as men about the qualities of grasses for the animals. . . . They drove the ox teams and collected pieces of dung . . . to fuel fires when there was no wood."[45] In addition to caring for their children, they

137. Albert Bierstadt. *The Landing of Columbus in San Salvador.*
1893. 80 x 120" (200.0 x 300.0 cm.). Plainfield Cultural and Heritage
Commission, Plainfield, New Jersey.

138. Emanuel Leutze. *Indians Attacking
a Wagon Train*. 1863. 40 x 70" (100.0 x
175.0 cm.). Dover Free Public Library,
Dover, New Jersey.

139. William T. Ranney. *Old Scout's Tale*. 1853. 13½ x 19½" (33.7 x 48.7 cm.). Thomas Gilcrease Institute of American History and Art, Tulsa, Oklahoma.

pitched tents, unloaded goods, yoked cattle, dug graves, headed households when men were away or had died. They often walked and helped push wagons up mountain trails to help preserve the strength of their animals. Indeed, animals were probably more pampered than women. Women also fought Indians, although evidence suggests that they cooperated with native Americans to a much greater extent than men did: battles were often avoided and passage from one area to another was considerably eased by their intervention.[46]

In view of our current knowledge, the image of the woman and child in William T. Ranney's *Old Scout's Tale* (plate 139) is a perversion of pioneer history. Ranney's woman is too posed, too pure: she recalls religious images of Mary and the infant Jesus, an association that idealizes her virtually right out of the campfire circle. The men talk to each other, but the woman stares into space or at the viewer, seemingly oblivious to the nature of their talk. She is not part of the pioneer experience; she represents instead a concept of motherhood and womanhood that did not exist and had no place on the trail.

The most famous painting of the western migration, Emanuel Leutze's *Westward the Course of Empire Takes Its Way* (plate 140), stereotypes not only women but native Americans and African Americans as well. The land in front of the advancing pioneers is empty of people (free of native inhabitants, in other words) and awaits their arrival. In the foreground, literally larger than life, a male pioneer envelops two women and a child in his

arms. Leutze described in his notes for the painting a "suffering wife" and "a lad who had been wounded probably in a fight with the Indians," but in typical mid-century fashion he did not reflect upon the suffering or wounds of the native populations.[47] In the version painted the following year, 1862, and now in the U.S. Capitol, Leutze added an African-American man leading a white woman on a mule. A contemporary critic guessed that Leutze by this addition wanted "to teach a new gospel to this continent, a new truth which this part of the world is to accept—that the Emigrant and the Freedman are the two great elements which are to be reconciled and worked with."[48] But Leutze admitted the African American to this group only in a subservient position. He is a freedman, it is true, but he is still a servant and therefore an inferior person, not an equal. The context of Leutze's times may not permit us to expect much else—but it was that very context that insisted on such marginalization.

Chapman saw Pocahontas in much the same way. In his discussion of *The Baptism of Pocahontas*, he wrote:

> [She] stands foremost in the train of those wandering children of the forest who have at different times . . . been snatched from the fangs of a barbarous idolatry, to become lambs in the fold of the Divine Shepherd. She therefore appeals to our religious as well as our patriotic sympathies, and is equally associated with the rise and progress of the Christian church, as with the political destinies of the United States.[49]

213

140. Emanuel Leutze. *Westward the Course of Empire Takes Its Way.* 1861. 33½ x 43⅜" (83.7 x 108.4 cm.). National Museum of American Art, Smithsonian Institution, Washington, D.C.; bequest of Sara Carr Upton.

141. Jerome Myers. *The Tambourine*.
1905. 22 x 32" (55.0 x 80.0 cm.). The
Phillips Collection, Washington, D.C.

142. George Luks. *The Spielers.* 1905.
36 x 26" (90.0 x 65.0 cm.). copyright
© Addison Gallery of American Art, Phillips
Academy, Andover, Massachusetts;
1931.9, gift of anonymous donor.

Historian Sherry L. Smith sees Chapman's Pocahontas differently, as a fictionalized and idealized noble Indian woman, the archetypal Indian "princess." "The Indian 'princess' was childlike, naturally innocent, beautiful and inclined toward civilization, Christianization, and to helping and mating with white men."[50] Like African Americans, she played an assigned role that reinforced the governing ideologies of race, territorial expansion, religion, and gender.

Artists who painted immigrant groups in the early twentieth century revealed the influences of pervasive hostility to minority groups and of then-popular assumptions of Anglo-Saxon superiority.[51] Although these painters sometimes endeavored to understand the textures of the lives of their subjects, their works suggest at times that a visit to the Lower East Side substituted for a trip to Italy or the Balkans to study the picturesque locals.

The language artists used in autobiographical statements and interviews also suggests as much and was no different from that found in both fictional and nonfictional writing throughout the turn-of-the-century decades. The observations of Basil and Isabel Marsh in William Dean Howells's *A Hazard of New Fortunes* (1890) is typical. In one scene set in Washington Square, the Marshes "met the familiar picturesque raggedness of southern Europe with the old kindly illusion that some-

how it existed for their appreciation and that it found adequate compensation for poverty in this." Mr. Marsh did not, as he said "find so much misery in New York. I don't suppose there's any more suffering here to the population than there is in the country. And they're so gay about it all." Nor did Mrs. Marsh "believe there's any *real* suffering—not really suffering—among these people; that is, it would be suffering from our point of view, but they've been used to it all their lives, and they don't feel their discomfort so much."[52]

In an 1893 *New York Times* article on the city's Jewish quarter, one commentator maintained, "It is impossible for a Christian to live there because he will be driven out. . . . Cleanliness is an unknown quantity to these people. They cannot be lifted up to a higher plane because they do not want to be."[53] Neither could Henry James find empathy for Lower East Side residents when he visited the area after living for years in London. Filled with self-pity when he found destroyed the house in which he was born—"the effect for me . . . was of having been amputated of half my history"—he could not even begin to imagine the effects of immigration on people who would not ever visit their old homes again and who had to function in a new language in a strange country. Instead, while musing on the geometric designs of fire escapes on the tenement buildings, he

217

likened them to "a little world of bars and perches and swings for human squirrels and monkeys . . . the inhabitants lead, like the squirrels and monkeys, all the merrier life." And observing an open space in a street, he saw "an ant-like population [darting] to and fro."[54]

So it comes as no surprise to find an artist such as Jerome Myers somehow overlooking the Lower East Side's incredibly crowded and squalid living conditions, high incidence of disease, and sweat shops in *The Tambourine* (plate 141). Rather, he found that his "love was my witness in recording these earnest, simple lives, these visions of the slums clothed in dignity, never to me mere slums but the habitations of a people who were rich in spirit and effort." Workers, he said, "came to me in gorgeous raiment of another world. . . . I was led to paint pictures in which these East Side scenes are lost in a tapestry of romance." He also believed that the slums, and only the slums, were the last preserves of individuality and were threatened by missions, settlement houses, and schools. "The slum folk are not to be pitied. Far from it. Generally speaking, they are better than we—better because genuine."[55] This is not unlike the romantic racialism of the mid-nineteenth century according to which African Americans were considered to be more truly Christian than whites because they were deferential. That is, they possessed a quality of character lacking in Anglo-Saxons.[56] So, too, slum dwellers possessed genuineness of character, a quality often lacking in the wealthier classes.

Myers's attitudes toward the slums were echoed by such other painters as William Glackens and George Luks. Glackens could not "see any sense in weeping over the people of the slums":

> A man who can be unconventional is apt to be more satisfied than one who cannot. I haven't noticed as much suffering in the slums as one hears about. It seems to me that the people down there have a pretty good time—assuming that they can stand the dirt. I can't see that they work so terribly hard. . . . They're probably more primitive than we are and less civilized, and they happen to make good subjects for pictures. . . . They do exactly as they please . . . and any one who can do that certainly ought to be far happier than the harassed businessman.[57]

Luks held that the only trait that distinguished the slums from wealthier districts was poverty. "Life in the slums," he wrote, "is precisely what it is uptown, save that uptown . . . has the advantage of a protective mantle of prosperity."[58] But, as if he felt it compensated for poverty, Luks thought the poor were more honest.

Still, even though Luks maintained that "a child of the slums will make a better painting than a drawing room lady gone over by a beauty shop," his comments do not intimate deep interest in or understanding of slum conditions.[59] His *Spielers* (plate 142) recalls images of African-American youth painted in the previous century. Granted, children do smile and play, but *The Spielers* ignores the larger truths of life in an immigrant ghetto. And like the critic of Clonney's painting, critics of Luks's work scrambled all over themselves to avoid confronting those truths. One said that it "was Luks's ideal to represent beggars and life realistically" and that "his two adorable 'Spielers' are . . . purely the product of the New York Streets."[60] Critic James Huneker found that "all happiness is not lost in those mean streets; a rift of wintry sunlight, a stray tune from some wheezy barrel organ, and two children waltz with unconscious zest of life."[61] And Everett Shinn, commenting on *The Spielers*, described the childish innocence of the two dancing girls, then speculated about their older sisters "hawking their wares at the Haymarket, a notorious beer garden and dance hall."[62] It is difficult to say here which is more glaring—Shinn's sexism or his insensitivity to immigrants, his assignment of these young girls and their older sisters to the feminine Other or his desire to construct a world of the immigrant Other.

By contrast, Jacob Riis better understood the effects of slum life and was more honest in his depiction of it, as his photograph *Two Ragamuffins Didn't Live Nowhere* (plate 143) attests. Unlike those nineteenth-century "experts" who blamed the marginalized for their marginality, Riis understood that the problem lay not in heredity but in the environment. Writing about slum dwellers, he said, "The bad environment becomes the heredity of the next generation." In effect, the poor did not create poverty; they were its victims.[63]

Riis was in fact one of the first white males in the history of American art to represent truthfully the subjects that had been and continued to be so easily marginalized. Robert Henri was another, even though not all of his fellow realists understood this. When Henri said, "If you want to be a historical painter, let your history be of your own time, of what you can get to know personally —of manners and customs within your own experience," his intention was not to say something with which earlier painters might have agreed. Henri asked for more than surveys of current prejudices or majoritarian beliefs. For him, painting was profoundly "the study of our lives, our environment. The American who is useful as an artist is one who studies his own life and records his experiences." Henri tried to observe each individual and not see stereotypes. "I am looking at each individual with the eager hope of finding something of the dignity of life, the humor, the humanity, the kindness," he said.[64] The kind of language both Henri and Riis used as well as the images they created denoted a new sensitivity to the marginalized in American art. Although the course of American art did not change abruptly, a corner had been turned.

143. Jacob Riis. *Two Ragamuffins Didn't
Live Nowhere.* ca. 1890. Photograph.
Museum of the City of New York, Jacob
A. Riis Collection.

144. Joe Rosenthal. *Raising the Flag on Iwo Jima.* February 23, 1945.
Photograph. Wide World Photos and George Eastman House,
Rochester, New York.

Afterword

History Pictures Past, Present, and Future

KENNETH L. AMES

History pictures are fascinating artifacts. Pictures, after all, don't just happen. They are produced because someone has a reason to send a message.[1] And history doesn't simply exist, either. It isn't just lying out there waiting to be discovered. History is constructed by people, usually toward a mixture of conscious and unconscious ends.[2] History pictures are neither inevitable nor accidental, nor are they simple statements of truth. They are messages typically sent by someone trying to use the past to affect the present in some way and often the future as well.

Not all history pictures depict subjects that were historic when the paintings were created. Some record contemporary events, events considered potentially historic, events around which history might be constructed. What these pictures have in common with those dealing with the past is that both normally carry heavy ideological baggage.

This realization provokes a critical look at history pictures and the ways they function in the society that creates them. Each history picture can be considered a cultural riddle of sorts, inviting a series of pertinent and sometimes impertinent questions. Who wants to send the message? Why do they want to send it? What will they gain by sending it? What exactly is the message? What is its text? What are its subtexts? What are its manifest functions? What are its latent functions? Why this episode of the past or present and not some other? Why presented this way and not some other? What people are in the picture? Where are they placed and what does it mean? What people are not in the picture? Why not? What assumptions inform the picture? What hierarchies are sustained or assaulted? What values are celebrated? What values are ignored or denigrated? And finally,

what is the net impact of this picture on society? Is it positive or negative? How does it affect me and what I believe in? Do I endorse or reject this picture and what it stands for and promotes?

This list of questions illuminates two critical points. First, history pictures are usually parts of social, political, and cultural strategies. They are not just stories. They are not simply inert truths. They are purposeful creations. They are arguments for a certain order, a certain structure, a certain cosmology. Second, although they are apparently intensely formal, history pictures are also often intensely personal. Often presented in superhuman and lofty terms, history pictures deal, albeit sometimes obliquely, with strongly held and deeply felt beliefs. There is no contradiction here. History pictures are statements about the way the world ought to be. It is difficult to find a topic about which there can be more intense feeling and more intense disagreement. The political, after all, is personal.

All of this makes history pictures more interesting than is usually recognized. For they are far more than elaborate formalist configurations, far more than great events of history preserved for posterity, far more than undisputed truths from the American past. They are a type of political rhetoric, with the word "political" understood in the broadest sense. For the intention behind most history pictures is to persuade and convince people of the fundamental correctness of the subject they portray[3] and the correctness of the social order that subject represents, celebrates, and promotes.

This is serious stuff. And this seriousness helps explain why, when academic artists of the seventeenth and eighteenth centuries laid out a hierarchy of imagery, they placed history paintings at the top. For history paintings were the most powerful of the painter's products. With history paintings, artists came closest to shaping the thinking, the beliefs, the values of those exposed to the images. Put bluntly, history paintings ranked at the top because they were most closely associated with and most obviously served the causes of power. It should come as little surprise, then, that this involvement with power was in turn played out in the subject matter of those same history paintings, where the celebration of power in its multifarious guises and disguises was the overwhelmingly dominant theme.

But the matter of power and history pictures is more complex than it may at first appear. For not only is the subject matter of these images conventionally concerned with commentary on and usually endorsement of certain patterns of power relations in human society, but the very medium has power—not the paint itself but the way it is manipulated to form mimetic images, images that create the illusion that we are looking at plausible reality.[4] No aesthetic distance sets them apart as a different or lesser experiential realm, a more obviously constructed or artificial reality capable of being held at arm's length and rationally and dispassionately examined. Pictures—however the word is understood—can be very real. They can be active, animating agents in the world.[5]

As active agents, images are capable of affecting people on a variety of conscious and unconscious levels. Many kinds of images can induce responses and reactions, but pictures of people, probably the most universally accessible of all the images humans create, are the most potent.[6] Religious imagery and what is called pornography are only two of the more obvious kinds of figural imagery known to evoke responses (reverence, arousal) and affect behavior. But history pictures also have power. Why else would people have gone to such considerable effort and expense over the years to create so many of them?

History pictures, then, are a powerful medium that often takes as its subject depictions of power. Control of these images is also a matter of power. Those who control images control thought and understanding. Those who control images may be able to shape behavior. This was true in times when images were scarce and remains true today. This is why advertising is a multibillion dollar industry. This is why there is so much concern about the types of images that appear on television. This is why pictorial propaganda becomes so important in wartime. This is why the press was tightly restricted during the war against Iraq. And this is why people attempting to take control of their lives engage in what is called "creative visualization," consciously putting images in their minds to direct their thought and behavior.[7]

It is also true that those who shape and structure

memory control our view of the past and can expand or limit what is perceived as possible in the present or the future. In defining what should be remembered, history pictures reify values and otherwise abstract or invisible cultural hierarchies. In defining what should be remembered from the past, history pictures define what should be valorized in the present.

As the essays in this book show, over time history pictures have addressed issues of central concern to American society. It is difficult to discuss these images without also discussing national, class, gender, racial, ethnic, regional, or cultural identity; the construction, reconstruction, or deconstruction of cultural myths and cosmologies; ideologies, hierarchies, and structures of wealth and power; values, changing concepts of heroism, personal worth, or the well-lived life; or understandings of the past and the uses of history. History pictures present these concerns in constantly shifting patterns, and studying them necessarily becomes the study of historical sociology and anthropology.

This book demonstrates the great variety and diversity of imagery that can be gathered together under the heading of American history pictures. The range of events, of times, of places, of personalities is notable and impressive. Beneath or within this apparent or surface diversity, however, lurks a surprisingly uniform and constant core of cultural values. Put differently, traditional American history paintings are remarkable for their severely limited perspective and how little of our national life and how few people they have actually depicted and served. We could almost say that for generations there was but one historical theme and that all history pictures were variations on that theme. Consider what Frederick Kemmelmeyer's *First Landing of Christopher Columbus* (plate 33), William Henry Powell's *Discovery of the Mississippi by De Soto* (plate 49), Emanuel Leutze's *Washington Crossing the Delaware* (plate 30), and Julian Scott's *Sheridan's Ride* have in common. These images and scores of others traditionally embraced in the genre of history painting all reveal a deep current of fascination, almost obsession, with power. They all glorify a monolithic model of behavior that centers on conquest and domination by "great," almost always white, men. This is not a new discovery. As feminist historians and as Voltaire, Marx, Veblen, Galbraith, and others have recognized, the dominant line of Western history and the dominant interpretation of heroic achievement have long centered on male activity. Patriarchal values have been dominant, supported by military and patriotic mythologies, not to mention orthodox religion. The conventional patriarchal definition of leadership has usually meant military exploit and conquest, and for many it still does.[8]

This comprehension of appropriate and laudable male behavior runs deep. Its own long history, the great mass of cultural production applauding it, and its undeniable cognates in animal behavior all make change difficult. Its repeated valorization in history pictures, especially when the multifaceted powers of those pictures are taken into account, reveals the vast cultural weight behind this prescription for heroic and worthy activity.

Thus it comes as little surprise that one of the most familiar history images of the nineteenth century is Emanuel Leutze's *Washington Crossing the Delaware*, a mythologizing depiction of military and political power staged with grand theatrical bravado. And it likewise comes as little surprise that one of the most familiar history images of this century is Joe Rosenthal's photograph of marines raising the American flag on Iwo Jima (plate 144). This image has all of the key elements of an archetypal history picture. The actors are all male. The event celebrated is a battle, this particular one taking more than twenty-eight thousand lives. And the centerpiece is the flag, sacred symbol of patriotic love of country. What makes this photograph even more archetypal as a history picture is the fact that its symbolic value and utility outweigh its literal truth or the strategic importance of the event depicted. Rosenthal's photograph does not record a moment in the midst of battle but an event a few hours later. It does not document the raising of the first American flag over Iwo Jima but documents, accurately, a later moment when the first, smaller flag was replaced by a larger flag, more visible to the troops.[9]

Most orthodox history pictures are carefully crafted presentations, intended in turn to influence those who see them. During the war and for years after, no image was more aggressively and successfully used to manipulate the American public to support the war, patriotism, and the Marine Corps than Rosenthal's Iwo Jima photograph. History pictures, then, sometimes experience long and powerful symbolic lives. When that occurs, it often means they have tapped firmly held beliefs and deep-seated, even unconscious, values.[10]

For some, male violence and the need to dominate are the stuff of great history, of real history, the only vein of human activity that really matters. For increasing numbers of others, however, male violence and the need to dominate are the central *problems* of the late twentieth century—at the interpersonal, the interethnic, and the international level.[11] Notions of war, patriotism, and masculinity are bound together not only etymologically (*pater, patria,* patriarchy, patriot) but emotionally and psychologically, each supporting and sustaining the other. Notions of white heterosexual male superiority— superiority over women, people of color, gays, others whomever they may be—reside at the core of American culture and seem particularly embedded in its political system. Orthodox history pictures have been part of this cultural package, limiting conceptions of the world and reinforcing old and, to many, injurious ways of thinking and acting.

As reflected in countless history paintings, most forms of male competitive accomplishment are manifestations of a more or less sublimated warrior motif. Warriors come in many guises. Some are warriors in the literal sense. But there are also industrialist warriors, politician warriors, even comedian warriors, and many others as well. The adversarial legal system depends on warriors. So do professional sports. In history paintings, often the warrior motif is flagrant, but sometimes it is subtle or only implied. E. L. Henry's *First Railroad Train on the Hudson and Mohawk Railroad* (plate 129) records the first passenger run of America's first railroad company: on August 9, 1831, the locomotive *DeWitt Clinton* and three passenger cars prepare to pull out of Albany and head for Schenectady. Henry's painting seems a straightforward record of technological innovation, but it also celebrates technology, a supremely competitive male-dominated area where the warrior motif is rarely far beneath the surface. Technology warriors simultaneously wage war on two fronts—against the physical laws and properties of nature (mother nature?) and against their competitors.

But this painting also suggests other patterns of male domination. For this picture, created sixty years after the event, depicts the progenitor of two great empires of the nineteenth century. One was the New York Central Railroad, which made the fortunes of the Cornings of Albany and of the Vanderbilts. The other was the giant American Locomotive Company, which made Schenectady a major industrial center. These are two different stories, but each, in its way, involves conquest and domination. And each endorses the warrior motif. Henry's celebration of the railroad is not a violent image, although the history of railroading had many violent episodes. Yet it is surprising how frequently violence and, even more significantly, mortality appear in or are alluded to in history pictures.[12] In the orthodox patriarchal mentality, death and greatness seem to be inseparable. Put in the crudest terms, the great seem either to kill or be killed. In history paintings, killings authorized by the great often remain implicit or off stage, but the death of the great frequently becomes the subject of history. History paintings such as *The Death of General Wolfe* (plate 17), *The Death of the Earl of Chatham* (plate 22), *La Salle Assassinated by Duhaut, The Burial of Desoto, The Death of General Sedgwick* (plate 86), and countless scenes of battle bear out the central role of glorious death or death for a glorious cause. Mortality even appears in symbolic guise, as in William W. Walcutt's image *Pulling Down the Statue of George III at Bowling Green* (plate 62). Thomas Hovenden's *Last Moments of John Brown* (plate 125) is a late example of this mode but hardly ends the genre.

145. Eastman Johnson. *Sugaring Off.* ca. 1861–66. 52¾ x 96½" (134.0 x 245.1 cm.). The Jesse H. Metcalf Fund.|Museum of Art, Rhode Island School of Design, Providence.

In addition to contemplating history pictures from the perspective of their dominant imagery—white male warriors or para-warriors—and the cosmology they reproduce, it is also crucial to be aware of those people not well served by orthodox history pictures, or who do not appear in them at all. The role of history pictures in promoting racism, sexism, and a hierarchical class structure has been recognized.[13] And because their utility as tools for hegemony is obvious and attractive, the role history pictures play in sustaining domination and the status quo is surely more often deliberate than inadvertent. "In any society the dominant groups are the ones with most to hide about the way society works"—and with the most to gain by disguising their motivations and vested interests.[14] History pictures, by providing negative or belittling images of some people and ignoring others, affect the way marginalized or disempowered people think about themselves and the way others think of them as well. In this way, history pictures often have been a form of oppression.

But historians have never focused solely on dominant males and their exploits. Even Herodotus was a student of cultural history and historical ethnography. And since at least the middle of the nineteenth century the practice of history at both the academic and grass-roots levels has diversified and gradually widened. Different understandings of history and different political constituencies with new agendas have meant different forms and different content for history pictures. The decline of painting's role in addressing shared social concerns and the concurrent rise of photography and photojournalism have meant not only changes of media but changes in audience, in distribution, in response, and, perhaps, in credibility as well.

One impulse for change in the definition of history came as a response to the increasing distance between urban and rural life, a distance intensified by the processes of industrialization and modernization. By the second half of the nineteenth century, sensitive people in most Western nations had become attentive to their own disappearing national or regional pasts. Their interest centered less on individuals or on conventional definitions of heroism than on the broad sweep of life, on customs and practices, on ordinary people and the character and conditions of their day-to-day, season-to-season, and year-to-year existence. One product of this emerging interest was the discipline called folklore.[15] Another was a different type of history picture.

In this country, Eastman Johnson was one of several painters who recorded and mythologized vanishing rural life.[16] Over several years, Johnson celebrated two great epics of New England, each revealing the distinctive flavor of a discreet regional culture, each exploring behaviors and ceremonies intimately tied to indigenous local foodways and, ultimately and mythically, to the land itself. One of these epics was the harvesting of maple sugar in western Maine in the late winter; the other, the harvesting of cranberries in southeastern Massachusetts in the fall. Copious sketches and paintings for each survive.

Johnson's *Sugaring Off* (plate 145) celebrates local color as it was disappearing before an expanding national, industrially produced culture. *Sugaring Off* eulogizes community in an age of increasing individuation. In this idyllic image, figures of both sexes and of all ages mingle as they participate in a recurring seasonal activity that simultaneously brings them together and reveals their connectedness to the changing seasons. The sugaring off and cranberrying pictures are also about sense of place, about vanishing customs and ways of life, about the ways rural peoples are connected to the land and each other. Both sets of pictures also helped create and sustain an emerging New England mystique, a mystique that endures to this day.[17] Strictly speaking, none of Johnson's rural images was a history picture as that term is usually understood, for the pictures dealt with contemporary subject matter. Seen from the vantage point of Johnson's midtown Manhattan studio, however, these people and their activities represented a kind of living past, surviving evidence of the way things used to be, of a world that had been left behind.

With this broadened view of history in the late nineteenth century came an interest in historical material culture. At about the time that affluent urban women were starting to spend warm summer days scouring rural New England for blue-and-white ceramics and that a few male antiquarians in Hartford, Boston, and elsewhere were collecting and studying seventeenth- and eighteenth-century furniture,[18] Johnson was painting his famous *Old Stage Coach* (plate 146). With this image, he again stretched the definition of history painting. For if the scene was contemporary, the key artifact in the image, the old coach, was not. Like every piece of old material culture, it was a persisting historical fact, a tangible product of past intentions and actions living on in a new and alien cultural order. Rendered obsolete by the rapid expansion of rail travel, *The Old Stage Coach* is a pendant to Henry's Hudson and Mohawk painting and a suitably ambiguous statement about the mixture of loss and gain that accompanies technological change. Viewed from another perspective, the old coach is an aged veteran of a battle lost.

The diversification of history has intensified in recent decades. Perhaps no period more decisively altered our understanding of the meaning and practice of history than the 1960s. Americans are still sorting out the impact of those years.[19] A decade of extraordinary disruption and unrest, of civil rights marches, Vietnam War protest, urban riots, assassinations, and powerful rock music, the sixties were also the period when the style of scholarship known as "the new history" came of age.[20] Like most allegedly new phenomena, the new history had plenty of documentable antecedents. But it was an assertively populist and alternative history for people deeply cynical about the established order.

The new history became deliberately a history of the ordinary, of the unsung, of the underdog, of the underside. It was history from below, history from the bottom up, in retaliation for years of history from the top down. It reached beyond the elites and the ruling classes and their perspectives to explore reality as experienced by those outside the circles of privilege. The new history was built, as one historian put it, upon "sympathy with the victims of historical processes and skepticism about the victors' claims."[21]

With the new history, the category of history pictures was once again stretched. Edward Kienholz's eerie assemblage called *The Wait* (plate 147) captures some of the spirit and concern of the sixties.[22] Surrounded by material culture from her own family past, a woman who is little more than a skeleton sits waiting for her own death. On a table beside her rest family photographs, democratizers of history and evocations of experiences and relationships that were once hers. The assemblage is bizarre, disturbing, unsettling, even macabre. It forces viewers to confront grim realities of

146. Eastman Johnson. *The Old Stage Coach*. 1871. 36¼ x 60⅛" (92.1 x 152.7 cm.). Milwaukee Art Museum, Milwaukee, Wisconsin; gift of Frederick Layton.

personal, interpersonal, and family history. It reminds viewers that most people live ordinary lives but that those lives are marked by positive and meaningful relationships with other people, by love, by warmth, by affection, as well as by loss, by pain, by sorrow, by dreams unfulfilled, by hopes unsustained. It asserts the fact that old people at the end of their lives are often alone, living on in a continually shrinking world made up of a few meaningful possessions and the lingering memories they evoke. Kienholz's use of surrealistic and decidedly uncomfortable forms pushes viewers to recognize the validity and the pervasiveness of the story this work tells.

The Wait is partially about pain and loss. But old people have no monopoly on pain and loss in this country. From the sixties until the present pained but increasingly confident and assertive voices—males outside the circles of dominance, people of color, women, gays and lesbians, and others—have found expression in an expanded and diversified history and in history pictures. The most significant of these perspectives, even if measured in quantitative terms alone, is feminism. Few intellectual, social, or political movements have had as much impact. Some wings of feminism endorse values that may ultimately transform a competitive, hierarchical, and exclusivist world. History has been dramatically reshaped by the introduction of feminist thinking,

which does not simply augment history but requires the entire rethinking of history and its premises. Feminist thought ultimately calls for the total transformation of knowledge.[23]

Probably the most famous feminist artwork, in large part because of the way it startles us into revisioning the world and rethinking basic premises, is Judy Chicago's richly complex cooperatively produced assemblage *The Dinner Party* (plate 148).[24] At this fantastic celebration of one of humankind's central rituals of bonding, the world's accomplished women appear as a series of imaginatively interpreted butterfly or vulvoid shapes. A complex creation that can be read on many levels, *The Dinner Party* reminds viewers provocatively about the centrality of sexuality to being, to identity, to self, of the many ways males have used sexuality and their fear of female sexuality as an excuse to shape and restrict women's lives and opportunities.[25] It is an alarming signal of the male tendency to objectify women and to appraise them as sexual objects and prospective sexual partners. And *The Dinner Party* presents an alternative expressive route that celebrates feminine achievements and perspectives long repressed and unvalued. *The Dinner Party* is also a feminist answer to such masculinist icons as *The Last Supper*, *The School of Athens* (plate 19) and *The Apotheosis of Homer*. In its openness it makes plain what is concealed in those pictures. In its

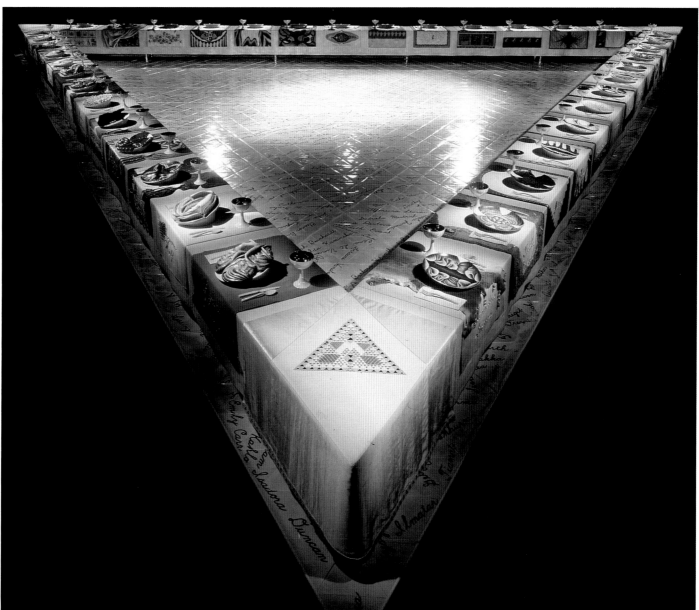

149. John Filo. *Kent State Shooting.* May 4, 1970. Photograph. © John Filo; private collection.

explicit femaleness it exposes what feminists call phallocentrism, the monistic view that evaluates and measures all things according to masculine standards. *The Dinner Party* is a legitimately historic history picture.

Despite their shared imagery and outlook, history pictures and history paintings are not quite the same. History paintings are a subset within the larger category of history pictures. At one time history paintings—and prints based on them—were dominant, but the advent of photography challenged their hegemony. Photography brought with it profound changes. Where major paintings took months to complete, photography allowed for the near-instantaneous capture of an image. Photography provided both a degree and a kind of detail often missing or excluded from paintings. As sanitized as they are now known to be, Brady, Gardner, and O'Sullivan photographs of the Civil War captured the grisly and desolate horror of battlefields dotted with decaying corpses more accurately than painters could or cared to. The advent of paper prints made possible the wide distribution of images, a multiplication of audience and ownership not possible within the more restrictive, more elitist, medium of painting. And the mere ease of operation made photography a skill attained much more readily than painting, which had historically relied

upon long periods of training and practice. As the century wore on, the price of cameras and supplies declined, enfranchising more and more people, of both sexes, as their own historians, as their own image takers. Photography democratized pictures, and it also democratized history.

History painters usually took pains to craft formalized renditions of allegedly famous or pivotal moments. The resulting images were rarely believed, either by painters or viewers, to reproduce the event accurately. Nor was that the point. Painters attempted to give to the subject an appropriate grandeur, majesty, and dignity, qualities that elevated and honored their subjects. The result might accurately be called a historical fantasy, loosely based on a theme but embellished in flattering ways.

Putting it in other terms, orthodox history pictures were conceived as what Irving Goffman has called "front" performances.[26] That is, they were ordered, controlled, carefully manipulated in order to manage the impression they made. Photography was capable of creating front images, as "photo ops" of celebrities and politicians and most official portraiture make clear, but it also showed a marked facility for capturing "back" images, those unplanned, unstructured, informal occasions when defenses are down and people act without pre-

150. Edward Adams. *Vietnamese Officer Shooting Suspected Vietcong.* February 1, 1968. Photograph. Wide World Photos, Associated Press, New York.

meditation. The candid snapshot is the prime manifestation of back imagery.

Cartoons had always claimed to depict the inglorious or back aspects of the rich, the powerful, and the pompous, but they were always obviously fabrications, projections at best. But a photograph had a degree of veracity that elevated it above other media. It was one thing to hear that Nelson Rockefeller made an obscene gesture to hecklers but another thing to see a photograph of him actually doing it. Like photographs of Lyndon Johnson displaying his scar and picking up his dogs by the ears, the Rockefeller photograph demystified the man. And by demystifying the powerful, photographs also demystified claims to power and authority.

Also from the 1960s came a new type of iconic image—one that laid bare abuses of power and moral corruption and demystified war as well as power and authority. From that period, it is not grandiose set pieces that stand out but certain unstaged images—images of Mary Ann Vecchio over the body of Jeff Miller, killed at Kent State (plate 149), images of children fleeing from napalm, images of a suspected Vietcong soldier being summarily shot by a South Vietnamese officer (plate 150). These images were products of changed thought about war, power, and violence, and they, in turn, were

instrumental in changing the way many people felt about behavior long taken for granted.

Another such history picture in this spirit is Mel Rosenthal's dramatic and moving—and thoroughly unstaged—photograph of a sick person collapsed on the street outside a New York City hospital (plate 151). This is not a self-congratulatory image, not a mystification of power or privilege. Rosenthal's photograph pushes people to think about the present social and political orders and their shortcomings. It is about callousness, about skewed priorities, about misallocation of resources and the imbalance of income that mocks claims that this land opens the golden door of opportunity. This is a harsh and outraged picture that cries out against the barbarism, the greed, the self-absorption that characterize much of late twentieth-century life. In the long tradition of history pictures, it is a dramatic and didactic image.[27]

Rising public skepticism almost seemed to have destroyed conventional history pictures, those elaborately staged historical panoramas of the past. Yet Richard Nixon is the subject of a new and massive traditional historical tableau, "one of the biggest oil paintings in the Los Angeles area," installed in 1992 at the Nixon Presidential Library in Yorba Linda, California (plate 152).[28]

What of history pictures in the future? We can hope

151. Mel Rosenthal. *Emergency,*
from *The Triage Project*. 1983.
Photograph. © Mel Rosenthal.

that the Nixon tableau stands out as an exception among history pictures of the present and the future, which increasingly promote humanistic values. Tomorrow's history pictures can be based on an understanding of history as a way of asking questions, not as a body of knowledge to be disseminated or, even less, as a series of grand assertions. History and history pictures can work to repair inequalities, to emancipate, to empower, to enlighten. They can operate under the premise that everyone matters.[29] They can envision and work to create a world with different priorities. In this reformed vision, heroism still has a place, but it takes on new meanings, as feminist philosopher Elizabeth Minnich has projected:

> Heroism can then cease to be a singular individual quality expressed in highly visible deeds and become a quality of character developed in a whole life, a life led

in relation to many others that expresses care, honesty, integrity, intimacy, constancy, as well as (even instead of) the ability to "win" through dramatic confrontations and adventures. And leadership can then be understood not in terms of dominance but as an ability to empower others.[30]

This history explores what it means to be human, what it means to live a responsible and caring life in the midst of other lives. As history and history pictures follow the paths of ordinary people, they make explicit what has been implicit; they make public and general what has been private and partial. In this way, history and history pictures can be disruptive in a positive sense. They can explore the ways people retain their dignity and self-respect in the face of difficulties and defeats. They can make vivid the drama of ordinary people's lives—their resistance, their resilience, and their resourcefulness.

230

152. Ferenc Daday. *Nixon at Andau.*
1971. 72 x 120" (180.0 x 300.0 cm.).
Richard Nixon Library & Birthplace,
Yorba Linda, California; photo by
Gamma Liaison.

Notes

Foreword

1. See David Levin, *History as Romantic Art: Bancroft, Prescott, Motley, and Parkman* (Stanford, Calif.: Stanford University Press, 1959); Arthur M. Schlesinger, Jr., "The Historian as Artist," *The Atlantic Monthly*, July 1963, 35–40; Peter Gay, *Style in History* (New York: Basic Books, 1974).

2. *In This Academy: The Pennsylvania Academy of the Fine Arts, 1805–1976* (Washington, D.C.: Museum Press, Inc., 1976), 101, 110.

3. See Daniel J. Boorstin, *The Genius of American Politics* (Chicago: University of Chicago Press, 1953); Irvin G. Wyllie, *The Self-Made Man in America: The Myth of Rags to Riches* (New Brunswick, N.J.: Rutgers University Press, 1954); John G. Cawelti, *Apostles of the Self-Made Man* (Chicago: University of Chicago Press, 1965); Henry Nash Smith, *Virgin Land: The American West as Symbol and Myth* (Cambridge, Mass.: Harvard University Press, 1950).

4. See Michael Kammen, *A Season of Youth: The American Revolution and the Historical Imagination* (New York: Alfred A. Knopf, 1978), 96–100 and figs. 22–27.

5. See Michael Kammen, *Mystic Chords of Memory: The Transformation of Tradition in American Culture* (New York: Alfred A. Knopf, 1991), 53, 240–42; Brian W. Dippie, *Custer's Last Stand: The Anatomy of an American Myth* (Missoula: University of Montana Press, 1976); Michael Kowalewski, "Imagining the California Gold Rush: The Visual Legacy," *California History* 71 (Spring 1992): 60–73.

6. Ralph Ellison, "Going to the Territory" (1979) in Ellison, *Going to the Territory* (New York: Random House, 1986), 123–24.

7. For an interesting contrast, see Joany Hichberger, "Old Soldiers," in *Patriotism: The Making and Unmaking of British National Identity*, ed. Raphael Samuel (London: Routledge, 1989), 3: 50–63. Hichberger finds that paintings of aged war veterans enjoyed considerable vogue in England for many decades after 1815. A prime example is David Wilkie's *Chelsea Pensioners Receiving the London Gazette Extraordinary of Thursday June 22nd 1815 Announcing the Battle of Waterloo*, first exhibited at the Royal Academy in 1822. Wilkie's painting emphasized working-class men, the "worthy poor," responding in a patriotic manner to the great victory. For the political complexities of what could (and could not) be shown in paintings of this sort, see 53–54.

8. David M. Potter, "The Historian's Use of Nationalism and Vice Versa," in Potter, *The South and the Sectional Conflict* (Baton Rouge: Louisiana State University Press, 1968), 68–83.

9. Mark Twain, *Life on the Mississippi* (1883; reprint, New York: New American Library, 1961), 254–55.

10. Michael Kammen, *Meadows of Memory: Images of Time and Tradition in American Art and Culture* (Austin: University of Texas Press, 1992), 138.

11. Kammen, *Meadows of Memory*, xv.

12. Robert Penn Warren, *The Legacy of the Civil War* (Cambridge, Mass.: Harvard University Press, 1961), 100.

Preface

1. Irma B. Jaffe, *Trumbull: The Declaration of Independence* (New York: The Viking Press, 1976), 97–100; *New York Daily Advertiser*, October 8, 1819. "Native Americans" as used here and by many other nineteenth-century writers refers to American citizens of European ancestry born in the United States; American Indians were not then given credit for being either "native" or "American."

2. *The Knickerbocker*, December 1851; *New York Evening Mirror*, November 7, 1851; *New York Observer*, February 5, 1852; *Literary World*, October 18, 1851; Raymond L. Stehle, "The Life and Works of Emanuel Leutze" (typescript, Washington, D.C., 1976), 29–33, Art and Architecture Collection, New York Public Library.

3. Henry James, *A Small Boy and Others* (London: Macmillan & Co., 1913), 279–80.

4. *New York Observer*, February 5, 1852; *Georgetown Advocate*, April 6, 1852; Stehle, "Life and Works of Emanuel Leutze," 35–39.

5. In some cases visual images reinforce written ones; at other times images and texts offer alternative visions—and in such instances the visual has often succeeded in obliterating competing considerations. With regard to another visual medium, the movies, Gore Vidal has observed that "we are both defined and manipulated by fictions of such potency that they are able to replace our own experience, often becoming the *sole* experience." See *Screening History* (Cambridge, Mass.: Harvard University Press, 1992), 32.

6. See Mark Thistlethwaite's essay in this volume.

7. The opposite tendency can be seen in many art museums, where an earlier generation of curators often relegated history paintings to storerooms because of their incongruence with the modernist aesthetic.

The History of History Painting

1. Allen Staley and Helmut von Erffa, *The Paintings of Benjamin West* (New Haven, Conn.: Yale University Press, 1986), 55. For an excellent discussion of West's *Death of General Wolfe*, see also Ann Uhry Abrams, *The Valiant Hero: Benjamin West and Grand-Style History Painting* (Washington, D.C.: Smithsonian Institution Press, 1985).

2. John Galt, *The Life, Studies and Works of Benjamin West, Esquire* (London: T. Cadell and W. Davies, 1820), 47, also quoted in Abrams, *Valiant Hero*, 14.

3. Galt, *Life, Studies and Works of West*, 48, also quoted in Staley and von Erffa, *Paintings of Benjamin West*, 57.

4. Edgar Wind, "The Revolution of History Painting," *Journal of the Warburg and Courtauld Institutes* 2 (1938–39): 117.

5. See Galt, *Life, Studies and Works of West*, 49, also quoted in Abrams, *Valiant Hero*, 14.

6. Galt, *Life, Studies and Works of West*, 49–50. See also Charles Mitchell, "Benjamin West's 'Death of General Wolfe' and the Popular History Piece," *Journal of the Warburg and Courtauld Institutes* 7 (1944): 21, and Abrams, *Valiant Hero*, 14.

7. See James A. Leith, *Art as Propaganda in France, 1750–1799: A Study in the History of Ideas* (Toronto: University of Toronto Press, 1965).

8. For example, see Abbe Jean Bernard Bernard Leblanc in *Lettre sur l'exposition des ouvrages de peinture* (1747), 154 passim, and *Dialogues sur la peinture*, 2d ed. (Paris, 1773), cited in Leith, *Art as Propaganda*, 8–9, 81, 82.

9. Warren E. Roberts, *Jacques-Louis David, Revolutionary Artist: Art, Politics and the French Revolution* (Chapel Hill and London: University of North Carolina Press, 1989), 32. Diderot's never-completed drama was titled *Traite de la poesie dramatique*.

10. See Anita Brookner, *Jacques-Louis David* (New York: Harper & Row, 1980), 37–38, 112, and Abrams, *Valiant Hero*, 58.

11. Brookner, *Jacques-Louis David*, 84.

12. Ibid., 83, 85.

13. Walter Pach, "The Heritage of J.-L. David," *Gazette des Beaux Arts* 45 (February 1955): 103.

14. Joshua Reynolds, "Discourse IV," *Discourses on Art*, ed. Robert R. Wark (San Marino, Calif.: Huntington Library, 1959), 59.

15. Rensselaer W. Lee, "Ut pictura poesis: The Humanistic Theory of Painting," *The Art Bulletin* 22, 4 (1940): 201.

16. Leon Battista Alberti, *Della Pittura*, trans. with an introduction and notes by John R. Spencer (New Haven, Conn.: Yale University Press, 1956), 75.

17. Lee, "Ut pictura poesis," 201.

18. Spencer, "Introduction," in Alberti, *Della Pittura*, 24.

19. Brian Pullan, *A History of Early Renaissance Italy* (London: Penguin Books Ltd., 1973), 309.

20. Matt. 17: 24–27.

21. *The Battle of San Romano* depicts Niccolo da Tolentino, one of the best-known *condottieri* of the day, directing the June 1, 1432, victory of the Florentines over the Sienese. It is one of three stages of the battle Uccello painted, the others being *The Unhorsing of Bernardino* (Uffizi, Florence) and *Micheletto da Cotignola Attacking the Sienese Rear* (Louvre, Paris). For a discussion of these works, see John Pope Hennessey, *Paolo Uccello*, 2d ed. (London and New York: Phaidon, 1969).

22. E. H. Gombrich, "Botticelli's Mythologies: A Study in the Neoplatonic Symbolism of his Circle," *Journal of the Warburg and Courtauld Institutes* 8 (1945): 16, 54.

23. Giorgio Vasari, *Lives of the Most Eminent Painters, Sculptors and Architects* (1568; reprint, New York: Macmillan and the Medici Society, 1912–15), 4, 217–18.

24. This notion was undoubtedly accepted by the French Academy, for one had to be a history painter in order to achieve its rank of professor. On Félibien, see André Félibien des Avaux, *Conference de L'Academie Royale de peinture et de sculpture*, reprinted in Theodore Besterman, ed., *The Printed Sources of Western Art* 8 (Portland, Ore.: Collegium Graphicum, 1972).

25. See Claire Pace, *Félibien's Life of Poussin* (London: A. Zwemmer, c. 1981).

26. Christopher Wright, *Poussin Paintings: A Catalogue Raisonné* (London: Harlequin Books, Ltd, 1985), 192. For another important study of the works of Poussin, see Sir Anthony Blunt, *The Paintings of Nicolas Poussin: A Critical Catalogue* (London: Phaidon, 1966).

27. Alfonso E. Perez Sanchez, "Velázquez and his Art," in *Velázquez* (New York: Harry N. Abrams, Inc., 1989), 32.

28. *The Surrender of Breda* is now in the collections of the Prado.

29. Jonathan Brown and J. H. Elliott, *A Palace for a King: The Buen Retiro and the Court of Philip IV* (New Haven, Conn., and London: Yale University Press, 1980), 178.

30. Antonio Rodriguez Villa, *Ambrosio Spinola, Primer Marques de Los Balbases* (Madrid, 1904), 432, quoted in Brown and Elliott, *A Palace for a King*, 176 n. 96.

31. Brown and Elliott, *A Palace for a King*, 181, 184.

32. Wind, "Revolution of History Painting," 116.

33. See Peter Cannon-Brookes et al., *The Painted Word: British History Painting: 1750–1830* (Woodbridge, Eng.: The Boydell Press, 1991), 17.

34. Simon Schama, *Dead Certainties* (New York: Alfred A. Knopf, 1991), 26, 32. Cannon-Brookes et al. in *Painted Word*, 17, state that West undoubtedly saw terracotta *Lamentation of the Dead Christ* groups in Naples and Bologna, which were presented in chapels as life-size *tableaux vivant*, painted in naturalistic colors and embellished with glass eyes and real hair.

35. Wind, "The Revolution in History Painting," 118.

36. Staley and von Erffa, *Paintings of Benjamin West*, 55.

37. See Reynolds, "Discourse IV."

38. Richard H. Saunders, "Genius and Glory: John Singleton Copley's *The Death of Major Peirson*," *The American Art Journal* 22, 3 (Autumn 1990): 8. On Copley, see also Jules David Prown, *John Singleton Copley*, 2 vols. (Cambridge, Mass.: Harvard University Press for the National Gallery of Art, 1966).

39. For a discussion of Trumbull's *Sortie Made by the Garrison at Gibraltar*, see Jules David Prown, "John Trumbull as a History Painter," in Helen A. Cooper, *John Trumbull: The Hand and Spirit of a Painter* (New Haven, Conn.: Yale University Art Gallery, 1982), 56–62.

40. Prown, "John Trumbull as a History Painter," 36–37.

41. Ibid., 35–37, 61. While planning this work, Trumbull made studies of both the *Dying Gaul* and the *Borghese Warrior*. Prown identifies the latter in the first painted version as the profile figure of a British soldier climbing the battery.

42. Charles F. Montgomery and Patricia E. Kane, eds., *American Art 1750–1800: Towards Independence* (Boston: New York Graphic Society, 1976), 99. On Trumbull, see also Prown, "John Trumbull as a History Painter," 22–92. On painters who traveled to London to study with West, see Dorinda Evans, *Benjamin West and His American Students* (Washington, D.C.: Smithsonian Institution Press, 1980). William H. Gerdts explains that Trumbull was the first of West's students to turn his attention to American history, a subject not available to West because of his service to the British Crown. See Gerdts, "On Elevated Heights: American Historical Painting and Its Critics," in William H. Gerdts and Mark Thistlethwaite, *Grand Illusions: History Painting in America* (Fort Worth, Tex.: Amon Carter Museum, 1988), 77.

43. See Montgomery and Kane, eds., *American Art 1750–1800*, 124.

44. Samuel Y. Edgerton, Jr., "The Murder of Jane McCrea: The Tragedy of an American *Tableau d'Histoire*," *The Art Bulletin* 47, 5 (December 1965): 482.

45. Edgerton, "Murder of Jane McCrea." See also Kathleen H. Pritchard, "Shorter Notes: John Vanderlyn and the Massacre of Jane McCrea," *The Art Quarterly* 12, 4 (Autumn 1949): 363–64. Pritchard noted that Vanderlyn was "an ardent worshiper at the Louvre where Napoleon's Galerie des Antiques displayed spoils from the Capitolene Museum and the Vatican"; there, he might have been exposed to these antique and neoclassical works.

46. Samuel F. B. Morse, *Lectures on the Affinity of Painting with the Other Fine Arts*, ed. Nicolai Cikovsky, Jr. (Columbia and London: University of Missouri Press, 1983), 46.

47. Daniel Fanshaw, "The Exhibition of the National Academy of Design, 1827. The Second," *The United States Review and Literary Gazette* 2, 4 (July 1827): 244. See also Gerdts, "On Elevated Heights," 71–72.

48. Fanshaw, "Exhibition of the National Academy," 245.

49. Carrie Rebora, "Robert Fulton's Art Collection," *The American Art Journal* 22, 3 (Autumn 1990): 43, 45. See also Kenneth C. Lindsay, *The Works of John Vanderlyn: From Tammany to the Capitol* (Binghamton: University Art Gallery, State University of New York, 1970), 141, catalog number 63.

50. For examples, see *National Academy of Design Record 1826–1860* (New York: New York Historical Society, 1943), and Maybelle Mann, *American Art-Union* (Otisville, N.Y.: ALM Associates, 1977).

51. "Review of New Books," *Graham's Magazine*, June 1843, 367.

See also Mark Thistlethwaite, "The Image of George Washington: Studies in Mid-Nineteenth-Century American History Painting" (Ph.D. diss., University of Pennsylvania, 1977), 16–19, for this reference as well as other contemporary pleas for historical veracity.

52. Gerdts, "The Düsseldorf Connection," in Gerdts and Thistlethwaite, *Grand Illusions*, 125.

53. Ibid., 125–68.

54. Ibid., 138.

55. For a history of the Düsseldorf Gallery, see R.L. Stehle, "The Dusseldorf Gallery of New York," *New-York Historical Society Quarterly* 58, 4 (October 1974): 305–14.

56. For example, Leutze sent a work titled *Henry VIII and Anne Boleyn* (currently unlocated) for exhibition in 1849.

57. See Barbara Groseclose, *Emanuel Leutze 1816–1868: Freedom is the Only King* (Washington, D.C.: Smithsonian Institution Press, 1976), 36, 40, and *Literary World*, November 1, 1851, 525.

The Landing of the Fathers

1. "The Landing of the Pilgrim Fathers in New England," *The Poetical Works of Felicia Hemans, Complete in One Volume* (Philadelphia: Porter and Coates, 1853), 495.

2. For basic definitions of history painting, see William H. Gerdts and Mark Thistlethwaite, *Grand Illusions: History Painting in America* (Fort Worth, Tex: Amon Carter Museum, 1988), 8–10, and Joshua Reynolds, *Discourses on Art*, ed. Robert R. Wark (San Marino, Calif.: Huntington Library, 1959).

3. Allen Staley, *Benjamin West: American Painter at the English Court* (Baltimore, Md.: The Baltimore Museum of Art, 1989), 52–54.

4. West left unfinished his only work relating to the Revolution, *The Peace Commissioners in 1782* (1783–84), a group portrait of the seven British and American individuals at the signing of the preliminary peace treaty.

5. Wendy Greenhouse, "Benjamin West and Edward III: A Neoclassical Painter and Medieval History," *Art History* 8, 2 (1985): 178–91.

6. Jules David Prown, *John Singleton Copley* (Cambridge, Mass.: Harvard University Press for the National Gallery of Art, 1966), 2: 343.

7. On the Historic Gallery, see T. S. R. Boase, "Macklin and Bowyer," *Journal of the Warburg and Courtauld Institutes* 26 (1963): 148–77.

8. Lillian B. Miller, "Paintings, Sculpture, and the National Character, 1815–1860," *The Journal of American History* 53, 4 (March 1967): 696–707. The utilitarian moral argument for the fine arts lasted well into the nineteenth century: see, for instance, "B.," "A Plea For Art," *Southern Literary Messenger*, September 1849, 624–26.

9. Quoted in Mark Thistlethwaite, "The Artist as Interpreter of American History," in *In This Academy: The Pennsylvania Academy of the Fine Arts, 1805–1976* (Philadelphia: The Pennsylvania Academy of the Fine Arts, 1976), 107.

10. See Ann Uhry Abrams's essay in this volume.

11. J. H. Plumb, *The Death of the Past* (Boston: Houghton Mifflin, 1970), 89.

12. Leonard Krieger, "European History in America," in *History*, ed. John Higham, The Princeton Studies in Humanistic Scholarship in America (Englewood Cliffs, N.J.: Prentice Hall, 1965), 239–40. For a fine general discussion of the New England sense of historical mission, see Frank Wesley Craven, *The Legend of the Founding Fathers* (New York: New York University Press, 1956), Chap. 1.

13. Craven, *Legend of the Founding Fathers*, 1–2.

14. See, for instance, Thomas W. Gilmer, "An Address before the Virginia Historical and Philosophical Society," *Southern Literary Messenger*, February 1837, 98–99.

15. See William H. Gerdts and Mark Thistlethwaite, *Grand Illusions: History Painting in America* (Fort Worth, Tex.: Amon Carter Museum, 1988), 45.

16. Indians, Roman Catholics, and other "aliens" to that mission, as defined by the mainstream culture, are typically depicted in such a way as to present a flattering contrast to superior white, Protestant civilization. See William H. Truettner et al., *The West as America* (Washington, D.C.: Smithsonian Institution, 1991), Introduction and Chaps. 1–3.

17. William H. Truettner convincingly demonstrates the link between scenes of American exploration and discovery and contemporary notions of progress and Manifest Destiny in his "The Art of History: American Exploration and Discovery Scenes, 1840–1860," *The American Art Journal* 14 (Winter 1982): 4–31. On the persistence of the millennialist conception of history from the Puritans into the nineteenth century, see Dorothy Ross, "Historical Consciousness in Nineteenth Century America," *American Historical Review* 89 (October 1984): 909–28, and Ernest L. Tuveson, *Redeemer Nation: The Idea of America's Millennial Role* (Chicago: University of Chicago Press, 1968).

18. Carl L. Crossman and Charles E. Strickland, "Early Depictions of the Landing of the Pilgrims," *Antiques*, November 1970, 777–81.

19. *The History of the Pilgrims; or, A Grandfather's Story of the First Settlers of New England* (Boston: Printed by J. R. Marvin, for the Massachusetts Sabbath School Union, 1831), 57–58.

20. Gilbert Tapley Vincent, "American Artists and the Changing Perceptions of American History, 1770–1940" (Ph.D. diss., University of Delaware, 1982), 42–43.

21. Gerdts and Thistlethwaite, *Grand Illusions*, 21.

22. Helen A. Cooper, *John Trumbull: The Hand and Spirit of the Painter* (New Haven, Conn.: Yale University Art Gallery, 1982), 76–81; Vincent, "American Artists," 35–39.

23. "J. G. Chapman, N.A.," *American Repertory of Arts, Science and Manufactures* 2 (January 1841): 435.

24. "American Works of Painting and Sculpture," *The Democratic Review*, January 1847, 60.

25. "Twenty-Sixth Exhibition of the National Academy of Design," *Bulletin of the American Art-Union*, May 1, 1851, 22.

26 *Morris's National Press*, May 9, 1846, 2.

27. Charles Lanman, "On the Requisites for the Formation of a National School of Historical Painting," *Southern Literary Messenger*, December 1848, 727–30.

28. "Twenty-Sixth Exhibition," 21.

29. An excellent summary of America's problematical relationship with the idea of the past is provided in David Lowenthal, "The Place of the Past in the American Landscape," in *Geographies of the Mind: Essays in Historical Geosophy in Honor of John Kirtland Wright*, ed. David Lowenthal and Martyn J. Bowden (New York: Oxford University Press, 1976), 89–117; see also Henry Steele Commager, "The Search for a Usable Past," *American Heritage*, February 1965, 4–9, 90–96; Michael Kammen, *A Season of Youth: The American Revolution and the Historical Imagination* (New York: Alfred A. Knopf, 1978), and Wilbur Zelinsky, *Nation into State: The Shifting Symbolic Foundations of American Nationalism* (Chapel Hill and London: University of North Carolina Press, 1988), 93.

30. It should be noted that the idea of America as a nation with little use for or interest in its past persisted well into the nineteenth century in certain quarters. See, for instance, *The Democratic Review* (1840) quoted in Kammen, *Season of Youth*, 4–5.

31. George H. Callcott, *History in the United States, 1800–1860: Its Practice and Purpose* (Baltimore, Md.: Johns Hopkins Press, 1970), 88.

32. Ruth Miller Elson, *Guardians of Tradition: American Schoolbooks of the Nineteenth Century* (Lincoln: University of Nebraska Press, 1964), 6–7.

33. Callcott, *History in the United States*, 88.

34. Lowenthal, "Place of the Past," 102–5.

35. "American Antiquities," *The Knickerbocker*, July 1837, 3.

36. Leslie W. Dunlap, *American Historical Societies 1790–1860* (Philadelphia: Porcupine Press, 1974), 18–20, 73–75. The American Antiquarian Society, for instance, was founded in 1812 mainly for the purposes of investigating Indian relics in Ohio; see Craven, *Legend of the Founding Fathers*, 66.

37. *The Democratic Review* (1842), quoted in W. R. B. Lewis, *The American Adam: Innocence, Tragedy and Tradition in the Nineteenth Century* (Chicago: University of Chicago Press, 1955), 159.

38. Dunlap, *American Historical Societies*, 8–9, 10–12; George Templeton Strong quoted in Kammen, *Season of Youth*, 12.

39. See Zelinsky, *Nation into State*, 71–73, 218–19; and Kammen, *Season of Youth*, Chap. 1.

40. This point is discussed further in Gail Husch's essay in this volume. See also Rush Welter, *The Mind of America 1820–1860* (New York and London: Columbia University Press, 1975), Chaps. 1–2.

41. Callcott, *History in the United States*, 25–26.

42. Quoted in Vincent, "American Artists," 58.

43. Emerson, *Nature*, in *Selected Writings of Ralph Waldo Emerson*, ed. Brooks Atkinson (New York: Modern Library, 1950), 3.

44. Lowenthal, "Place of the Past," 98–101.

45. Donald Ringe, *The Pictorial Mode: Space and Time in the Art of Bryant, Irving and Cooper* (Lexington: University of Kentucky Press, 1971); Harry B. Henderson III, *Versions of the Past: The Historical Imagination in American Fiction* (New York: Oxford University Press, 1974).

46. On Scott's treatment of the past see Avrom Fleishman, *The English Historical Novel, Walter Scott to Virginia Woolf* (Baltimore, Md.: The John Hopkins University Press, 1971); David Daiches, "Walter Scott and History," *Études Anglaises* 24 (October–December 1971): 458–77; P. D. Garside, "Scott, the Romantic Past and the Nineteenth Century," *The Review of English Studies* 23 (May 1972): 147–61; and Boris G. Reizov, "History and Fiction in Walter Scott's Novels," *Neohelicon* 2 (1974): 165–75. On Scott's influence on British and French artists, see Catherine M. Gordon, "Scott's Impact on Art," *Apollo Magazine* (July 1973): 36–39, and Beth Segal Wright, "Scott's Historical Novels and French Historical Painting 1815–1855," *Art Bulletin* 63 (June 1981): 268–87. No study exists of American illustrations to Scott, but an examination of exhibition records reveals comparable interest on this side of the Atlantic in Scott as an artistic source.

47. Frank Luther Mott, *Golden Multitudes: The Story of Best Sellers in the United States* (New York: Macmillan Co., 1947).

48. See Roy Strong, *Recreating the Past: British History and the Victorian Painter* (New York: Thames and Hudson, 1978), and Wright, "Scott's Historical Novels."

49. Quoted in David D. Van Tassel, *Recording America's Past: An Interpretation of the Development of Historical Studies in America, 1607–1884* (Chicago: University of Chicago Press, 1960), 115.

50. Gerdts and Thistlethwaite, *Grand Illusions*, 40–41.

51. *The American Monthly Magazine*, February 1, 1835, 338–39. On Bancroft and his fellow Brahmin historians, see David Levin, *History as Romantic Art: Bancroft, Prescott, Motley, and Parkman* (New York; AMS Press, Inc., 1967).

52. Russell B. Nye quoted in Mason Wade, "The Literary Historians: The Brahmins Contemplate the Past," in *American Classics Reconsidered: A Christian Appraisal*, ed. Harold C. Gardiner, S.J. (New York: Scribner, 1958), 266.

53. Carl Bode, *The Anatomy of American Popular Culture, 1840–1861* (Berkeley: University of California Press, 1959), 249; Commager, "Search for a Usable Past," 90.

54. See Krieger, "European History in America," 240–41; and Wendy Greenhouse, "The American Portrayal of Tudor and Stuart History" (Ph.D. diss., Yale University, 1989).

55. Levin, *History as Romantic Art*, 12–19.

56. Truettner, ed., *West as America*, 68.

57. Gerdts, "On Elevated Heights," in Gerdts and Thisthethwaite, *Grand Illusions*, 125–68.

58. Barbara Groseclose, "Washington Crossing the Delaware: The Political Context," *American Art Journal* 7 (November 1975): 70–78.

59. Washington, notes Mark Thistlethwaite, was likened by at least one midcentury writer to Moses, uniting and leading his people out of bondage. See Thistlethwaite, *The Image of George Washington: Studies in Mid-Nineteenth-Century American History Painting* (New York and London: Garland Publishing, Inc., 1979), 92.

60. Kammen, *Season of Youth*, 28–30, 50–57, 155–56. On southern uses for the rhetoric of '76, see also William R. Taylor, *Cavalier and Yankee: The Old South and American National Character* (Garden City, N.Y.: Anchor Books, 1963), Chap. 8.

61. See, for instance, the critical review of the first volume of Bancroft's *History* in *The Southern Literary Messenger*, June 1835, 587–91. On the rise of local history, see Craven, *Legend of the Founding Fathers*, 67–85.

62. "Exhibitions. 'The First Day of Worship,' by Schwartze," *The Crayon* 7 (May 1860): 147.

63. John W. Venable to L. M. Charles, January 8, 1840, John W. Venable Papers, Archives of American Art, Smithsonian Institution (microfilm reel number 1321); Lanman, "On the Requisites," 729. According

to a contemporary observer, on the other hand, Weir's picture represented the Puritans, Vanderlyn's Roman Catholicism, Chapman's Episcopalianism, and a bas-relief of Penn's treaty with the Indians represented Quakerism. Stephen Greenleaf Bulfinch, *A Discourse Suggested by Weir's Picture of the Embarkation of the Pilgrims: Delivered in the Unitarian Church. Washington: December 31st, 1843 by S.G. Bulfinch. Published by Request* (Washington: Printed by Giles and Seaton, 1844), 6–7.

64. *The Picture of the Embarcation of the Pilgrims from Delft-Haven, in Holland; Painted by Robt. W. Weir, In Conformity to an Act of Congress for Filling the Vacant Panels in the Rotunda of the Capitol at Washington* (New-York: Piercy & Reed, Printers, 1843), 6.

National Paintings and American Character

1. I wish to thank Vivien Green Fryd for sharing her manuscript of *Art & Empire: The Politics of Ethnicity in the United States Capitol, 1815–1860* (New Haven, Conn.: Yale University Press, 1992), and Elizabeth Johns and Anne Palumbo for their helpful suggestions.

2. See Charles Lanman, "Our National Paintings," *The Crayon*, February 28, 1855, 136.

3. James Fenimore Cooper to William Cullen Bryant and William Leggett (for the *Evening Post*, December 1834), in *The Letters and Journals of James Fenimore Cooper*, ed. James Franklin Beard (Cambridge, Mass.: Harvard University Press, 1964), 3, 80.

4. For a more complete discussion of this issue, see Lillian B. Miller, *Patrons and Patriotism: The Encouragement of the Fine Arts in the United States, 1790–1860* (Chicago: The University of Chicago Press, 1966), 3–84.

5. Harold Kirker, *The Architecture of Charles Bulfinch* (Cambridge, Mass.: Harvard University Press), 325–26.

6. For more information about Trumbull, see Helen A. Cooper, *John Trumbull: The Hand and Spirit of a Painter* (New Haven, Conn.: Yale University Art Gallery, 1982); Irma Jaffe, *John Trumbull: Patriot Artist of the American Revolution* (Boston: New York Graphic Society, 1975); and Theodore Sizer, ed., *The Autobiography of Colonel John Trumbull, Patriot-Artist, 1756–1843* (New Haven, Conn.: Yale University Press, 1953).

7. *Annals of Congress*, 14th Cong., 2d sess., January 27, 1817, 762.

8. *Annals of Congress*, 15th Cong., 2d sess., February 9, 1819, 1142–43.

9. *Annals of Congress*, 18th Cong., 2d sess., February 18, 1825, 624. Also see George R. Neilson, "Paintings and Politics in Jacksonian America," *Capitol Studies* 2 (Spring 1972): 88.

10. Sizer, ed., *Autobiography*, 257–61, Irma B. Jaffe, *Trumbull: The Declaration of Independence* (New York: Viking Press, 1976), 61–67 passim; Miller, *Patrons and Patriotism*, 45–46; and Jaffe, *John Trumbull: Patriot Artist*, 234–36.

11. See Cooper, *John Trumbull*, 76–81; Jaffe, *John Trumbull: Patriot Artist*, 97–122 passim; Jaffe, *Trumbull: The Declaration of Independence*; and Michael Kammen, *A Season of Youth: The American Revolution and the Historical Imagination* (New York: Oxford University Press, 1980), 80–81 passim. For a discussion of American ideals, see Robert E. Shalhope, "Toward a Republican Synthesis: The Emergence of an Understanding of Republicanism in American Historiography," *William and Mary Quarterly* 29 (January 1972): 49–80, and "Republicanism and Early American Historiography," *William and Mary Quarterly* 39 (April 1982): 334–56; Joyce Appleby, "Republicanism in Old and New Contexts," *William and Mary Quarterly* 43 (January 1986): 20–34, and "Republicanism and Ideology," *American Quarterly* 37 (Fall 1985): 461–73; Colin Gordon, "Crafting a Usable Past: Consensus, Ideology and Historians of the American Revolution," *William and Mary Quarterly* 46 (October 1989): 670–695; and Bernard Bailyn, *The Ideological Origins of the American Revolution* (Cambridge, Mass.: Harvard University Press, 1967).

12. Quoted in Linda K. Ferber, "The Republican Ideology of the Revolutionary Generation," *American Quarterly* 37 (Fall 1985): 475. See also Edgar Wind, "The Revolution of History Painting," *Journal of the Warburg and Courtauld Institutes* 2 (1938–39): 116–27; Jaffe, *John Trumbull, Patriot Artist*, 242–43, and Jaffe, *Trumbull: Declaration of*

Independence, 78–87.

13. Quoted in William Kelby, *Notes on American Artists, 1754–1820* (New York: New-York Historical Society, 1922), 53.

14. See Garry Wills, *Cincinnatus, George Washington and the Enlightenment* (Garden City, N.Y.: Doubleday & Co., 1984), 3–84.

15. *Annals of Congress*, 18th Cong., 2d sess., February 18, 1825, 624.

16. Quoted in Cooper, *John Trumbull*, 90 and Sizer, ed., *Autobiography of Colonel John Trumbull*, 258.

17. For details about the creation of *Burgoyne* and *Cornwallis*, see Cooper, *John Trumbull*, 82–87.

18. See, for example, Benjamin Franklin's listed "virtues" in *The Autobiography of Benjamin Franklin*, ed. Leonard W. Labaree et al. (New Haven, Conn.: Yale University Press, 1973), 149–50; and James Madison's *Federalist* No. 47 of 1788 describing the "Distribution of Powers," in *The Forging of American Federalism: Selected Writings of James Madison*, ed. Saul K. Padover (New York: Harper & Row, 1953), 161–68 passim.

19. Morse's plan is in S. F. B. Morse to G. C. Verplanck, December 21, 1826, Verplanck Papers, New-York Historical Society. Also see "Designs of Paintings," H. Rept. 8, 19th Cong., 2d sess., December 19, 1826. For information on the founding of the NAD, see Thomas S. Cummings, *Historic Annals of the National Academy of Design* (Philadelphia, 1865).

20. For details of the debate, see *Gales & Seaton's Register of Debates in Congress*, vol. 4, pt. 1, 20th Cong., 1st sess., January 8 & 9, 1828, 930–52; Fryd, *Art & Empire*, 45–46; Neilson, "Paintings and Politics," 89–92; Miller, *Patrons and Patriotism*, 45–57; and Kent Aherns, "Nineteenth-Century History Painting and the United States Capitol," *Records of the Columbia Historical Society of Washington, D.C.* 15 (1980): 191–201.

21. *Gales & Seaton's Register*, 946.

22. For the contest among artists, see Jared B. Flagg, *The Life and Letters of Washington Allston* (New York: Charles Scribner's Sons, 1892), 229–38; Paul Staiti, *Samuel F. B. Morse* (Cambridge: Cambridge University Press, 1989), 175–76 passim; Miller, *Patrons and Patriotism*, 51–52, 247 n.14; and Carleton Mabee, *The American Leonardo: A Life of Samuel F. B. Morse* (New York: Alfred A. Knopf, 1943), 184–85. For a summary of that debate, see Miller, *Patrons and Patriotism*, 52–54; Fryd, *Art & Empire*, 46; and William Pardee Campbell, unfinished manuscript, Campbell Papers, Archives of American Art.

23. *Annals of Congress, Register of Debates*, 12, pt. 4, Appendix, 24th Cong., 1st sess., June 23, 1836, Resolution 8, xxiii.

24. Cummings, *Historic Annals*, 144–46; Mabee, *American Leonardo*, 245–47; Staiti, *Samuel F. B. Morse*, 208–12; Harry B. Wehle, *Samuel F. B. Morse, American Painter* (New York: Metropolitan Museum of Art, 1932), 25–26; Beard, ed., *Letters of Cooper*, 3, 259; and Fryd, *Art & Empire*, 46–47.

25. *New York Mirror*, September 2, 1837, 80.

26. Frances Mossiker, *Pocahontas: The Life and the Legend* (New York: Alfred A. Knopf, 1976); Jay B. Hubbell, "The Smith-Pocahontas Story in Literature," *The Virginia Magazine of History and Biography* 65 (July 1957): 275–312; Philip Young, "The Mother of Us All: Pocahontas Reconsidered," *Kenyon Review* 24 (Summer 1962): 397; and Philip L. Barbour, *Pocahontas and Her World* (Boston: Houghton Mifflin, 1970).

27. Barbour, *Pocahontas*, passim; and Edward Arber, ed., *Travels and Works of Captain John Smith* (Edinburgh: John Grant, 1910), 38, 400–401, 410, 436, 455, 460, 498, 511–12, 514, 525, 529, 530–35.

28. See Elemire Zolla, *The Writer and the Shaman: A Morphology of the American Indian*, trans. Raymond Rosenthal (New York: Harcourt, Brace, Jovanovich, 1969), 20–24.

29. For information on the image of native Americans in the nineteenth century, see Ronald N. Satz, *American Policy in the Jacksonian Era* (Lincoln: University of Nebraska Press, 1975), 1–63; Robert F. Berkhofer, Jr., *The White Man's Indian: Images of the American Indian from Columbus to the Present* (New York: Alfred A. Knopf, 1978), 157–64 passim; Richard Slotkin, *Regeneration through Violence: The Mythology of the American Frontier, 1600–1860* (Middletown, Conn.: Wesleyan University Press, 1983); Julie Schimmel, "Inventing 'the Indian,'" in *The West as America: Reinterpreting Images of the Frontier, 1820–1920*, ed. William H. Truettner (Washington, D.C.: Smithsonian Institution Press for the National Museum of American Art, 1991), 149–89; and Louise K.

Barnett, *The Ignoble Savage: American Literary Racism, 1790–1890* (Westport, Conn.: Greenwood Press, 1975).

30. Anne Norton, *Alternative Americas: A Reading of Antebellum Political Culture* (Chicago: University of Chicago Press, 1986), 148.

31. For information on Chapman, see William P. Campbell, *John Gadsby Chapman* (Washington, D.C.: National Gallery of Art, 1962); Georgia S. Chamberlain, *John Gadsby Chapman, 1808–1889* (privately printed, 1963) and "The Baptism of Pocahontas," *The Iron Worker* 23 (Summer 1959): 18–19; William J. Dickman, "John Gadsby Chapman: Alexandria's Foremost 19th Century Painter," *Northern Virginia Heritage* (February 1980): 15–18; Edward F. Heite, "Painter of the Old Dominion," *Virginia Cavalcade*, Winter 1968, 11–29; and William P. Campbell, Chapman MS, Archives of American Art.

32. Quoted in Chamberlain, "Baptism of Pocahontas," 21.

33. *The Picture of the Baptism of Pocahontas. Painted by the Order of Congress for the Rotundo of the Capitol, by J.G. Chapman, of Washington* (Washington: Peter Force, 1840), 4–5.

34. Stephen Greenleaf Bulfinch, *A Discourse Suggested by Weir's Picture of the Embarkation of the Pilgrims: Delivered in the Unitarian Church. Washington: December 31st, 1843 by S. G. Bulfinch. Published by Request* (Washington, D.C.: Printed by Giles and Seaton, 1844).

35. Quoted in Irene Weir, *Robert W. Weir, Artist* (New York: House of Field-Doubleday, Inc., 1947), 83; for further evidence of the New England emphasis, see *The Picture of the Embarcation of the Pilgrims from Delft-Haven, in Holland; Painted by Robt. W. Weir, in Conformity to an Act of Congress for Filling the Vacant Panels in the Rotunda of the Capitol at Washington* (New-York: Piercy & Reed, Printers, 1843).

36. For additional information on Weir's career, see William H. Gerdts, "Robert Weir: Artist and Teacher of West Point," in *Robert Weir: Artist and Teacher of West Point* (West Point, N.Y.: Cadet Fine Arts Forum of the United States Corps of Cadets, 1976), 9–23, and Michael E. Moss, ed., *Robert W. Weir of West Point: Illustrator, Teacher and Poet* (West Point, N.Y.: United States Military Academy, 1976).

37. *The Writings and Speeches of Daniel Webster* (Boston: Little, Brown & Co., 1903), 1, 184. Also see Paul D. Erickson, "Daniel Webster's Myth of the Pilgrims," *New England Quarterly* 57 (March 1984): 44–64.

38. [Jacob Abbott] The American Popular Library, *New England and Her Institutions by One of Her Sons* (Boston, 1835), 245–46. For other contemporaneous opinions, see "Immigration," *North American Review* 40 (April 1835): 460–61, and "The New England Character," *North American Review* 44 (January 1837): 237–38. For information on nineteenth-century anti-Catholicism, see Ray Allen Billington, *The Origins of Nativism in the United States, 1800–1844* (New York: Arno Press, 1974), 49–110, and Ira M. Leonard and Robert D. Parmet, *American Nativism, 1830–1860* (New York: Van Nostrand Reinhold Co., 1971).

39. See Perry Miller, *Errand into the Wilderness* (Cambridge, Mass.: The Belknap Press of Harvard University Press, 1956), 1–15; Sacvan Bercovitch, *The American Jeremiad* (Madison: The University of Wisconsin Press, 1978); Bercovitch, "Rhetoric and History in Early New England: The Puritan Errand Reassessed," in *Toward a New Literary History*, ed. L. J. Budd et al. (Durham, N.C.: Duke University Press, 1980), 54–68; Bercovitch, "New England's Errand Reappraised," in *New Directions in American Intellectual History*, ed. John Higham and Paul K. Conklin (Baltimore, Md.: Johns Hopkins University Press, 1979), 85–104; Theodore Dwight Bozeman, "The Puritan's 'Errand into the Wilderness' Reconsidered," *New England Quarterly* 59 (June 1986): 231–51, and Bozeman, "The Reinvention of New England, 1691–1770," *New England Quarterly* 59 (September 1986): 315–40; Daniel Walker Howe, *The Political Culture of the American Whigs* (Chicago and London: The University of Chicago Press, 1979), 71.

40. Bulfinch, *Discourse*.

41. *Daily National Intelligencer*, October 3, 1846, 3; and *The Boston Daily Advertiser*, April 3, 1837, typescript of the clippings, Archives of the Architect of the Capitol; George C. Hazelton, Jr., *The National Capitol: Its Architecture Art and History* (New York, 1897), 121; and Lanman, "Our National Paintings," 136–37.

42. Washington Irving, *The Life and Voyages of Christopher Columbus*, ed. John Harmon McElroy (Boston: Twayne Publishers, 1981), 564–65.

43. See, for example, Jeremy Belknap, *A Discourse Intended to Com-*

memorate the Discovery of America by Christopher Columbus (Boston, 1792).

44. See the sketches in Kenneth C. Lindsay, *The Works of John Vanderlyn: From Tammany to the Capitol* (Binghamton: University Art Gallery, State University of New York, 1970), 96–102.

45. Eliza Robbins, *American Popular Lessons . . .* (New York, 1829), 206. For more information on nineteenth-century texts, see Ruth Miller Elson, *Guardians of Tradition: American Schoolbooks of the Nineteenth Century* (Lincoln: University of Nebraska Press, 1964).

46. *Putnam's Magazine*, January 1854, 118; and Henry Stuart, *William H. Powell's Historical Picture of the Discovery of the Mississipi by De Soto . . .* New York, 1854), 2.

47. Dawn Glanz, *How the West Was Drawn: American Art and the Settling of the Frontier* (Ann Arbor, Mich.: UMI Research Press, 1982), 1–25.

48. "Filling the Panels of the Capitol with National Pictures," *Literary World*, November 20, 1848, 385; Miller, *Patrons and Patriotism*, 66–84; and G. Kemble to M.C. Meigs, February 3, 1853, and other letters and clippings in the Archives of the Architect of the Capitol.

49. George H. Callcott, *History in the United States, 1800–1860: Its Practice and Purpose* (Baltimore, Md.: Johns Hopkins Press, 1970), 160–66, and Fred Somkin, *Unquiet Eagle: Memory and Desire in the Idea of American Freedom, 1815–1860* (Ithaca, N.Y.: Cornell University Press, 1967), 55–90.

50. For the diversity of scholarship on the subject, see Thomas P. Slaughter, "The Historian's Quest for Early American Culture(s)," *American Studies International* 24 (April 1986): 29–59.

51. R. Laurence Moore, "Religion, Secularization, and the Shaping of the Culture Industry in Antebellum America," *American Quarterly* 41 (June 1989): 216–37.

52. Fryd, *Art & Empire*, and Architect of the Capitol, *Art in the United States Capitol* (Washington, D.C.: U.S. Government Printing Office, 1978).

"Freedom's Holy Cause"

1. "The Spirit of the Age," *United States Catholic Magazine*, December 1845, 750.

2. "The Coming Age," *The Independent*, 16 January 1851, 10.

3. Lewis G. Clark, "Freedom's Holy Cause," *The Odd-Fellows' Offering, for 1851* (New York: Edward Walker, 1850), 292.

4. Clark, "Freedom's Holy Cause," 291–92.

5. "Popular Institutions," *Graham's Magazine*, March 1851, 189.

6. *The Spirit of Peace* was produced as part of a pair: its pendant is *The Spirit of War*, in the collections of the National Gallery of Art, Washington, D.C.

7. Michael Kammen, *A Season of Youth: The American Revolution and the Historical Imagination* (New York: Alfred A. Knopf, 1978), 49, 51. According to Kammen, the year 1832, which marked the centennial of George Washington's birth and the death of Charles Carroll, the last signer of the Declaration of Independence, was a watershed in America's sense of tradition and its relationship to the Revolutionary past.

8. Ernest R. Sandeen, "Millennialism," in Edwin S. Gaustad, ed., *The Rise of Adventism: Religion and Society in Mid-Nineteenth-Century America* (New York: Harper and Row, 1974), 116.

9. George H. Callcott, *History in the United States, 1800–1860: Its Practice and Purpose* (Baltimore, Md.: Johns Hopkins Press, 1970), 18.

10. James H. Moorhead, "Between Progress and Apocalypse: A Reassessment of Millennialism in American Religious Thought, 1800–1880," *Journal of American History* 71 (December 1984): 524–42.

11. "Editor's Department," *The Nineteenth Century* 2 (1848): 171.

12. David N. Lord, "Millennial State of the Church," *Theological and Literary Journal* 2 (April 1850): 657.

13. Albert Barnes, *The Casting Down of Thrones: A Discourse on the Present State of Europe Delivered in the First Presbyterian Church, Philadelphia, May 14, 1848* (Philadelphia: William Sloanaker, 1848), 3.

14. Durand took the subject of *God's Judgment upon Gog* from the first through the fourth verses of the thirty-ninth chapter of the Book of Ezekiel, which also serves as a type of the final battle of good and evil—of Gog and Magog—described in Revelations 20:8. The painting, not dated, was exhibited for the first time in April 1852.

15. John Durand, *The Life and Times of Asher B. Durand* (New York: Charles Scribner's Sons, 1894), 174.

16. *New York Times*, 30 November 1874, 5. The name "Jonathan Sturges" appears on a list dated 1843 of managers of the New York Association for Improving the Condition of the Poor, published in James Grant Wilson, ed., *Memorial History of the City of New-York and the Hudson River Valley*, vol. 3 (New York: New-York History Company, 1892), 436, and as vice president of the Whig Party for New York's Ward 3 on a list published in the *New York Tribune*, 9 April 1846, 2. For other biographical information, see Mary Cady [Mrs. Jonathan] Sturges, *Reminiscences of a Long Life* (New York: F. E. Parrish and Company, 1894).

17. Notebooks of Virginia Reed Osborn (née Sturges), New-York Historical Society.

18. John Greenleaf Whittier, "The Peace of Europe," *Littel's Living Age*, 13 March 1852, 522.

19. John Greenleaf Whittier to William Lloyd Garrison, May 1852, in *Letters of John Greenleaf Whittier*, ed. John B. Pickard (Cambridge, Mass.: The Belknap Press of Harvard University Press, 1975), 2: 191.

20. Harriet Beecher Stowe, *Uncle Tom's Cabin; or, Life Among the Lowly* (1852; reprint, Franklin Center, Pa.: The Franklin Library, 1984), 477–78. For a discussion of the relationship of the Fugitive Slave Law to apocalyptic language in Herman Melville's *Moby Dick*, see Carolyn L. Karcher, *Shadow over the Promised Land: Slavery, Race and Violence in Melville's America* (Baton Rouge: Louisiana State University Press, 1980), 78.

21. Sturges's address honoring William Cullen Bryant was published in Parke Godwin, *A Biography of William Cullen Bryant with Extracts from His Private Correspondences* (New York: Russell and Russell, 1883), 2:348.

22. See Ezek. 39:21–29.

23. "The Fine Arts. Exhibition of the National Academy of Design, No. III," *The Literary World*, 8 May 1852, 331.

24. Kammen, *Season of Youth*, 13.

25. *Address of the American Republican Association of Hamilton County, Published by Order of the Committee* (Cincinnati: n.p., 1845), 4.

26. On Bingham's political beliefs and for recent interpretations of *County Election*, see Barbara Groseclose, "The 'Missouri Artist' as Historian," in *George Caleb Bingham* (New York: Harry N. Abrams, 1990); Gail E. Husch, "George Caleb Bingham's 'The County Election': Whig Tribute to the Will of the People," *The American Art Journal* 19, 4 (1987): 4–22; Elizabeth Johns, *American Genre Painting: The Politics of Everyday Life* (New Haven, Conn., and London: Yale University Press, 1991); and Nancy Rash, *The Painting and Politics of George Caleb Bingham* (New Haven, Conn., and London: Yale University Press, 1991).

27. Elizabeth Johns also notes a timely relationship between the European revolutions and the theme of American democracy in Bingham's *County Election* in *American Genre Painting*, 94.

28. Johns, *American Genre Painting*, 93.

29. For discussions of this painting, see Francis S. Grubar, "Richard Caton Woodville: An American Artist, 1825 to 1855" (Ph.D. diss., The Johns Hopkins University, 1966), 135–42, and Johns, *American Genre Painting*, 108. Woodville offered a similar confrontation in his *War News from Mexico* of 1848.

30. An article in the *Bulletin of the American Art-Union*, June 1850, 46, identifies the portrait as that of the old man in his youth.

31. Johannsen, *To the Halls of the Montezumas*, 57.

32. "War and Its Conclusion," *The Home Journal*, 22 July 1848, 2.

33. Johannsen, *To the Halls of the Montezumas*, 283–84.

34. D. H. Barlow, "Mission of America," *Graham's Magazine*, January 1851, 48.

35. According to Kammen, this question was "the most constant refrain of these decades [1830s, 1840s, and 1850s], repeatedly invoked with reference to the Revolutionary tradition. . . . It recurs continuously in odes and orations . . . in the South as well as in the North." *Season of Youth*, 49.

36. "A New Feature in Our Plan," *Philadelphia Art Union Reporter* 1 (March/April 1851): 39.

37. Quoted from an explanatory pamphlet and key to the painting

prepared by the Philadelphia Art Union in June 1852 to accompany Rothermel's painting and its resultant print. The quotation is credited to and paraphrased from William Wirt's popular biography, *Sketches of the Life and Character of Patrick Henry*, first published in 1817; a ninth edition of Wirt's book appeared in 1845.

38. The identities of Rothermel's figures are taken from the Philadelphia Art Union key to the painting.

39. Two preliminary drawings in the collection of Red Hill, the Patrick Henry National Memorial in Brookneal, Virginia, illustrate the development of Rothermel's composition. One drawing, apparently the earlier of the two, uses a horizontal format which presents a more accurate picture of the House of Burgesses in Williamsburg than the final painting. This drawing is perhaps also related to an illustration of the same subject that appeared in Benson Lossing's popular book, *Seventeen Hundred and Seventy-Six; or, The War of Independence* (New York: Edward Walker, 1847). An obviously later and more complete drawing shows Rothermel's shift to a vertical format.

40. In notes he made for the painting, Rothermel marveled at Henry's height—"nearly *6 feet*"—and observed that the "text [probably William Wirts's standard account] does not justify putting upon him a cloak," a distinguished article of clothing for lawyers and statesmen. See notes in collection of Red Hill, Patrick Henry National Memorial. In fact, Henry did not own a bright red cloak like the one he wears in Rothermel's painting until he became the American governor of Virginia in 1776. Information concerning Henry's characteristic dress comes from Mark Couvillon at Red Hill.

41. Rothermel was married in a Presbyterian church in Philadelphia on 27 May 1844, according to his marriage certificate in the Rothermel Papers, Archives of American Art. This is not to claim a direct connection between Rothermel's painting and Barnes's sermon, but rather to acknowledge that they are almost contemporary products of a similar social and religious milieu.

42. Barnes, *Casting Down of Thrones*, 4–5, 24, 21, 10–11.

43. Mark E. Thistlethwaite, "Peter F. Rothermel: A Forgotten History Painter," *Antiques*, November 1983, 1019. Thistlethwaite also cites Rubens' *Mystical Marriage of St. Catherine* and Washington Allston's *Belshazzar's Feast* as other possible influences.

44. "The Academy of the Fine Arts," *Graham's Magazine*, March 1851, 269.

45. Ibid.

46. Letter from Vincent Colyer published in the *New York Times*, 18 November 1851, 2, and in the *Bulletin of the American Art-Union* 4 (December 1851): 149.

47. Groseclose, "Washington Crossing the Delaware: The Political Context," *The American Art Journal* 7 (November 1975): 70–78, 75.

48. Arthur S. Marks, "The Statue of King George III in New York and the Iconology of Regicide," *The American Art Journal* 13 (Summer 1981): 78–81. Walcutt produced an earlier version of this painting in 1854.

49. "The Philadelphia Art-Union," *Graham's Magazine*, March 1852, 326.

50. Barnes, *Casting Down of Thrones*.

51. "The Philadelphia Art Union," 326.

52. Nicholas B. Wainwright, "Joseph Harrison, Jr., A Forgotten Art Collector," *Antiques*, October 1972, 660.

53. Joseph Harrison, Jr., to Henry Harrison, 30 January 1849, Harrison Letterbooks, vol. 1, Historical Society of Pennsylvania.

Historic Reportage and Artistic License

1. James Goodwyn Clonney painted a similar picture, *Mexican News*, in 1847, a year before Woodville's image; it is now in the collections of the Munson-Williams-Proctor Institute, Utica, N.Y. See Wayne Craven and Richard Martin, *Two Hundred Years of American Art: The Munson-Williams-Proctor Institute* (Seattle: University of Washington Press, 1986).

2. Martha A. Sandweiss, Rick Stewart, and Ben W. Huseman, *Eyewitness to War: Prints and Daguerreotypes of the Mexican War, 1846–1848* (Washington, D.C.: Smithsonian Institution Press and Amon Carter Museum, 1989), 16–17.

3. Michael Twyman, *Lithography, 1800–1850: The Techniques of Drawing on Stone in England and France and Their Application in Works of Topography* (London: Oxford University Press, 1970), 3–57.

4. Harry T. Peters, *Currier & Ives, Printmakers to the American People* (Garden City: Doubleday, Doran & Co., Inc., 1942), and Sandweiss et al., *Eyewitness to War*, 19.

5. Sandweiss et al., *Eyewitness to War*, 17. Following a clash on April 25, General Taylor wrote President Polk that "hostilities may now be considered as commenced." See K. Jack Bauer, *The Mexican War, 1846–1848* (New York: Macmillan Publishing Co., Inc., 1974), 48, 66–69. For examples of these prints, see Donald H. Mugridge and Helen F. Conover, *An Album of American Battle Art, 1755–1918* (1947; reprint, New York: Da Capo Press, 1972), 127–63.

6. Ronnie C. Tyler, *The Mexican War: A Lithographic Record* (Austin: Texas State Historical Association, 1973), 2, 6–12.

7. Henry Clay to H. R. Robinson, Ashland, Ky., December 24, 1847, Document S-517/C578, Beinecke Rare Book and Manuscript Library, Yale University, New Haven, Conn. Clay's letter was published in the *Daily National Intelligencer* (Washington, D.C.), January 28, 1848.

8. *The American Flag*, August 14, 1846, 1; Sandweiss et al., *Eyewitness to War*, 115–21, contains the count. See also New Orleans *Bee*, August 6–7, 1847, 1: 3; New Orleans *Picayune*, July 6, 1847, 2: 2, August 3, 1847, 2: 4, and September 7, 1847, 2: 1 and 3: 1; and *Daily National Intelligencer*, September 17, 1847, 3: 2 and September 27, 1847, 3: 3, 5. Brown's painting of Taylor and his officers is now in the collections of the National Portrait Gallery, Smithsonian Institution.

9. Sandweiss et al., *Eyewitness to War*, 10–12, 105–9. See also Thomas Bangs Thorpe, *"Our Army" on the Rio Grande* (Philadelphia: Carey and Hart, 1846), and William Seaton Henry, *Campaign Sketches of the War with Mexico* (New York: Harper and Brothers, 1847). Most of the best-known prints of the Mexican War were initially paintings, though some were sketches drawn in the field.

10. *Niles' National Register*, quoted in Sandweiss et al., *Eyewitness to War*, 101; Napoleon J. T. Dana to his wife, February 16, 1847, Archives of the U.S. Military Academy, West Point, N.Y., quoted in ibid., 102.

11. Ibid., 102.

12. Quoted in ibid., 122.

13. Quoted in ibid., 30–31.

14. Ibid., 10, 158.

15. Ibid., 14, 19, 31–32, 267–68, 271–74, 275, 279–91; K. Jack Bauer, *Surfboats and Horse Marines: U.S. Naval Operations in the Mexican War, 1846–48* (Annapolis, Md.: United States Naval Institute, 1969), 83–122; Nicholas B. Wainwright, *Philadelphia in the Romantic Age of Lithography: An Illustrated History of Early Lithography in Philadelphia with a Descriptive List of Philadelphia Scenes Made by Philadelphia Lithographers before 1866* (Philadelphia: The Historical Society of Pennsylvania, 1958), 30–45, 61–74.

16. Audrey Gardner Wright, "Henry Walke, 1809–1896: 'Romantic Painter, and Naval Hero'" (M. A. thesis, George Washington University, 1971), 3, 10, 41; Sandweiss et al., *Eyewitness to War*, 31–32.

17. Sandweiss et al., *Eyewitness to War*, 271–74. For an assessment of the accuracy of Walke's prints, see Samuel Eliot Morison, *"Old Bruin": Commodore Matthew C. Perry, 1794–1858* (Boston: Atlantic Monthly Press, 1967), 209, 215, 217, 219, 226–27, 230–36.

18. Phillips is usually listed as the author/artist of the portfolio, although Alfred Rider is also given credit on the title page. The portfolio was issued in two editions—deluxe, in half morocco portfolio with colored lithographs on thick cards, and regular, with smaller, uncolored plates. See R. V. Tooley, *English Books with Coloured Plates, 1790 to 1860: A Bibliographical Account of the Most Important Books Illustrated by English Artists in Colour Aquatint and Colour Lithography* (London: B. T. Batsford Ltd., 1987), 296; Sandweiss et al., *Eyewitness to War*, 301.

19. See Carl Nebel, *Voyage pittoresque et archéologique dans la partie la plus interessante du Mexique* (Paris: M. Moench and M. Gau, 1836). A Spanish-language edition was issued in 1840.

20. Sandweiss et al., *Eyewitness to War*, 111.

21. Ibid., 130, 323–25. Despite the fact that the soldiers in *Pass in the Sierra Madre* appear to be Mexican, the flag in the Amon Carter Museum version of the view is red, white, and blue. See also ibid., 302, which relates the story of a Mexican captured in the act of making a

"taking a draft of our encampment." Suspected of being a spy, the prisoner turned out to be an artist who was impressed with "the form of our encampment."

22. Marian R. McNaughton, "James Walker—Combat Artist of Two American Wars," *Military Collector & Historian* 9 (Summer 1957): 31–32. See also Nebel, *Voyage pittoresque*, and [John James Peck], *The Sign of the Eagle: A View of Mexico—1836 to 1855*, ed. Richard F. Pourade (San Diego, Calif.: A Copley Book, 1970), 165.

23. *Daily American Star* (Mexico City), October 26 [25?], 1847, 1: 4, 2: 1. This perspective was the one that Walker used when he was commissioned to paint the battle for the House Military Committee Room in the Capitol in 1857; the painting now hangs above the railing of the Senate staircase. See also McNaughton, "James Walker," 31–35; *Army & Navy Journal* 18, 21 (December 25, 1880): 411; 18, 32 (March 12, 1881): 657; Architect of the Capitol, *Art in the United States Capitol* (Washington, D.C.: U.S. Government Printing Office, 1978), 146.

24. *North American*, November 30, 1847, 3: 2; "C.C." reported in the New Orleans *Picayune*, December 7, 1847, 1: 7, that the view is "exceedingly correct."

25. Fayette Copeland, *Kendall of the Picayune* (Norman: University of Oklahoma Press, 1943), 84, 170, 188–89. Some have theorized that Nebel returned to Europe after publication of his *Voyage pittoresque* and remained there until Kendall found him and employed him to do the pictures for his portfolio. However, he was in Mexico in 1840, when he went on a photographic expedition with Fanny Calderón de la Barca. See her *Life in Mexico: The Letters of Fanny Calderón de la Barca*, ed. and annotated by Howard T. Fisher and Marion Hall Fisher (Garden City, N.Y.: Doubleday & Company, Inc., Anchor Books, 1970), 357. Nebel was in Mexico again in 1847, when he was spotted on the street. See James Duncan to George Wilkins Kendall, Mexico City, November 22, 1847, in George Wilkins Kendall Papers, Special Collections Division, University of Texas at Arlington Library, Arlington, Tex.

26. New York *Herald*, December 23, 1850; *New Orleans Picayune* (New Orleans), June 4, 1851.

27. George Wilkins Kendall, *The War between the United States and Mexico Illustrated* (New York: D. Appleton and Company, 1851), [iii]; New York *Herald*, December 23, 1850; Sandweiss et al., *Eyewitness to War*, 109.

28. *Daily American Star* (Mexico City), November 25, 1847, 2: 4. Mexican lithographers P. Guerleti and Manuel Murguía advertised their panorama of Mexico in the *Daily American Star*, May 25, 1848, 2: 4, hoping that Americans would buy it as a souvenir. One Mexican lithographer even made a print showing American soldiers buying items in the market. See Eugenia Meyer, coordinadora, *Museo nacional de las intervenciones, 1829–1917* (Mexico: Ex Convento de Churubusco, Instituto Nacional de Antropología e Historia, 1981), 63.

29. New Orleans *Picayune*, quoted in Sandweiss et al., *Eyewitness to War*, 122.

30. See Tyler, *Mexican War*, 12–20, 80, 84; Morison, *"Old Bruin"*, 209, 215, 217, 219, 226–27, 230–36; and Robert W. Johannsen, *To the Halls of the Montezumas: The Mexican War in the American Imagination* (New York and Oxford: Oxford University Press, 1985), 223–28.

31. *North American*, December 3, 1847, 2: 1.

32. Captain George T. M. Davis (aide-de-camp to Quitman), quoted in Sandweiss et al., *Eyewitness to War*, 333, 334.

33. Ibid., 334.

34. Ibid., 159.

35. W. M. Albin to George B. Claver, Matamoros, Mexico, January 15, 1846, document S-987/A113, Beinecke Rare Book and Manuscript Library, Yale University; *The Picket Guard* (Saltillo), May 3, 1847, 4: 2.

36. There are, of course, prints of the war that depict the Mexican point of view. Six such images are included in a portfolio published by Julio Michaud y Thomas, *Album Pintoresco de la Republica Méxicana* (ca. 1850). Most probably were copied from European or American sources and produced by French artists and lithographers. See Sandweiss et al., *Eyewitness to War*, 127, 149, 297, 315, 334, 341–43.

37. Kendall, *War between the United States and Mexico*, [iii].

38. Albert Boime, *The Magisterial Gaze: Manifest Destiny and American Landscape Painting c. 1830–1865* (Washington, D.C.: Smithsonian Institution Press, 1991).

39. Leutze is quoted in William H. Truettner, ed., *The West as America: Reinterpreting Images of the Frontier, 1820–1920* (Washington, D.C.: Smithsonian Institution Press for the National Museum of American Art, 1991), 62.

40. William H. Prescott, *The History of the Conquest of Mexico*, abridged and ed. by C. Harvey Gardiner (Chicago: University of Chicago Press, 1966), 369.

41. Truettner, ed., *West as America*, 61–62.

42. Ibid., 59–63, discusses various aspects of this painting. Samuel Y. Edgerton, Jr., offered additional observations in a letter to the editor of the *New York Times*, June 16, 1991.

43. Elizabeth Johns, *American Genre Painting: The Politics of Everyday Life* (New Haven, Conn., and London: Yale University Press, 1991), 180, discusses both Woodville paintings. See also Brian Wolf, "All the World's a Code: Art and Ideology in Nineteenth-Century American Painting," *Art Journal* 44, 4 (Winter 1984): 330–33.

Painting the Civil War as History, 1861–1910

1. Other key nineteenth-century illustrated histories of the war include Evert A. Duyckinck, *National History of the War for the Union* (New York: Johnson, Fry & Company, 1861–65); Harper & Brothers, *Harper's Pictorial History of the Great Rebellion* (New York, Harper & Brothers, 1866); Edwin Forbes, *Life Studies of the Great Army* (New York: E. Forbes, 1876); Benson John Lossing, *The Pictorial Field Book of the Civil War in the United States of America*, 3 vols. (New Haven, Conn.: George S. Lester, 1878–80); and Rossiter Johnson, *Campfire and Battlefield: An Illustrated History of the Campaigns and Conflicts of the Great Civil War* (New York: Bryan, Taylor & Co., 1896). Two monumental photographic histories of the war were published in the early years of the twentieth century to commemorate the fiftieth anniversary of the war's beginning: Francis Trevelyan Miller, ed., *The Photographic History of the Civil War*, 10 vols. (New York: Review of Reviews, 1911); and Benson John Lossing, *Mathew Brady's Illustrated History of the Civil War, 1861–65* (New York: The War Memorial Association, 1912).

2. Among the illustrators of *Battles and Leaders* were many of the artist-reporters who had worked for the illustrated newspapers during the war—Winslow Homer, Theodore Russell Davis, Edwin Forbes, and the Waud brothers, Alfred and William. The works of such Confederate soldier-artists as Allen C. Redwood, William Ludwell Sheppard, and John Adams Elder appear, as do representatives of a younger generation of painters and illustrators—Bror Thure de Thulstrup, William Gilbert Gaul, Julian Scott, William Brooke Thomas Trego, Xanthus R. Smith, James Earl Taylor, and Edwin J. Meeker. There are also a few surprises in the roster of illustrators for *Battles and Leaders*; the presence of works by Otto Henry Bacher, Edward Lamson Henry, William Morris Hunt, William Langston Lathrop, Thomas Moran, Joseph Pennell, and Irving Ramsey Wiles indicates that the editors of *The Century* sought a uniformly high level of artistic talent.

3. Lossing, *Pictorial Field Book*, 3.

4. According to Edwin B. Coddington, "To lead up to and complement the big scene of Pickett's charge, Rothermel painted five smaller pictures which show other memorable but less decisive episodes during the three days of battle." See his *Rothermel's Paintings of the Battle of Gettysburg*, reprint from *Pennsylvania History, Quarterly Journal of the Pennsylvania Historical Association* 27, 1 (January 1960): 1. The full set of Rothermel's Gettysburg paintings is illustrated in color in Champ Clark and the editors of Time-Life Books, *Gettysburg: The Confederate High Tide* (Alexandria, Va.: Time-Life Books, 1985), 88–97.

5. Among the most familiar of these are William Wehner and the American Panorama Company of Milwaukee's *Cyclorama of the Battle of Atlanta*, begun in 1883 (now owned by the City of Atlanta and exhibited in its own building in Grant Park), and Paul Dominique Philippoteaux's *Cyclorama of the Battle of Gettysburg* (1883), on permanent view at Gettysburg National Military Park. Both of these works toured the country upon their completion, as did a now-lost *Cyclorama of the Battles of Vicksburg* (ca. 1886), painted by Joseph Bertrand and Lucien Sergent.

6. Coddington, *Rothermel's Paintings*, 6. Even then, the artist had to select from the often conflicting testimonies of the participants and, Coddington has noted, "took advantage of the opening and chose the

version best suited to his purpose" (14).

7. The Rev. P. C. Croll, "Peter F. Rothermel," *The Pennsylvania-German* 5, 3 (July 1904): 106.

8. Coddington, *Rothermel's Paintings*, 17.

9. Mark Thistlethwaite, "The Most Important Themes: History Painting and Its Place in American Art," in William H. Gerdts and Mark Thistlethwaite, *Grand Illusions: History Painting in America* (Fort Worth, Tex: Amon Carter Museum, 1988), 48. According to Thistlethwaite, while "the painting awes the viewer with its overwhelming quantity of persons and details, [it] fails to convey effectively any quality of high-minded purpose or value. Rothermel's elephantine canvas completely eschews idealism for realism; inspired fiction gives way to herculean reportage."

10. William A. Frassanito, *Gettysburg: A Journey in Time* (New York: Charles Scribner's Sons, 1975), 186–92. This title for the photograph appears in Alexander Gardner, *Gardner's Photographic Sketch Book of the Civil War* (1866; reprint, New York: Dover Publications, Inc., 1959), plate 41. Gardner's caption for the plate continued, "Some mother may yet be patiently watching for the return of her boy, whose bones lie bleaching, unrecognized and alone, between the rocks at Gettysburg."

11. Bingham painted a second version of *Order No. 11* between 1869 and 1870 in order to promote an engraving of the first version then being worked on by John Sartain in Philadelphia. This later painting is now in the collections of the State Historical Society of Missouri in Columbia. Ewing was Sherman's brother-in-law as well as commander of the federal forces in Missouri.

12. Nancy Rash, *The Painting and Politics of George Caleb Bingham* (New Haven, Conn., and London: Yale University Press, 1991), 184–215. For a popular and immensely readable version of the events leading up to and following the painting's execution, see Lew Larkin, *Bingham: Fighting Artist* (Kansas City, Mo.: Burton Publishing Company, Inc., 1954). Masaccio's *Explusion of Adam and Eve* is in the Brancacci Chapel in Florence.

13. George Caleb Bingham, *An Address to the Public Vindicating a Work of Art Illustrative of the Federal Military Policy in Missouri during the Late Civil War* (Kansas City, 1871), 5, quoted in Rash, *Painting and Politics*, 202–3.

14. Bruce W. Chambers, *The World of David Gilmour Blythe (1815–1865)* (Washington, D.C.: Smithsonian Institution Press for the National Collection of Fine Arts, 1980), 75.

15. Beard enlisted in the Union Army at the outbreak of the war and served for a time in the corps of General Lew Wallace (later of Ben Hur fame), attaining the rank of captain. See John Howard Brown, ed., *Lamb's Biographical Dictionary of the United States* (Boston: James H. Lamb Company, 1900), 1: 237–38. Blythe may also have accompanied Union troops as far south as Chattanooga in 1863. See Chambers, *World of Blythe*, 98.

16. Chambers, *World of Blythe*, 95–97. Milo Naeve of the Art Institute of Chicago noted the connection to Wise in his typescript, "'Old Virginia Home': David Gilmour Blythe's Allegory on Manumission and the Union."

17. Hope's monumental 5½-by-12-foot version of this work is now in the collection of the Antietam National Battlefield. Captain of the Second Vermont Volunteers, Hope had already had nineteen years' experience as a painter before he enlisted in the Union cause in June 1861. During his year and a half of service (he was discharged for medical reasons in December 1862), he fought at both battles of Bull Run, at Fredericksburg, and at Antietam. This painting was one of a series of five Hope painted of the battle.

18. George Inness's *Peace and Plenty* shows a landscape after the storm; painted in 1865, it declared the Union's return to peace and prosperity.

19. Holmes as quoted in Arlene Jacobowitz, *James Hamilton, 1819–1878: American Marine Painter* (Brooklyn, N.Y.: The Brooklyn Museum, 1966), 49.

20. Bruce W. Chambers, "The Southern Artist and the Civil War," *The Southern Quarterly* 24, 1–2 (Fall–Winter 1985): 89–90.

21. Among Chapman's colleagues in this duty was the painter John Ross Key, whose *Bombardment of Fort Sumter* (1863) was long misrepresented as a work by Albert Bierstadt. According to Alfred Harrison, Key's biographer, Key and Chapman visited the ruins of Fort Sumter together on December 7, 1863 (telephone conversation with the author, April 13, 1985). Chapman's father honored his close friend Governor Wise in naming his son.

22. For an expanded discussion of this and other of Chapman's Sumter paintings, see Chambers, "Southern Artist," 85–88, 90–91.

23. Mark E. Neely, Jr., Harold Holzer, and Gabor S. Boritt, *The Confederate Image: Prints of the Lost Cause* (Chapel Hill and London: University of North Carolina Press, 1987), ix–xii.

24. Henry T. Tuckerman, *Book of the Artists: American Artist Life* (New York: Putnam, 1867), 543.

25. This description appears in a pamphlet issued by the Chicago Opera House Association on the occasion of its exhibition of *Recognition* in June 1866 (Chicago: Chicago Opera House Association, 1866). Born in France between 1829 and 1832, Mayer studied at Ecole des Beaux-Arts and with Léon Cogniet before emigrating to the United States in 1857 and setting up a studio in New York City. In 1866, he won admission to the National Academy of Design as an associate member. Despite his new status as an American citizen, Mayer continued to travel to Paris regularly, exhibiting frequently at the Salon after 1865 and being elected Chevalier of the Legion of Honor in 1869. In 1895 he returned permanently to France and died in Paris in 1911.

26. William H. Gerdts, "On Elevated Heights: American Historical Painting and Its Critics," in Gerdts and Thistlethwaite, *Grand Illusions*, 106.

27. Quoted in Marc Simpson, *Winslow Homer Paintings of the Civil War* (San Francisco: The Fine Arts Museums of San Francisco, with Bedford Arts, Publishers, 1988), 242. Simpson acknowledges the assistance of Alfred Harrison, Jr., in locating this review.

28. Among those who reported on the horrors of the prison were two soldier-artists who had been imprisoned at Andersonville—the Pittsburgh painter Capt. John Donaghy of the 103rd Pennsylvania Volunteers, who had escaped in April 1864, and the New York illustrator and topographical engineer Robert K. Sneden of the 40th New York Regiment, whose view of the prison was published in *Leslie's* in April 1865.

29. Simpson, *Winslow Homer*, 244.

30. Thistlethwaite, "The Most Important Themes," 49.

31. For more information on the role of the artist-reporter during the war, see W. Fletcher Thompson, Jr., *The Image of War: The Pictorial Reporting of the American Civil War* (New York and London: Thomas Yoseloff, 1960).

32. For Scott's biography, I have used John Howard Brown, ed., *Lamb's Biographical Dictionary of the United States* (Boston: Federal Book Company of Boston, 1903), 6: 655; James E. Tracy, "Memoirs of a Famous Vermont Artist," *Vermonter*, n.s., 11 (1906): 155; and Robert J. Titterton, "A Soldier's Sketchbook," *Civil War Times Illustrated*, September–October 1991, 54–57, 59–60. Titterton also curated an exhibition of Scott's work at the Dibden Gallery of Johnson State College in Vermont in 1989.

33. Titterton, "Soldier's Sketchbook," 56–57.

34. Bvt. Maj.-Gen. Martin T. McMahon, "The Death of General John Sedgwick," in *Battles and Leaders of the Civil War*, ed. Robert Underwood Johnson and Clarence Clough Buel (New York: The Century Company, 1888), 4: 175.

35. It is generally acknowledged today that the Spanish-American War of 1898 marked another turning point, insofar as it was the first time since the Mexican War of 1848 that both northern- and southern-born troops fought together against a common enemy, thereby healing a lot of old wounds.

36. Robert W. Chambers, "Special Messenger," *Harper's New Monthly Magazine*, February 1905, 344–53; the illustration based on Pyle's painting appears on 345.

37. Thistlethwaite used this term in reference to a similar work by Edwin Blashfield. See "Most Important Themes," 54. See also William C. Brownell, "The Younger Painters of America. Second Paper," *Scribner's Monthly*, July 1880, 326.

Picturing Lincoln

1. Robert N. Bellah, Richard Madsen, William M. Sullivan, Ann Swi-

dler, and Steven M. Tipton, *Habits of the Heart* (New York: Harper and Row, 1985), 152–55.

2. Cited in Mark Thistlethwaite, "The Most Important Themes: History Painting and Its Place in American Art," in William H. Gerdts and Mark Thistlethwaite, *Grand Illusions: History Painting in America* (Fort Worth, Tex.: Amon Carter Museum, 1988), 14.

3. Idealism and frequent deviation from historical records in grand-style paintings of Lincoln distinguish them from other mid-nineteenth-century works, most of which conformed strictly to the realist canon. For details, see Mark Thistlethwaite, *The Image of George Washington: Studies in Mid-Nineteenth-Century American History Painting* (New York and London: Garland Publishing, Inc., 1979), 1–39.

4. Stephen B. Oates, *Lincoln: The Man behind the Myths* (New York: Harper and Row, 1984), 17.

5. Stephen B. Oates, *With Malice toward None* (New York: Harper and Row, 1977), 436.

6. *New-York Tribune*, April 19, 1865, 4; George W. Briggs, *Eulogy on Abraham Lincoln* (Salem, Mass., 1865), 28; George Templeton Strong, *Diary of George Templeton Strong*, ed. Allen Nevins and Milton H. Thomas (1865; reprint, New York: Macmillan, 1952), 3:580.

7. Quoted by Don E. Fehrenbacher, *Lincoln in Text and Context* (Stanford, Calif.: Stanford University Press, 1987), 175.

8. *Illinois State Journal*, September 24, 1862, 1.

9. In still another (allegorical) depiction titled *Emancipation Proclamation* (1863), A. A. Lamb showed Lincoln on horseback waving his great document beside America's "Emancipation Chariot."

10. Francis Bicknell Carpenter, *Six Months at the White House* (New York: Hurd and Houghton, 1867), 11.

11. Ibid., 26.

12. Thistlethwaite, "The Most Important Themes," 20.

13. Chappel's depiction of the physical setting and the cabinet members' proximity to the president bears no relation to Carpenter's, which is based on Lincoln's own recollection. See Carpenter, *Six Months at the White House*, 28.

14. The legal basis of emancipation is detailed in William Whiting's *War Powers of the President* and Joseph Story's *Commentary on the Constitution*, which lay on the floor nearest Attorney General Edward Bates. In *Six Months at the White House*, Carpenter explained his decision to include the *New-York Tribune* and the Story and Whiting books as accessories; see 152, 353. He did not discuss the inclusion of Simon Cameron's portrait, but he applauded Cameron's radicalism and character (136–38, 253). On the other hand, Carpenter never mentioned Andrew Jackson, whose location in his painting is interpretable only in terms of Jackson's presidential policies and political attitudes.

15. David Kertzer, *Ritual, Politics, and Power* (New Haven, Conn.: Yale University Press, 1988), 72, 76.

16. *Reception at the White House* (1864), attributed to Carpenter, shows Lincoln playing the same symbolic role. In one of the Civil War era's best portrayals of the hyperbole of power, Lincoln ritually affirms himself as leading representative of the nation's political elite.

17. On the linkage between national crisis, collective arousal, mourning, and deification, see Emile Durkheim, *The Elementary Forms of the Religious Life* (1912; reprint, New York: The Free Press, 1965), 235–72, 434–61.

18. The details of this meeting are described in Admiral Porter's diary.

19. William T. Sherman, *Memoirs of General William T. Sherman* (1875; reprint, Bloomington: Indiana University Press, 1957), 322–80. See especially 328–31.

20. John G. Nicolay and John Hay, *Abraham Lincoln: A History* (New York: The Century Company, 1890), 10:218.

21. *Boston Journal* reprinted in *Littell's Living Age* (Boston), April 22, 1865, 138.

22. In contrast, Thomas Nast's illustration of *Lincoln Entering Richmond* (1868) may have underestimated the number of white people welcoming him.

23. *New York Times*, April 8, 1865, 1.

24. Barry Schwartz, "Mourning and the Making of a Sacred Symbol: Durkheim and the Lincoln Assassination," *Social Forces* 70 (December 1991): 343–66.

25. Durkheim, *Elementary Forms of the Religious Life*, 445.

26. Gideon Welles, *Diary of Gideon Welles* (Boston: Houghton Mifflin Co., 1909), 2:285–86.

27. No other Lincoln deathbed scene contains so many figures. John H. Littlefield's *The Death of Lincoln*, depicting twenty-four visitors, ranks second on this score behind the Bachelder/Chappel view.

28. Andrew Johnson was sworn into office later in the day by the new U.S. Chief Justice Salmon P. Chase.

29. Barry Schwartz, "The Reconstruction of Abraham Lincoln, 1900–1920" in *Collective Remembering*, ed. David Middleton and Derek Edwards (London: Sage, 1990), 81–107.

30. Henry Steele Commager, *The American Mind* (New Haven, Conn.: Yale University Press, 1950), 41; Richard Hofstadter, ed., *The Progressive Movement* (Englewood Cliffs, N.J.: Prentice-Hall, 1963), 15, 36.

31. Patricia Hills, *Eastman Johnson* (New York: Clarkson N. Potter, 1972 in association with The Whitney Museum of American Art), 50.

32. Pyle prepared his illustration for William H. Crooks's "Lincoln's Last Day," *Harper's Monthly*, September 1907, 519–30.

33. In March 1864, six years after this debate, the conflict over race came to a head as Charleston's confederate sympathizers confronted unionists in one of the war's bloodiest riots.

34. Abraham Lincoln, "Fourth Debate," in *The Collected Works of Abraham Lincoln*, ed. Roy Basler (New Brunswick, N.J.: Rutgers University Press, 1953), 3:145–46.

35. For a clearer example of the genrification of Lincoln's image, see Harvey Dunn's *Lincoln-Douglas Debate* (1929).

36. Marvin Meyers, *The Jacksonian Persuasion* (New York: Vintage, 1960); Alexis de Tocqueville, *Democracy in America*, vol. 2 (New York: Alfred A. Knopf, 1946); Daniel Walker Howe, *The Political Culture of the American Whigs* (Chicago: University of Chicago Press, 1979); Richard Ellis and Aaron Wildavsky, *Dilemmas of Presidential Leadership: From Washington through Lincoln* (New Brunswick, N.J.: Transaction, 1989).

Paintings for the People

1. For a discussion of the Centennial and its display of art, see Lillian Miller, "Engines, Marbles and Canvases, The Centennial Exposition of 1876," *Indiana Historical Society. Lectures 1972–1973* (Indianapolis: Indiana Historical Society, 1973), 3–29.

2. See Richard Guy Wilson, "Presence of the Past," in *The American Renaissance: 1876–1917*, ed. Richard Guy Wilson, Dianne H. Pilgrim, and Richard N. Murray (Brooklyn, N.Y.: Brooklyn Museum, 1976), 39–55.

3. Edward King, "In the Good Old Colony Times," *The Monthly Illustrator*, May 1895, 135.

4. "Historical Art in the United States," *Appleton's Journal of Popular Literature, Science and Art*, April 10, 1869, 45–46, quoted in William H. Gerdts, "On Elevated Heights: American Historical Painting and its Critics," in William H. Gerdts and Mark Thistlethwaite, *Grand Illusions: History Painting in America* (Fort Worth, Tex.: Amon Carter Museum, 1988), 110.

5. S.N.C., *The Art Journal*, American ed., 2, 21 (September 1876): 284.

6. For an overview of the history of nineteenth-century criticism in relation to history painting, see Gerdts, "On Elevated Heights," 61–123.

7. For discussions of this work, see Ann Uhry Abrams's essay in this book and Jules David Prown, "John Trumbull as a History Painter," in Helen A. Cooper, *John Trumbull: The Hand and Spirit of a Painter* (New Haven, Conn., and London: Yale University Art Gallery, 1982), 76–81.

8. On Ferris, see Barbara J. Mitnick, "Jean Leon Gerome Ferris: America's Painter Historian" (Ph.D. diss., Rutgers: The State University of New Jersey, 1983).

9. A major example is John Marshall, *Life of George Washington* (Philadelphia: C. P. Wayne, 1804–1807). Marshall, the first authorized biographer of Washington, clearly maintained an iconic view of the leader.

10. Quoted in Henry T. Tuckerman, *Book of the Artists: American*

Artist Life (New York: G.P. Putnam & Son, 1867), 14.

11. For a recent study of American early nineteenth-century patronage and collecting, see Wayne Craven, "Patronage and Collecting in America, 1800–1835," in *Mr. Luman Reed's Picture Gallery: A Pioneer Collection of American Art* (New York: Harry N. Abrams with the New-York Historical Society, 1990), 11–18. On West, see Allen Staley and Helmut von Erffa, *The Paintings of Benjamin West* (New Haven, Conn.: Yale University Press, 1986); Dorinda Evans, *Benjamin West and His American Students* (Washington, D.C.: Smithsonian Institution Press, 1980) and Ann Uhry Abrams, *The Valiant Hero: Benjamin West and Grand-Style History Painting* (Washington, D.C.: Smithsonian Institution Press, 1985). On Copley, see Jules David Prown, *John Singleton Copley, 1738–1815*, 2 vols. (Cambridge, Mass.: Harvard University Press for the National Gallery of Art, 1966).

12. See Mark E. Thistlethwaite, *The Image of George Washington: Studies in Mid-Nineteenth Century American History Painting* (New York and London: Garland Publishing, Inc., 1979) for a study of the effect of Jacksonian democracy on the development of humanistic images of Washington. On Jackson and his presidency, see Robert Remini, *Andrew Jackson and the Course of the American Empire* (New York: Harper & Row, [1977]).

13. See Herman Warner Williams, Jr., *Mirror to the American Past: A Survey of American Genre Painting, 1750–1900* (Greenwich, Conn.: New York Graphic Society, 1973).

14. *National Academy of Design Record 1826–1860* (New York: New-York Historical Society, 1943), 2:19, no. 218. Matteson's *Spirit of 1776* has recently been rediscovered in a private collection.

15. For visual references to the domestication of the image of Washington, see Margaret Brown Klapthor and Howard Alexander Morrison, *G. Washington; A Figure upon the Stage* (Washington, D.C.: National Museum of American History, 1982), 62–69. Mount Vernon's restoration began in 1858 when Ann Pamela Cunningham chartered the Mount Vernon Ladies' Association to raise money for the project.

16. See, for example, Marshall, *Life of George Washington*, 2:52, and Aaron Bancroft, *An Essay on the Life of George Washington* (Worcester, Mass.: Thomas and Sturvetant, 1807), 38.

17. Examples of exhibited history paintings include Robert W. Weir, *The Landing of Hendrick Hudson* (1835); Emanuel Leutze, *The Return of Columbus in Chains to Cadiz* (1843); and Tompkins H. Matteson, *The First Sabbath of the Pilgrims* (1847). See *National Academy of Design Record* 2:191, no. 223; 1:293, no. 100; 2:19, no. 142. On the Knoedler lithograph and other images of Washington, see Barbara J. Mitnick, *The Changing Image of George Washington* (New York: Fraunces Tavern Museum, 1989).

18. *National Academy of Design Record*, 2:139, no. 348.

19. Horatio Hastings Weld, *The Life of George Washington* (Philadelphia: Lindsay & Blakiston, 1845), 146, quoted in Thistlethwaite, *The Image of George Washington*, 146 n. 19. Aaron Bancroft made a similar observation about Washington's agricultural activity in *An Essay on the Life of George Washington*, reiterated but not expanded upon in his *Life of George Washington* (Boston: T. H. Carter & Co., 1833).

20. See Barbara Groseclose, *Emanuel Leutze, 1816–1868: Freedom Is the Only King* (Washington, D.C.: Smithsonian Institution Press, 1976), 83, 34–37. See also *Literary World* 10 (November 1, 1851): 525, quoted in Groseclose, *Emanuel Leutze*, 40.

21. Willard Rouse Jillson, *The Mayflower Compact: Bright Torch of Liberty and Freedom* (Frankfort, Ky.: Roberts Printing Company, 1966), 13.

22. On Darley, see Christine Anne Hahler, introduction in *"...illustrated by Darley"* (Wilmington: Delaware Art Museum, 1978). On Chappel, see Barbara J. Mitnick and David Meschutt, *The Portraits and History Paintings of Alonzo Chappel* (Chadds Ford, Pa.: Brandywine River Museum, 1992).

23. For information on the kinds of historical paintings Chappel saw in New York early in his career, see Barbara J. Mitnick, "The History Paintings," in *Portraits and History Paintings of Alonzo Chappel*, 41–44.

24. See Mitnick, "History Paintings," 44.

25. John Frederick Schroeder, *Life and Times of Washington*, 2 vols. (New York: Johnson, Fry, and Company, 1857). Chappel also illustrated several other sets of historical books.

26. Schroeder, *Life and Times of Washington*, 2:291. Earlier biogra-

phers who mentioned the moving embrace include John Marshall, *Life of George Washington*, 4:106; Jared Sparks, *The Life of Washington*, vol. 1 of *The Writings of George Washington*, ed. Jared Sparks (Boston: Little, Brown, 1855), 371; and John Frost, *The Pictorial Life of Washington* (Philadelphia: Thomas Cowperthwait, 1848), 468.

27. Tuckerman, *Book of the Artists*, 24; Mary E. Nealy, "The Real and the Ideal in Art," *The Art Journal* 2, 21 (September 1876): 287.

28. Most history painters in the postwar period were male. Jennie Brownscombe (1851–1936) was a notable exception.

29. Richard McLanathan, foreword, *The Brandywine Heritage* (Greenwich, Conn.: The New York Graphic Society Ltd., 1971), 7.

30. See Rowland Elzea, "Howard Pyle and Late 19th-Century American Illustration," in *Howard Pyle: Works in the Collection of the Delaware Art Museum* (Wilmington: Delaware Art Museum, 1971), 9.

31. On Pyle, see Charles D. Abbott, *Howard Pyle: A Chronicle* (New York and London: Harper and Brothers, 1925), Henry Clarence Pitz, *Howard Pyle: Writer, Illustrator, Founder of the Brandywine School* (New York: Bramhall House, 1965), and McLanathan, *Brandywine Heritage*. Pyle's books of historical illustration include *The Merry Adventures of Robin Hood* (New York: Charles Scribner's Sons, 1883), *The Rose of Paradise* (New York: Harper & Brothers, 1888), *Otto of the Silver Hand* (New York: Charles Scribner's Sons, 1888), and Robert Louis Stevenson's *Kidnapped* (New York: Charles Scribner's Sons, 1895). For a complete bibliography of books Pyle wrote and illustrated, see Pitz, *Howard Pyle*, 231–44.

32. For a complete list of Howard Pyle's students, see Pitz, *Howard Pyle*, 228.

33. See *The Moran Family* (Huntington, N.Y.: Heckscher Museum, 1965) for works produced by other members of this notable family. Percy Moran is known to have created a number of works dealing with colonial and Revolutionary War history; many remain unlocated. Edward Moran's series is in the collections of the United States Naval Academy, Annapolis, Md. See Paul D. Schweizer, *Edward Moran: American Marine and Landscape Painter* (Wilmington: Delaware Art Museum, 1979), 66.

34. On Schussele, see George W. Dewey, "C. Schussele," *Sartain's Union Magazine of Literature and Art* 10, 6 (June 1852): 462.

35. On Gérôme's influence on Ferris, see Mitnick, "Jean Leon Gerome Ferris," 44, and, on Gérôme, see Will H. Low, "J. L. Gérôme," in *Modern French Masters*, ed. John C. Van Dycke (New York: The Century Co., 1896), 31–43. Ferris's statement is in Jean Leon Gerome Ferris, "Autobiography," 1, Archives of 76, Cleveland, Ohio.

36. Mitnick, "Jean Leon Gerome Ferris," 331–32.

37. Clarence Cook, "Artists as Historians," *The Monthly Illustrator*, January 1895, 103.

38. See Ferris, "Autobiography," 2.

39. Wilfred Jordan to George E. Datesman, Director of Public Works, City of Philadelphia, May 5, 1916, quoted in Mitnick, *Jean Leon Gerome Ferris*, 161.

40. On Deming, see Thomas G. Lamb, *Eight Bears: A Biography of E. W. Deming 1860–1942* (Oklahoma City: Griffin Books, Inc., 1978), and Mitnick, "Edwin Willard Deming: A Rediscovered Painter of American History," forthcoming.

41. This information is revealed in a series of letters Deming wrote to his family in the 1880s, now in the collections of the New York Public Library Manuscript Division.

42. Deming to his family, January 31, 1885, New York Public Library Manuscript Division.

43. Therese Osterheld, Deming's wife, wrote several books on native Americans that Deming illustrated, all issued by New York publisher Frederick A. Stokes: *Indian Pictures* and *Indian Child Life* (1899), *Red Folk and White Folk* (1902), *American Animal Life* (1916), and *Many Snows Ago* (1929). Osterheld also compiled a group of Deming's letters and reviews in *Edwin Willard Deming: His Work* (New York: The Riverside Press, 1925).

44. See auction catalog, *Indians and the West: The Library of Edwin Willard Deming, Painter and Sculptor of American Indian Life* (New York: Swann Auction Galleries, November 5, 1941), lot 193.

45. Ella E. Clark and Margot Edmonds, *Sacagawea of the Lewis and Clark Expedition* (Berkeley, Los Angeles, and London: University of California Press, 1979). Sacajawea's image later became a symbol of the

struggle for women's suffrage.

46. These paintings have been recently rediscovered. See Mitnick, "Edwin Willard Deming," forthcoming.

47. Florence Seville Berryman, "Dunsmore's Epic of the American Revolution," *Daughters of the American Revolution Magazine* 60, 11 (November 1926): 652, 649.

48. George A. Zabriskie donated thirty-nine of Dunsmore's historical paintings to Fraunces Tavern Museum in New York City on October 26, 1936. See Sons of the Revolution in the State of New York, *Reports and Proceedings, July 1, 1936–June 30, 1937*, 18–19.

49. Douglas Allen and Douglas Allen, Jr., *N.C. Wyeth: The Collected Paintings, Illustrations, and Murals* (New York: Crown Publishers, Inc., 1972), 15.

50. Wyeth illustrated Edwin Markham, "The Romance of the C.P.," *Success,* March 1903, and John M. Oskison, "Working for Fame," *Leslie's Popular Monthly,* August 1903. On the western trip, see Allen and Allen, Jr., *N. C. Wyeth*, 31.

51. Allen and Allen, Jr., *N. C. Wyeth*, presents a complete bibliography of Wyeth's published works beginning on 193.

52. In 1740, the bank's site was the location of the residence of Lewis Morris, Royal Governor of New Jersey; an iron factory and a tavern later occupied the spot. In 1837, the original structure was demolished in order to build the Mechanics and Manufacturers Bank. See *The Trentonian,* April 19, 1989, B-11.

53. Quoted in *Philadelphia Public Ledger,* Sunday edition, 1932, undated clipping in the collections of the Brandywine River Museum Archives, Chadds Ford, Pennsylvania.

A Fall from Grace

1. In his recent book, Michael Kammen argues for an expanded notion of what constitutes history painting, in particular that it includes contemporary art and that it has too long been defined "in conventional terms of tragic, noble, or heroic events set somewhere in a detached past that is clearly discrete from the present" (121). This view, supported fundamentally by Courbet's belief that "historical art is by nature contemporary" (71), reflects part of the modernist attitude that I discuss here as nearly ending the traditional concept of history painting. While I, in fact, agree with Kammen, my essay examines how critics during the transition to modernism dealt with the mode of painting that had held, and for some still did, the elevated position in the realm of art because of its expression of significant human emotions, values, and events. See Michael Kammen, *Meadows of Memory: Images of Time and Tradition in American Art and Culture* (Austin: University of Texas Press, 1992).

2. William Ordway Partridge, "The Demands of Art in This New Republic," *The Arena* 30 (September 1903): 225; Frederic Harrison, "Art and Shoddy: A Reply to Criticism," *The Forum,* August 1893, 718; "American Painting Reflects American Character," *The Outlook,* January 4, 1908, 10.

3. "Art as the Handmaid of Literature," *The Forum,* May 1901, 370; F. D. Millet, "What Are Americans Doing In Art?" *The Century Magazine,* November 1891, 47.

4. See, for instance, George Parson Lathrop, "The Book of American Figure Painters," *Lippincott's Magazine,* December 1886, 754; W. Lewis Fraser, "Decorative Painting at the World's Fair," *The Century Magazine,* May 1893, 14; and Millet, "What Are Americans Doing In Art?" 46.

5. "Educational Influence of Art," *National Repository,* February 1877, 177.

6. Samuel Isham, *The History of American Painting,* new ed., with supplemental chapters by Royal Cortissoz (1905; reprint, New York: The Macmillan Company, 1936), 291.

7. S. S. Conant, "The Progress of the Fine Arts," *Harper's New Monthly Magazine,* April 1876, 701.

8. Frank H. Norton, *Illustrated Register of the United States Centennial Exposition and of the Exposition Universelle, Paris, 1878* (New York: The American News Company, 1879), 179.

9. S. N. C., "Art at the Exhibition," *Appleton's Journal,* June 31, 1876,

10. See William H. Gerdts, "On Elevated Heights: American Historical Painting and Its Critics," in William H. Gerdts and Mark Thistlethwaite, *Grand Illusions: History Painting in America* (Fort Worth, Tex.: Amon Carter Museum, 1988), for a discussion of the critical reception to history painting before the Civil War.

11. John V. Sears, "Art in Philadelphia," *The Aldine* 8 (June 1876): 196.

12. Clarence Cook, "A Centennial Blunder," *New-York Tribune,* May 4, 1876, 2.

13. C.C. [Clarence Cook], "The Art Department [of the Centennial]," *New-York Tribune,* June 17, 1876, 4.

14. The Editor, "The Progress of Painting in America," *The North American Review,* May 1877, 458–59.

15. "The Fine Arts in America," *New York Times,* October 15, 1877, 5.

16. Keith F. Davis, "'A Terrible Distinctness,'" in *Photography in Nineteenth-Century America,* ed. Martha Sandweiss (Fort Worth, Tex.: Amon Carter Museum, and New York: Harry N. Abrams, Inc., Publishers, 1991), 133.

17. For a discussion of the connections and differences between popular illustrations and photographs of the Civil War, see Alan Trachtenberg, *Reading American Photography* (New York: Hill and Wang, 1989), 84–88, 95–96.

18. Davis, "'A Terrible Distinctness,'" 134.

19. For a discussion of the traits of painting compared and contrasted with those of photographs, see Trachtenberg, *Reading American Photography,* 72–84.

20. Robert Penn Warren, *The Legacy of the Civil War* (New York: Random House, 1961), 85.

21. Davis, "'A Terrible Distinctness,'" 150.

22. Ibid., 152.

23. *Pan-American Exposition. Catalogue of the Exhibition of Fine Arts* (Buffalo: David Gray, 1901).

24. R. S. [Russell Sturgis], "The Paris Exposition—XV. The United States Fine-Art Exhibit," *The Nation,* November 28, 1878, 331.

25. G. A. R., "American Genre Painters," unidentified clipping in New York Public Library Art Scrapbooks. The clipping indicates that the author is "our Special Correspondent" and carries the dateline, "Paris, August 1, 1878."

26. Mrs. Mary E. Nealy, "Art at the Capitol," *The Aldine* 9 (May 1878): 146.

27. "The Academy Exhibition," *New York Times,* April 14, 1878, 7.

28. "The Metropolitan Museum Re-Opening," *The Art Amateur* 34 (December 1895): 3.

29. S. G. W. Benjamin, *Art in America* (1880; reprint, New York and London: Garland Publishing, Inc., 1976), 89–90.

30. "Washington Crossing the Delaware," *New York Times,* January 1, 1897, 6.

31. Isham, *History of American Painting,* 295.

32. Caffin regarded Leutze's brushwork as plodding and constrained and noted that "with Leutze the attempt of American painters to execute large historical subjects ceased, not to be revived until nearly fifty years later, when it reappeared in [Edwin] Abbey." See Charles H. Caffin, *The Story of American Painting* (New York: Frederick A. Stokes Company, 1907), 105–7.

33. "Washington Crossing the Delaware," *New York Times,* January 22, 1897, 6.

34. John F. Weir, "John Trumbull," *Scribner's Magazine,* November 1913, 661.

35. Benjamin, *Art in America,* 130, 23.

36. Ibid., 88, 126. Other critics praised this work when it appeared at the annual exhibition of the National Academy of Design in 1878. One wrote that it shows "some excellent work; the picture is interesting and we thank the artist for his attempt at reproducing the historic scene"; another found favor in Thompson not making the figures "pretty and impossible; neither is their raggedness overdone." See "Fine Arts—National Academy of Design," unidentified newspaper clipping, New York Public Library Art Scrapbooks, 1878; "The Academy Exhibition," *New York Times,* April 10, 1878, 2.

37. Benjamin, *Art in America,* 126. A review of the work when it appeared in the 1879 National Academy of Art exhibition noted the subject itself gave the picture a "serious character," although this value

"artists like to characterize with the slightly disparaging adjective, literary." The writer then laments "how few of our painters attempt such [war] scenes." See "Budding Academicians," *New York Times*, April 20, 1879, 10. Scott's *In the Cornfield at Antietam* has not been located.

38. William A. Coffin, "A Word About Painting," *Scribner's Magazine*, April 1894, 503.

39. "Art Notes," *Boston Evening Transcript*, November 3, 1882, 4; "Art and Artists," *Boston Evening Transcript*, April 3, 1883, 6.

40. For a detailed discussion of this event, see my "Patronage Gone Awry: The Temple Historical Painting Competition of 1883," *The Pennsylvania Magazine of History and Biography* 112 (October 1988): 545–78. The competition rules are cited in "Prospectus for Temple Competition of Historical Painting," Pennsylvania Academy of The Fine Arts Archives.

41. "Mr. Clarke's Exhibition," *New York Times*, December 28, 1883, 5.

42. H. Barbara Weinberg, "Thomas B. Clarke: Foremost Patron of American Art from 1872 to 1899," *The American Art Journal* 8 (May 1976): 71–83.

43. "The Academy of Design," *New-York Tribune*, April 5, 1884, 5.

44. R., "Men, Women, and Pictures," *New York Times*, May 18, 1884, 6.

45. Lee M. Edwards, "Noble Domesticity: The Paintings of Thomas Hovenden," *American Art Journal* 19 (1987): 14–19.

46. "The Society of American Artists," *The Art Amateur* 17 (June 1887): 5; "Spring at the Academy," *New York Times*, March 30, 1889, 4.

47. "The Academy Exhibition," *Art Age* 7 (June 1888): 95.

48. "The Academy Paintings," *New York Times*, April 7, 1889, 5.

49. "This Week in the Art World," *New York Times*, March 26, 1898, Saturday Review of Books and Art, 196.

50. Philip Rodney Paulding, "Illustrators and Illustrating," *Munsey's*, May 1895, 152.

51. William Herbert Hobbs, "Art as the Handmaid of Literature," *The Forum*, May 1901, 371–72.

52. Ibid., 375.

53. Paulding, "Illustrators and Illustrating," 152.

54. Ibid., 155–56.

55. Christian Brinton, "Art in America III. American Figure-Painters," *Woman's Home Companion*, April 1911, 17.

56. "Art and Portraits," *New York Times*, February 10, 1898, 6.

57. Isham, *History of American Painting*, 504.

58. Russell Sturgis, "Painting," *The Forum*, January 1903, 406.

59. William Walton, "Mural Painting in This Country since 1898," *Scribner's Magazine*, November 1906, 637.

60. Russell Sturgis, "Mural Painting," *The Forum*, January 1906, 370.

61. Sturgis, "Mural Painting," 374.

62. Will H. Low, "The Mural Painter and His Public," *Scribner's Magazine*, February 1907, 256.

63. Ibid.

64. Sturgis, "Mural Painting," 380–81.

65. Edwin Howland Blashfield, *Mural Painting in America* (New York: Charles Scribner's Sons, 1913), 191.

66. Ibid., 175, 199, 193.

67. Arthur Hoeber, "Unrest in Modern Art," *The Forum*, June 1909, 528.

68. Kenyon Cox, *The Classic Point of View* (New York: Charles Scribner's Sons, 1911), 36, 47.

69. Ibid., 59–60, 66.

70. Ibid., 67–68.

71. Ibid., 68, 70.

72. Ibid., 71.

73. Millet, "What Are Americans Doing In Art?" 46. See also W. J. Stillman, "The Revival of Art," *Atlantic Monthly*, August 1892, 251.

74. Charles H. Caffin, "The Art of Edmund C. Tarbell," *Harper's Monthly Magazine*, June 1908, 65, 66.

75. Oliver S. Tonks, "The Modernist Movement in Painting," *Scribner's Magazine*, August 1922, 253.

76. Willard Huntington Wright, "The Truth about Painting," *The Forum*, October 1915, 446, 447, 454.

77. Caffin, *The Story of American Painting*, 194, 197.

78. Leo Stein, "If Rubens Were Born Again," *The New Republic*, June 1, 1918, 145.

79. Lucia Fairchild Fuller, A.N.A., "E.L. Henry, N.A. An Appreciation," *Scribner's Magazine*, August 1920, 256.

80. Brinton, "American Figure-Painters," 17.

81. "The Futility of American Art," *The Independent*, January 30, 1908, 268.

82. Birge Harrison, "The Future of American Art," *North American Review*, January 1909, 33.

83. Leila Mechlin, "Trend of American Art," *Cosmopolitan Magazine*, June 1906, 182; George H. Roeder, Jr., *Forum of Uncertainty: Confrontations with Modern Painting in Twentieth-Century America* (Ann Arbor, Mich.: UMI Research Press, 1980), 60.

84. C. Grant La Farge, "The Education of the Artist," *Scribner's Magazine*, August 1915, 257; Allan McLane Hamilton, "Insane Art," *Scribner's Magazine*, April 1918, 488.

85. Herbert Adams, "The War's Influence on Art," *The Forum*, January 1919, 71.

86. For a diagram of *Massacre at Dinant* showing the initial divisions of Dynamic Symmetry, see Michael Quick et al., *The Paintings of George Bellows* (Fort Worth, Tex.: Amon Carter Museum; Los Angeles: Los Angeles County Museum of Art; and New York: Harry N. Abrams, Inc., 1992), 64.

87. "Paintings by George Bellows," *New York Times*, April 6, 1919, III: 4; "George Bellows' Work on Exhibition," *New York Times*, November 11, 1918, IV: 4.

88. "Walt Kuhn's Indian Subjects," *New York Times*, March 28, 1920, VI: 6.

89. Thomas Craven, "Men of Art. American Style," *The American Mercury*, December 1925, 428, 432.

90. Ibid., 432, 431.

91. Henry Adams, *Thomas Hart Benton: An American Original* (New York: Alfred A. Knopf, 1989), 129.

92. Lewis Mumford, "An American Epic in Paint," *The New Republic*, April 4, 1927, 197.

93. "Thomas H. Benton Conceives a New Style of Mural Painting," *Art Digest*, March 1, 1927, 7.

94. Ibid.

On the Margins of American History

1. From the *Catalogue of the Second Annual Exhibition* (Philadelphia: Artists' Fund Society, 1836), 5, cited in Mark Thistlethwaite, "The Artist as Interpreter of American History," in *In This Academy: The Pennsylvania Academy of the Fine Arts, 1805–1976* (Philadelphia: Pennsylvania Academy of the Fine Arts, 1976), 101.

2. Joel Kovel, *White Racism: A Psychohistory* (New York: Columbia University Press, 1970), 13. I want to thank James Livingston of the Rutgers University history department for calling this book to my attention.

3. Sacvan Bercovitch, "The Problem of Ideology in American Literary History," *Critical Inquiry* 12 (Summer 1986): 635.

4. Raymond Williams, *Marxism and History* (New York: Oxford University Press, 1977), 115, 116.

5. Sir Joshua Reynolds, *Discourses on Art*, ed. Robert Wark (San Marino, Calif.: Huntington Library, 1959). "Discourse 4," 55.

6. Theodore Sizer, ed., *The Autobiography of Colonel John Trumbull, Patriot-Artist, 1756–1843* (New Haven, Conn.: Yale University Press, 1953), 339–40.

7. Trumbull to Thomas Jefferson, 1789, in Sizer, ed., *Autobiography*, 160.

8. Kenneth A. Silverman, *A Cultural History of the American Revolution* (New York: Thomas Y. Crowell, 1976), 279; and Reynolds, *Discourses on Art*, 57.

9. For various accounts of this work, see Albert Boime, *The Art of Exclusion* (Washington, D.C.: Smithsonian Institution Press, 1990), 21; Hugh Honour, *The Image of the Black in Western Art*, vol. 4, part 1 (Cambridge, Mass.: Harvard University Press, 1989), 42; Irma Jaffe, *John Trumbull: Patriot Artist of the American Revolution* (Boston: New York Graphic Society, 1975), 85; Jules David Prown, "John Trumbull as History Painter," in Helen A. Cooper, *John Trumbull: The Hand and Spirit of a Painter* (New Haven: Yale University Art Gallery, 1982), 31; and Theodore Sizer, *The Works of Colonel John Trumbull: Artist of the*

American Revolution (New Haven: Yale University Press, 1967), caption for fig. 151.

10. Joseph T. Wilson, *The Black Phalanx: A History of the Negro Soldiers of the United States in the Wars of 1775–1812, 1861–1865* (1890; reprint, New York: Arno Press, 1968), 33–34, 38.

11. "Art and Artists of America, *Christian Examiner*, July 1863, 116, cited in William H. Gerdts and Mark Thistlethwaite, *Grand Illusions: History Painting in America* (Fort Worth, Tex.: Amon Carter Museum, 1988), 18.

12. Henry Louis Gates, Jr., "The Face and Voice of Blackness," in Guy C. McElroy, *Facing History: The Black Image in American Art, 1710–1940* (Washington, D.C.: Corcoran Gallery of Art, 1990), xxix.

13. George M. Frederickson, *The Black Image in the White Mind* (New York: Harper and Row, 1971), 2.

14. *African Repository*, June 1828, 118, cited in Frederickson, *Black Image in the White Mind*, 17.

15. Clergyman Michael Hammett's statement of 1833 is mentioned in David M. Striefford, "The American Colonization Society: An Application of Republican Ideology to Early Antebellum Reform," *Journal of Southern History* 45, 2 (1979): 216, cited in Elizabeth Johns, *American Genre Painting: The Politics of Everyday Life* (New Haven, Conn., and London: Yale University Press, 1991), 101.

16. Frederickson, *Black Image in the White Mind*, Chap. 3; Reginald Horsman, *Race and Manifest Destiny: The Origins of American Racial Anglo-Saxonism* (Cambridge, Mass.: Harvard University Press, 1981), Chap. 7. The American school included Dr. Josiah C. Nott, Dr. Samuel George Morton, and George R. Gliddon, among others. Studies of head sizes and shapes include Samuel George Morton, *Crania Americana* (1839); and Orson S. and Lorenzo N. Fowler, *Phrenology Proved, Illustrated, and Applied* (1846).

17. Karen Mary Adams, "Black Images in Nineteenth-Century American Painting and Literature" (Ph.D. diss., Emory University, 1977), 46, and Johns, *American Genre Painting*, 131, 103.

18. Frederickson, *Black Image in the White Mind*, 78, 52.

19. For a different interpretation, see Thistlethwaite, "The Artist as Interpreter," 107.

20. Kovel, *White Racism*, 36.

21. From James Kirke Paulding, *Slavery in the United States* (1836), 176, cited in Johns, *American Genre Painting*, 101.

22. Houston A. Baker, Jr., *Modernism and the Harlem Renaissance* (Chicago: University of Chicago, 1987), 21, 22; see also Eric Lott, "'The Seeming Counterfeit': Racial Politics and Early Blackface Minstrelsy," *American Quarterly* 43 (June 1991): 223–54. I want to thank Kathryn Grover for calling to my attention this essay.

23. Barry D. Adams, *The Survival of Domination: Inferiorization and Everyday Life* (New York: Elsevier, 1978), 93. I want to thank Judith Gerson of the Rutgers University sociology department for calling this book to my attention.

24. "The Fine Arts: Review of Exhibition," *The Knickerbocker*, July 1841, 87, cited in McElroy, *Facing History*, 39.

25. See Boime, *Art of Exclusion*, 106; Adams, "Black Images," 127–38; Mary Ann Calo, "Winslow Homer's Visit to Virginia during Reconstruction," *The American Art Journal* 12 (Winter 1980): 10; and McElroy, *Facing History*, xvii.

26. Frederick C. Hoffman, *Race Traits and Tendencies of the American Negro*, (New York: Macmillan and the American Economic Association, 1896), 311. For other, similar-minded authors, see Frederickson, *Black Image in the White Mind*, 98–101; Frederick Merk, *Manifest Destiny and Mission in American History: A Reinterpretation* (New York: Vintage Books, 1963), Chap. 11; and Ernest L. Tuveson, *Redeemer Nation: The Idea of America's Millennial Role* (Chicago: University of Chicago Press, 1968), 137–38, 165–70. See also Josiah Strong, *Our Country: Its Possible Future and Its Present Crisis* (New York: Baker and Taylor, 1885) and his *The New Era; or, The Coming Kingdom* (New York: Baker and Taylor, 1893); and John Fiske, *American Political Ideas* (New York: Harper and Brothers, 1865). For psychological studies, see Adams, *Survival of Domination*, 97.

27. Hoffman, *Race Traits and Tendencies*, 312.

28. Some of the material in this section is taken directly from my "Territory, Race, Religion: Images of Manifest Destiny," *Smithsonian Studies in American Art* 4 (Summer/Fall 1990): 3–21.

29. Francis Jennings, *The Invasion of America: Indians, Colonialism, and the Cant of Conquest* (New York: W. W. Norton, 1975), 146, cited in Julie Schimmel, "Inventing 'the Indian,'" in *The West as America: Reinterpreting Images of the Frontier, 1820–1920*, ed. William H. Truettner (Washington, D.C.: Smithsonian Institution Press, 1991), 162.

30. See my "Territory, Race, Religion" and my *Albert Bierstadt* (New York: Watson-Guptill, 1981), 9–10.

31. [John L. O'Sullivan], "The True Title," [New York] *Morning News*, December 27, 1845. The full text is reproduced in Conrad Cherry, ed., *God's New Israel: Religious Interpretations of American Destiny* (Englewood Cliffs, N.J.: Prentice-Hall, 1971), 128–30.

32. Horace Greeley, *An Overland Journey from New York to San Francisco in the Summer of 1859* (1860; reprint, New York: Alfred A. Knopf, 1969), 120.

33. "Our Relations with Mexico," *American Review: A Whig Journal* 4 (July 1846): 14.

34. Horsman, *Race and Manifest Destiny*, 190.

35. Fowler and Fowler, *Phrenology Proved*, 29–31, cited in Horsman, *Race and Manifest Destiny*, 145.

36. On Remington, see Harold McCracken, *Frederic Remington: Artist of the Old West* (Philadelphia: Lippincott, 1947), 66; on Miller, see Carol Clark, "A Romantic Painter in the American West," in *Alfred Jacob Miller: Artist on the Oregon Trail*, ed. Ron Tyler (Fort Worth, Tex.: Amon Carter Museum, 1982), 56.

37. George Catlin, *Letters and Notes on the Manners, Customs, and Conditions of the North American Indians* (1841; reprint, New York: Dover Publications, 1973), 2: 148, 1: 261–62.

38. "Review of National Academy of Design," *The Knickerbocker*, July 1853, 95.

39. "Our Indian Policy," *The United States Magazine and Democratic Review*, February 1844, 169, and "Desultory Thoughts on the Philosophy and the Process of Civilization," *The Knickerbocker*, July 1840, 2.

40. Merk, *Manifest Destiny*, 354–57.

41. Susan Armitage, "Through Women's Eyes: A New View of the West," in *The Women's West*, ed. Susan Armitage and Elizabeth Jameson (Norman: University of Oklahoma Press, 1987), 9.

42. I want to thank Mary Jane Melendez for letting me use some material she developed in her undergraduate honors paper, "Women on the Trail: Image and Reality" (Rutgers: The State University of New Jersey, 1991).

43. Robert L. Griswold, "Anglo Women and Domestic Ideology in the American West in the Nineteenth and Early Twentieth Centuries," in *Western Women: Their Land, Their Lives*, ed. Lillian Schlissel et al. (Albuquerque: University of New Mexico Press, 1988), 16, 18.

44. Barbara Welter, "The Cult of True Womanhood: 1820–1850," *American Quarterly* 18 (Summer 1966): 151–74. This article is constantly cited in the literature.

45. Lillian Schlissel, *Women's Diaries of the Westward Journey* (New York: Schocken Books, 1982), 13.

46. Schlissel, *Women's Diaries*, 15–16, 30–40. See also Armitage, "Woman and Western American History" (working paper 134, Wellesley College Center for Research on Women, 1984); and Corlann Gee Bush, "The Way We Weren't: Images of Women and Men in Cowboy Art," in Armitage and Jameson, eds., *Women's West*, 29.

47. Cited in Dawn Glanz, *How the West Was Drawn: American Art and the Settling of the Frontier* (Ann Arbor, Mich.: UMI Research Press, 1982), 82.

48. Anne Brewster, "Emmanuel [sic] Leutze, the Artist," *Lippincott's Magazine*, November 1868, 536, cited in Glanz, *How the West Was Drawn*, 80, and in Patricia Hills, "Picturing Progress in the Era of Westward Expansion," in Truettner, ed., *West as America*, 119.

49. John Gadsby Chapman, *The Picture of the Baptism of Pocahontas* (1840), cited in William H. Truettner, "Prelude to Expansion: Repainting the Past," in Truettner, ed., *West as America*, 71.

50. Sherry L. Smith, "Beyond Princess and Squaw: Army Officers' Perceptions of Indian Women," in Armitage and Jameson, eds., *Women's West*, 64.

51. See the works cited in note 26.

52. William Dean Howells, *A Hazard of New Fortunes* (1890; reprint, New York: New American Library, 1980), 48, 54, 60.

53. "East Side Street Vendors," *New York Times*, July 30, 1893, cited

in Allen Schoenered, *Portal to America: The Lower East Side, 1870–1925* (New York: Holt, Rinehart and Winston, 1967), 57–58.

54. Henry James, *The American Scene* (1907; reprint, New York: St. Martin's Press, 1987), 65, 96.

55. Jerome Myers, *Artist in Manhattan* (New York: American Artists' Group, 1940), 48, 49; and Louis Baury, "The Message of the Proletaire," *The Bookman* 34 (December 1911): 409. See also my "Notes on Realistic Painting and Photography, Circa 1900–1910," *Arts Magazine* 55 (May 1981): 141 43.

56. Frederickson, *Black Image in the White Mind*, 101–6.

57. Baury, "Message of the Proletaire," 410.

58. Ibid., 400.

59. Stanley L. Cuba, "George Luks (1866–1933)" in *George Luks: An American Artist* (Wilkes-Barre, Pa.: Wilkes College Sordoni Art Gallery, 1987), 42.

60. William B. M'Cormick, "George Luks, Agitator," *Arts and Decoration* 4 (July 1914): 336, 337.

61. From the catalog of an exhibition of Luks's work at the Newark Museum, 1934, in Judith H. O'Toole, "George Luks: an American Artist," in *George Luks*, 20. Able only to fictionalize the reality of the streets, Huneker wrote about searching those streets for Luks-like subject matter—for, as he said, "a regular Luks." See James Huneker, *The New Cosmopolis* (New York: Scribner's and Sons, 1915), 20.

62. "Everett Shinn on George Luks: An Unpublished Memoir," *The Archives of American Art Journal* 6 (April 1966): 2.

63. Jacob Riis, *The Battle with the Slum* (New York: Macmillan, 1902), 1; and Ferenc M. Szasz and Ralph F. Bogardus, "The Camera and the American Social Conscience: The Documentary Photography of Jacob A. Riis," *New York History* 55 (October 1974): 436.

64. Robert Henri, *The Art Spirit* (1923; reprint, Philadelphia: Lippincott, 1960), 218, 116; and Rose Henderson, "Robert Henri," *The American Magazine of Art* 21 (January 1, 1930): 10.

Afterword

I am grateful to Bill Ayres and Kathryn Grover for editorial assistance and to Janet Francendese for suggesting helpful readings.

1. This idea is explored in Maurice Berger, *How Art Becomes History: Essays on Art, Society, and Culture in Post-New Deal America* (New York: HarperCollins, 1992).

2. For a recent assessment of people's understanding of differences between the past and history, see "The Pilot Study Report: People and the Past," *Mosaic: The Newsletter of the Center on History-Making in America* 1, 2–3 (Spring/Summer 1992).

3. On art used for persuasion and conviction, see Alan Gowans, *Learning to See: Historical Perspectives on Modern Popular/Commercial Arts* (Bowling Green, Ohio: Bowling Green University Popular Press, 1981), 363–461.

4. See David Freedberg, *The Power of Images: Studies in the History and Theory of Response* (Chicago: University of Chicago Press, 1989).

5. Pictures can also be "affecting presences." See Robert Plant Armstrong, *The Affecting Presence* (Urbana: University of Illinois Press, 1971).

6. I use the term "pictures" loosely in this essay. I mean by it mimetic images in both two and three dimensions. Thus, I would call both French's statue of the Minute Man and Saint-Gaudens's Shaw Memorial history pictures. On universals, see Donald E. Brown, *Human Universals* (Philadelphia: Temple University Press, 1991).

7. A classic text on creative visualization is Shakti Gawain, *Creative Visualization* (New York: Bantam, 1979).

8. It could also be argued that military exploit and domination, often cloaked as service to god and country, in turn mask or mystify economic exploit and domination. See John Kenneth Galbraith, *The Age of Uncertainty* (Boston: Houghton Mifflin, 1977).

9. This photograph, the events leading up to it, and its history are explored in Karal Ann Marling and John Wetenhall, *Iwo Jima: Monuments, Memories, and the American Hero* (Cambridge, Mass.: Harvard University Press, 1991). Rosenthal's image was unposed, but its serendipitous conformity to the conventions of previous history paintings helps to account for its impact and positive reception.

10. Symbols share many of the properties of rituals and are often incorporated in them. See David I. Kertzer, *Ritual, Politics, and Power* (New Haven, Conn.: Yale University Press, 1988).

11. Myriam Miedzian, *Boys Will Be Boys: Breaking the Link between Masculinity and Violence* (New York: Doubleday, 1991).

12. On mortality, see Elizabeth Kamarck Minnich, *Transforming Knowledge* (Philadelphia: Temple University Press, 1990), 132–36.

13. See, for example, Matthew Baigell, "Territory, Race, Religion: Images of Manifest Destiny," *Smithsonian Studies in American Art* 4 (Summer/Fall 1990): 3–21, and William H. Truettner, ed., *The West as America: Reinterpreting Images of the Frontier, 1820–1920* (Washington, D.C.: Smithsonian Institution Press for the National Museum of American Art, 1991).

14. Barrington Moore, Jr., quoted in Harvey J. Kaye, *The Powers of the Past: Reflections on the Crisis and the Promise of History* (Minneapolis: University of Minnesota Press, 1991), 153. This idea surfaces repeatedly in Galbraith, *Age of Uncertainty.*

15. See Simon J. Bronner, ed., *Folklife Studies from the Gilded Age* (Ann Arbor, Mich.: UMI Research Press, 1987).

16. On Johnson, see Patricia Hills, *Eastman Johnson* (New York: Clarkson N. Potter in association with the Whitney Museum of American Art, 1972).

17. Expressions of the New England mystique are abundant. For an example from the mid-twentieth century, see Bertha Damon, *A Sense of Humus* (New York: Simon & Schuster, 1943). For contemporary evidence, see *Yankee* and *Down East* magazines. For a study of the mythologizing of rural life, see Sarah Burns, *Pastoral Inventions: Rural Life in Nineteenth-Century American Art and Culture* (Philadelphia: Temple University Press, 1989).

18. On early collecting and interest in historic material culture, see Elizabeth Stillinger, *The Antiquers* (New York: Alfred A. Knopf, 1980).

19. See, for example, Todd Gitlin, *The Sixties: Years of Hope, Days of Rage* (New York: Bantam, 1987).

20. For a personal perspective on the new history, see Kaye, *Powers of the Past*, 1–6, 21–39.

21. Barrington Moore, Jr., quoted in Kaye, *Powers of the Past*, 30.

22. Kienholz also created a piece that comments on the flag raising on Iwo Jima. See Marling and Wetenhall, *Iwo Jima*, 202–4.

23. This assertion is the subject of Minnich, *Transforming Knowledge.*

24. The ideas behind this assemblage and the process of creating it are described at length in Judy Chicago, *The Dinner Party: A Symbol of Our Heritage* (Garden City, N.Y.: Anchor/Doubleday, 1979). Chicago explains her artistic and personal evolution in *Through the Flower: My Struggle as a Woman Artist* (Garden City, N.Y.: Doubleday, 1975).

25. Men's fear of women is explored in Sam Keen, *Fire in the Belly* (New York: Bantam, 1991), 11–24.

26. Formulated in Erving Goffman, *The Presentation of Self in Everyday Life* (Garden City, N.Y.: Doubleday Anchor, 1959).

27. In the space of half an hour, Rosenthal made three separate attempts to rouse hospital staff to attend to the person on the sidewalk. A nurse entering the hospital was finally able to summon aid from those inside.

28. Seth Mydans, "Painting of Heroic Size Shows Nixon to Match," *New York Times*, August 13, 1992, A16.

29. Kaye, *Powers of the Past*, 145–69.

30. Minnich, *Transforming Knowledge*, 35; see also Gloria Steinem, *Revolution from Within* (Boston: Little, Brown, 1992), 338.

Selected Bibliography

Abrams, Ann Uhry. *The Valiant Hero: Benjamin West and Grand-Style History Painting*. Washington, D.C.: Smithsonian Institution Press, 1985.

Adams, Barry D. *The Survival of Domination: Inferiorization and Everyday Life*. New York: Elsevier, 1978.

Aherns, Kent. "Nineteenth-Century History Painting and the United States Capitol." *Records of the Columbia Historical Society* 15 (1980): 191–222.

———. "Robert Weir's 'Embarkation of the Pilgrims.'" *Capitol Studies* 1 (Fall 1972): 59–71.

Allen, Douglas, and Douglas Allen, Jr. *N.C. Wyeth: The Collected Paintings, Illustrations, and Murals*. New York: Crown Publishers, Inc., 1972.

Architect of the Capitol. *Art in the United States Capitol*. Washington, D.C.: U.S. Government Printing Office, 1978.

Armitage, Susan, and Elizabeth Jameson, eds. *The Women's West*. Norman: University of Oklahoma Press, 1987.

Baigell, Matthew. "Territory, Race, Religion: Images of Manifest Destiny." *Smithsonian Studies in American Art* 4 (Summer/Fall 1990): 3–21.

Bauer, K. Jack. *The Mexican War, 1846–1848*. New York: Macmillan Publishing Co., Inc., 1974.

Bercovitch, Sacvan. *The American Jeremiad*. Madison: University of Wisconsin Press, 1978.

Berger, Maurice. *How Art Becomes History: Essays on Art, Society, and Culture in Post–New Deal America*. New York: HarperCollins, 1992.

Berkhofer, Robert F., Jr. *The White Man's Indian: Images of the American Indian from Columbus to the Present*. New York: Alfred A. Knopf, 1978.

Bjelajac, David. *Millennial Desire and the Apocalyptic Vision of Washington Allston*. Washington, D.C., and London: Smithsonian Institution Press, 1988.

Blashfield, Edwin Howland. *Mural Painting in America*. New York: Charles Scribner's Sons, 1913.

Bloch, E. Maurice. *The Paintings of George Caleb Bingham: A Catalogue Raisonné*. Columbia: University of Missouri Press, 1986.

Bode, Carl. *The Anatomy of American Popular Culture, 1840–1861*. Berkeley: University of California Press, 1959.

Boime, Albert, *The Art of Exclusion*. Washington, D.C.: Smithsonian Institution Press, 1990.

———. *The Magisterial Gaze: Manifest Destiny and American Landscape Painting c. 1830–1865*. Washington, D.C.: Smithsonian Institution Press, 1991.

Callcott, George H. *History in the United States 1800–1860: Its Practice and Purpose*. Baltimore: Johns Hopkins Press, 1970.

Campbell, William P. *John Gadsby Chapman*. Washington, D.C.: National Gallery of Art, 1962.

Cannon-Brookes, Peter, et al. *The Painted Word: British History Painting: 1750–1830*. Woodbridge, Eng.: The Boydell Press, 1991.

Chamberlain, Georgia S. *John Gadsby Chapman, 1808–1889*. Privately printed, 1963.

Chambers, Bruce W. *The World of David Gilmour Blythe (1815–1865)*. Washington, D.C.: Smithsonian Institution Press for the National Collection of Fine Arts, 1980.

Cooper, Helen A. *John Trumbull: The Hand and Spirit of a Painter*. New Haven, Conn., and London: Yale University Art Gallery, 1982.

Craven, Frank Wesley. *The Legend of the Founding Fathers*. New York: New York University Press, 1956.

Craven, Wayne. "Patronage and Collecting in America, 1800–1835." In *Mr. Luman Reed's Picture Gallery: A Pioneer Collection of American Art*. New York: Harry N. Abrams, Inc., with the New-York Historical Society, 1990: 11–18.

Danly, Susan. *Telling Tales: Nineteenth-Century Narrative Painting from the Collection of the Pennsylvania Academy of the Fine Arts*. New York and Philadelphia: The American Federation of the Arts and the Pennsylvania Academy of the Fine Arts, 1991.

Devine, Michael J. "The Historical Paintings of William Henry Powell." *Ohio History* (Winter 1980): 65–77.

Dickman, William J. "John Gadsby Chapman: Alexandria's Foremost 19th Century Painter." *Northern Virginia Heritage* (February 1980): 15–18.

Edgerton, Samuel Y., Jr. "The Murder of Jane McCrea: The Tragedy of an American *Tableau d'Histoire*." *Art Bulletin* 47, 5 (December 1965): 481–92.

Edwards, Lee M. "Noble Domesticity: The Paintings of Thomas Hovenden." *The American Art Journal* 19 (1987): 14–19.

Elson, Ruth Miller. *Guardians of Tradition: American Schoolbooks of the Nineteenth Century.* Lincoln: University of Nebraska Press, 1964.

Evans, Dorinda. *Benjamin West and His American Students.* Washington, D.C.: Smithsonian Institution Press, 1980.

Fehrenbacher, Don E. *Lincoln in Text and Context.* Stanford, Calif.: Stanford University Press, 1987.

Ferguson, Russell, et al., eds. *Out There: Marginalization and Contemporary Culture.* Cambridge, Mass.: MIT Press, 1990.

Freedberg, David. *The Power of Images: Studies in the History and Theory of Response.* Chicago: University of Chicago Press, 1989.

Gardner, Alexander. *Gardner's Photographic Sketch Book of the Civil War.* 1866. Reprint, New York: Dover Publications, Inc., 1959.

Gerdts, William H., and Mark Thistlethwaite. *Grand Illusions: History Painting in America.* Fort Worth, Tex.: Amon Carter Museum, 1988.

Glanz, Dawn. *How the West Was Drawn: American Art and the Settling of the Frontier.* Ann Arbor, Mich.: UMI Research Press, 1982.

Gowans, Alan. *Learning to See: Historical Perspectives on Modern Popular/Commercial Arts.* Bowling Green, Ohio: Bowling Green University Popular Press, 1981.

Greenhouse, Wendy. "Benjamin West and Edward III: A Neoclassical Painter and Medieval History." *Art History* 8, 2 (1985): 178–91.

Groseclose, Barbara. *Emanuel Leutze 1816–1868: Freedom is the Only King.* Washington, D.C.: Smithsonian Institution Press, 1976.

———. "'Washington Crossing the Delaware': The Political Context." *The American Art Journal* 7 (November 1975): 70–78.

Handlin, Oscar. *Truth in History.* Cambridge, Mass., and London: The Belknap Press of Harvard University Press, 1979.

Harris, Neil. *The Artist in American Society.* New York: Braziller, 1966.

Hazelton, George C., Jr. *The National Capitol: Its Architecture Art and History.* New York: J. Little & Co., 1897.

Heite, Edward F. "Painter of the Old Dominion." *Virginia Cavalcade* (Winter 1968): 11–29.

Henderson, Harry B., III. *Versions of the Past: The Historical Imagination in American Fiction.* New York: Oxford University Press, 1974.

Hills, Patricia. *Eastman Johnson.* New York: Clarkson N. Potter in association with the Whitney Museum of American Art, 1972.

Honour, Hugh. *The Image of the Black in Western Art.* 4 vols. Cambridge, Mass.: Harvard University Press, 1989.

Horsman, Reginald. *Race and Manifest Destiny: The Origins of American Racial Anglo-Saxonism.* Cambridge, Mass.: Harvard University Press, 1981.

Howe, Daniel Walker. *The Political Culture of the American Whigs.* Chicago and London: University of Chicago Press, 1979.

In This Academy: The Pennsylvania Academy of the Fine Arts, 1805–1976. Washington, D.C.: Museum Press, Inc., 1976.

Jaffe, Irma. *John Trumbull: Patriot Artist of the American Revolution.* Boston: New York Graphic Society, 1975.

———. *Trumbull: The Declaration of Independence.* New York: Viking Press, 1976.

Johannsen, Robert W. *To the Halls of the Montezumas: The Mexican War in the American Imagination.* New York and Oxford: Oxford University Press, 1985.

Johns, Elizabeth. *American Genre Painting: The Politics of Everyday Life.* New Haven, Conn., and London: Yale University Press, 1991.

Kammen, Michael. *A Season of Youth: The American Revolution and the Historical Imagination.* New York: Alfred A. Knopf, 1978.

——— *Meadows of Memory: Images of Time and Tradition in American Art and Culture.* Austin: University of Texas Press, 1992.

———. *Mystic Chords of Memory: The Transformation of Tradition in American Culture.* New York: Alfred A. Knopf, 1991.

Kaye, Harvey J. *The Powers of the Past: Reflections on the Crisis and the Promise of History.* Minneapolis: University of Minnesota Press, 1991.

Kertzer, David. *Ritual, Politics, and Power.* New Haven, Conn.: Yale University Press, 1988.

Klapthor, Margaret Brown, and Howard Alexander Morrison. *G. Washington; A Figure upon the Stage.* Washington, D.C.: National Museum of American History, 1982.

Lanman, Charles. "On the Requisites for the Formation of a National School of Historical Painting." *Southern Literary Messenger,* December 1848, 727–30.

———. "Our National Paintings." *The Crayon,* February 28, 1855, 136.

Levin, David. *History as Romantic Art: Bancroft, Prescott, Motley, and Parkman.* Stanford, Calif.: Stanford University Press, 1959.

Lewis, W. R. B. *The American Adam: Innocence, Tragedy and Tradition in the Nineteenth Century.* Chicago: University of Chicago Press, 1955.

Lindsay, Kenneth C. *The Works of John Vanderlyn: From Tammany to the Capitol.* Binghamton: University Art Gallery, State University of New York, 1970.

Lossing, Benson John. *The Pictorial Field Book of the Civil War in the United States of America.* 3 vols. New Haven, Conn.: George S. Lester, 1878–80.

———. *Mathew Brady's Illustrated History of the Civil War, 1861–65.* New York: The War Memorial Association, 1912.

Marks, Arthur S. "The Statue of George III in New York and the Iconology of Regicide." *The American Art Journal* 13 (Summer 1981): 61–82.

Marling, Karal Ann, and John Wetenhall. *Iwo Jima: Monuments, Memories, and the American Hero.* Cambridge, Mass.: Harvard University Press, 1991.

McElroy, Guy C. *Facing History: The Black Image in American Art, 1710–1940.* Washington, D.C.: Corcoran Gallery of Art, 1990.

McNaughton, Marian R. "James Walker—Combat Artist of Two American Wars." *Military Collector & Historian* 9 (Summer 1957): 31–32.

Middleton, David, and Derek Edwards, eds. *Collective Remembering.* London: Sage, 1990.

Miller, Lillian B. *Patrons and Patriotism: The Encouragement of the Fine Arts in the United States, 1790–1860.* Chicago: University of Chicago Press, 1966.

———. "Paintings, Sculpture, and the National Character, 1815–1860." *Journal of American History* 53, 4 (March 1967): 696–707.

Mitnick, Barbara J. *The Changing Image of George Washington.* New York: Fraunces Tavern Museum, 1989.

———. "Jean Leon Gerome Ferris: America's Painter Historian." Ph.D. diss., Rutgers, the State University of New Jersey, 1983.

Mitnick, Barbara J., and David Meschutt. *The Portraits and History Paintings of Alonzo Chappel*. Chadds Ford, Pa.: Brandywine River Museum, 1992.

Montgomery, Charles F., and Patricia E. Kane, eds. *American Art 1750–1800: Towards Independence*. Boston: New York Graphic Society, 1976.

Moorhead, James H. "Between Progress and Apocalypse: A Reassessment of Millennialism in American Thought, 1800–1880." *Journal of American History* 71 (December 1984): 524–42.

Morse, Samuel F. B. *Lectures on the Affinity of Painting with the Other Fine Arts*. Ed. Nicolai Cikovsky, Jr. Columbia and London: University of Missouri Press, 1983.

Moss, Michael E., ed. *Robert W. Weir of West Point: Illustrator, Teacher and Poet*. West Point, N.Y.: United States Military Academy, 1976.

Moure, Nancy, and Donelson F. Hoopes. *American Narrative Painting*. Los Angeles, Calif.: Los Angeles County Museum of Art, 1974.

Neely, Mark E., Jr., Harold Holzer, and Gabor S. Boritt. *The Confederate Image: Prints of the Lost Cause*. Chapel Hill and London: University of North Carolina Press, 1987.

Neilson, George R. "Paintings and Politics in Jacksonian America." *Capitol Studies* 2 (Spring 1972): 87–92.

Norton, Anne. *Alternative Americas: A Reading of Antebellum Political Culture*. Chicago: University of Chicago Press, 1986.

Oates, Stephen B. *Lincoln: The Man behind the Myths*. New York: Harper and Row, 1984.

———. *With Malice toward None*. New York: Harper and Row, 1977.

Pitz, Henry Clarence. *Howard Pyle: Writer, Illustrator, Founder of the Brandywine School*. New York: Bramhall House, 1965.

Plumb, J. H. *The Death of the Past*. Boston: Houghton Mifflin, 1970.

Potter, David M. *The South and the Sectional Conflict*. Baton Rouge: Louisiana State University Press, 1968.

Pritchard, Kathleen. "Shorter Notes: John Vanderlyn and the Massacre of Jane McCrea." *The Art Quarterly* 12, 4 (Autumn 1949): 363–64.

Prown, Jules David. *John Singleton Copley, 1735–1815*. 2 vols. Cambridge, Mass.: Harvard University Press for the National Gallery of Art, 1966.

Quick, Michael, et al. *The Paintings of George Bellows*. Fort Worth, Tex.: Amon Carter Museum; Los Angeles: Los Angeles County Museum of Art; and New York: Harry N. Abrams, Inc., 1992.

Rash, Nancy. *The Painting and Politics of George Caleb Bingham*. New Haven, Conn., and London: Yale University Press, 1991.

Reynolds, Joshua. *Discourses on Art*. Ed. Robert R. Wark. San Marino, Calif.: Huntington Library, 1959.

Richardson, Edgar P., Brooke Hindle, and Lillian Miller. *Charles Willson Peale and His World*. New York: Harry N. Abrams, Inc., 1983.

Ringe, Donald. *The Pictorial Mode: Space and Time in the Art of Bryant, Irving and Cooper*. Lexington: University of Kentucky Press, 1971.

Ross, Dorothy. "Historical Consciousness in Nineteenth Century America." *American Historical Review* 89 (October 1984): 909–28.

Sandweiss, Martha A., Rick Stewart, and Ben W. Huseman. *Eyewitness to War: Prints and Daguerreotypes of the Mexican War, 1846–1848*. Washington, D.C.: Smithsonian Institution Press and Amon Carter Museum, 1989.

Sandweiss, Martha A., ed. *Photography in Nineteenth-Century America*. Fort Worth, Tex.: Amon Carter Museum and Harry N. Abrams, Inc., 1991.

Satz, Ronald N. *American Policy in the Jacksonian Era*. Lincoln: University of Nebraska Press, 1975.

Saunders, Richard H. "Genius and Glory: John Singleton Copley's *The Death of Major Peirson*." *The American Art Journal* 22, 3 (Autumn 1990): 4–39.

Schama, Simon. *Dead Certainties*. New York: Alfred A. Knopf, 1991.

Schlissel, Lillian, et al., eds. *Western Women: Their Land, Their Lives*. Albuquerque: University of New Mexico Press, 1988.

Schoonmaker, Marius. *John Vanderlyn: Artist, 1775–1852*. Kingston, N.Y.: The Senate House Assoc., 1950.

Schudson, Michael. "The Present in the Past versus the Past in the Present." *Communication* 11 (1989): 105–13.

Schwartz, Barry. *George Washington: The Making of an American Symbol*. New York: The Free Press, 1987.

———. "Iconography and Collective Memory: Lincoln's Image in the American Mind." *Sociological Quarterly* 32 (Fall 1991): 301–19.

Sellers, Charles Coleman. *Charles Willson Peale*. New York: Charles Scribner's Sons, 1969.

Silverman, Kenneth A. *A Cultural History of the American Revolution*. New York: Thomas Y. Crowell, 1976.

Simpson, Marc. *Winslow Homer Paintings of the Civil War*. San Francisco: The Fine Arts Museums of San Francisco, with Bedford Arts, Publishers, 1988.

Sizer, Theodore, ed. *The Autobiography of Colonel John Trumbull: Patriot-Artist, 1756–1843*. New Haven, Conn.: Yale University Press, 1953.

Slotkin, Richard. *Regeneration through Violence: The Mythology of the American Frontier, 1600–1860*. Middletown, Conn.: Weslyan University Press, 1973.

Somkin, Fred. *Unquiet Eagle: Memory and Desire in the Idea of American Freedom, 1815–1860*. Ithaca, N.Y.: Cornell University Press, 1967.

Staley, Allen. *Benjamin West: American Painter at the English Court*. Baltimore, Md.: Baltimore Museum of Art, 1989.

Staley, Allen, and Helmut von Erffa. *The Paintings of Benjamin West*. New Haven, Conn.: Yale University Press, 1986.

Stehle, R.L. "The Düsseldorf Gallery of New York." *New-York Historical Society Quarterly* 58, 4 (October 1974): 305–14.

Strong, Roy. *Recreating the Past: British History and the Victorian Painter*. New York: Thames and Hudson, 1978.

Taylor, William R. *Cavalier and Yankee: The Old South and American National Character*. Garden City, N.Y.: Anchor Books, 1963.

Thistlethwaite, Mark E. *The Image of George Washington: Studies in Mid-Nineteenth-Century American History Painting*. New York and London: Garland Publishing, Inc., 1979.

———. "Patronage Gone Awry: The 1883 Temple Competition of Historical Paintings." *The Pennsylvania Magazine of History and Biography* 112 (October 1988): 545–78.

———. "Peter F. Rothermel: A Forgotten History Painter," *Antiques*, November 1983, 1016–22.

Thompson, W. Fletcher, Jr. *The Image of War: The Pictorial Reporting of the American Civil War*. New York and London: Thomas Yoseloff, 1960.

Trachtenberg, Alan. *Reading American Photography*. New York: Hill and Wang, 1989.

Truettner, William H. "The Art of History: American Exploration and Discovery Scenes, 1840–1860." *The American Art Journal* 14 (Winter 1982): 4–31.

Truettner, William H., ed. *The West as America: Reinterpreting Images of the Frontier, 1820–1920.* Washington, D.C., and London: Smithsonian Institution Press for the National Museum of American Art, 1991.

Tuveson, Ernest Lee. *Redeemer Nation: The Idea of America's Millennial Role.* Chicago: University of Chicago Press, 1968.

Tyler, Ronnie C. *The Mexican War: A Lithographic Record.* Austin: Texas State Historical Association, 1973.

Van Tassel, David D. *Recording America's Past: An Interpretation of the Development of Historical Studies in America, 1607–1884.* Chicago: University of Chicago Press, 1960.

Welter, Barbara. "The Cult of True Womanhood: 1820–1850." *American Quarterly* 18 (Summer 1966): 151–74.

Welter, Rush. *The Mind of America 1820–1860.* New York and London: Columbia University Press, 1975.

Williams, Herman Warner, Jr. *Mirror to the American Past: A Survey of American Genre Painting, 1750–1900.* Greenwich, Conn.: New York Graphic Society, 1973.

Wilson, Richard Guy, Dianne H. Pilgrim, and Richard N. Murray, eds. *The American Renaissance: 1876–1917.* Brooklyn, N.Y.: The Brooklyn Museum, 1976.

Wind, Edgar. "The Revolution of History Painting." *Journal of the Warburg and Courtauld Institutes* 2 (1938-1939): 116–127.

Zelinsky, Wilbur. *Nation into State: The Shifting Symbolic Foundations of American Nationalism.* Chapel Hill and London: University of North Carolina Press, 1988.

Index

251